Into the World of the New Testament

Into the World of the New Testament

Greco-Roman and Jewish Texts and Contexts

Daniel Lynwood Smith

B L O O M S B U R Y

LONDON • NEW DELHI • NEW YORK • SYDNEY

Bloomsbury T&T Clark

An imprint of Bloomsbury Publishing Plc

50 Bedford Square	1385 Broadway
London	New York
WC1B 3DP	NY 10018
UK	USA

www.bloomsbury.com

Bloomsbury is a registered trade mark of Bloomsbury Publishing Plc

First published 2015

British Library Cataloguing-in-Publication Data
A catalogue record for this book is available from the British Library.

ISBN: HB: 978-0-56765-703-9
PB: 978-0-56765-702-2
ePDF: 978-0-56765-704-6
ePub: 978-0-56765-742-8

Library of Congress Cataloging-in-Publication Data
A catalog record for this book is available from the Library of Congress.

Typeset by RefineCatch Limited, Bungay, Suffolk
Printed and bound in India

constudentibus meīs

Contents

Part III Reading Old Words

Acknowledgments

Some people get by with only a little help from their friends, I hear. I am not among them. When I think of the ways in which my friends (and family members and colleagues and students and mentors) have helped me in the creation of this book, I find that I owe many a debt. Dozens of eyes have read this manuscript at various stages, and these many readings have led me to make many additions, subtractions, and other modifications to this book. I assume responsibility for the final product, but I do so with humility and with gratitude for all those who have joined me on the way. The dedication aims to capture something of this sense of appreciation for my fellow *studentēs*. The Latin verb *studēre* means "to be zealous for" or "to strive after" (not simply "to study"); in bringing this project to fruition, I have not striven alone.

I must begin by acknowledging my teachers and fellow students at the University of Notre Dame, where I spent nearly a decade investigating Jews and Christians in their ancient contexts. It may still be some time before I fully appreciate all that I gained from the wise men and women that I encountered in Malloy Hall.

Next, I must thank my editor, Dominic Mattos. This book was a faint intuition in the back of my mind until Dominic's question over lunch in Bannister House on a spring day in 2013. That idea became a proposal, then a manuscript, and now, at last, a book. Along with Miriam Cantwell and Joshua Pawaar, Dominic has cheerfully and competently guided me through this process. I am grateful.

Finally, I must thank the many readers who have improved this book along the way. The staff members and incarcerated students of the ERDCC—whom I taught as part of the Saint Louis University Prison Program—served both as the first readers of my complete draft chapters and as the inspiration for my continued efforts. My THEO 220 03H students of Spring 2014 then read draft chapters and offered useful feedback. I am also grateful to friends and colleagues whose comments, corrections, and collaboration have improved this book in countless ways: Yvonne Angieri, Matt Bates, Doug Boin, Michal Beth Dinkler, Peter Martens, Geoff Miller, Scott Moringiello,

Randy Rosenberg, Eric Rowe, Sarah Smith, Matt Thiessen, Abram Van Engen, Marc Vorih, Jeff Wickes, Rick Yaw, and the anonymous external reviewer. In the final stages, Paul King, my copy editor, impressed me with his eye for detail. Each of you has given me (and the readers of this book) more than a little help. Thank you.

Sarah, Ezra, Agnes, Isaiah, Nathan, and Ezekiel, thank you for your patience with me and your love for me. You have taught me so much.

Daniel Lynwood Smith
Saint Louis University
Holy Week 2014
Ad maiōrem Deī glōriam

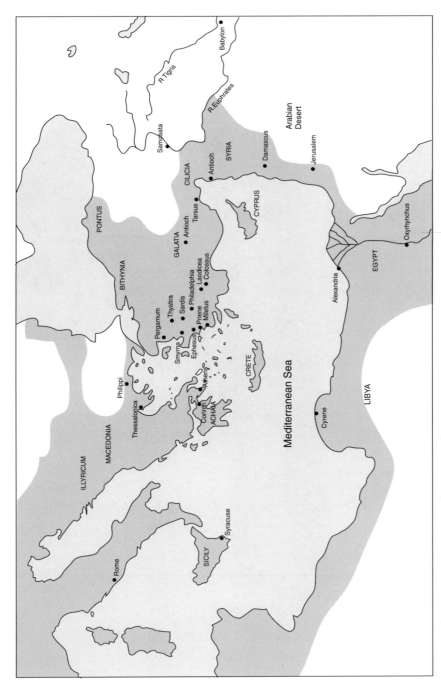

Map 1 The Roman Empire in the Time of Augustus

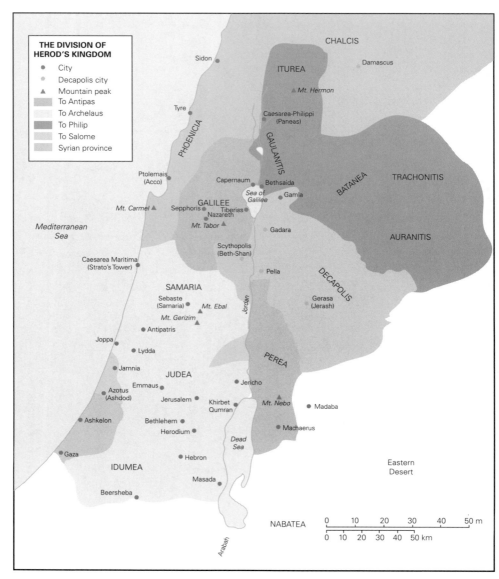

Map 2 Israel-Palestine in 30 C.E.

Abbreviations

Books of the Tanakh (Christian Old Testament)

Gen	Genesis
Exod	Exodus
Lev	Leviticus
Num	Numbers
Deut	Deuteronomy
Josh	Joshua
Judg	Judges
Ruth	Ruth
1–2 Sam	1–2 Samuel
1–2 Kgs	1–2 Kings
1–2 Chr	1–2 Chronicles
Ezra	Ezra
Neh	Nehemiah
Esth	Esther
Job	Job
Ps (Pss)	Psalms
Prov	Proverbs
Eccl	Ecclesiastes
Song	Song of Songs (Song of Solomon)

Isa	Isaiah
Jer	Jeremiah
Lam	Lamentations
Ezek	Ezekiel
Dan	Daniel
Hos	Hosea
Joel	Joel
Amos	Amos
Obad	Obadiah
Jonah	Jonah
Mic	Micah
Nah	Nahum
Hab	Habakkuk
Zeph	Zephaniah
Hag	Haggai
Zech	Zechariah
Mal	Malachi

Selected Apocrypha

Jdt	Judith
1–2 Macc	1–2 Maccabees
3–4 Macc	3–4 Maccabees
Sir	Sirach/Ecclesiasticus
Tob	Tobit
Wis	Wisdom of Solomon

Books of the New Testament

Matt	Matthew
Mark	Mark
Luke	Luke
John	John
Acts	Acts
Rom	Romans
1–2 Cor	1–2 Corinthians
Gal	Galatians
Eph	Ephesians
Phil	Philippians
Col	Colossians
1–2 Thess	1–2 Thessalonians
1–2 Tim	1–2 Timothy
Tit	Titus
Phlm	Philemon
Heb	Hebrews
Jas	James
1–2 Pet	1–2 Peter
1–3 John	1–3 John
Rev	Revelation

Other abbreviations

ANF   *The Ante-Nicene Fathers.* Edited by Alexander Roberts and James Donaldson. 1885–1887. 10 vols. Repr. Peabody, Mass.: Hendrickson, 1994.

B.C.E.	Before the Common Era (= B.C.)
ca.	*circa* (Latin word meaning "approximately")
C.E.	Common Era (= A.D.)
e.g.	*exempli gratia* (Latin expression meaning "for example")
esp.	especially
LCL	*Loeb Classical Library*. Edited by Jeffrey Henderson, George P. Goold, T. E. Page, Edward Capps, L. A. Post, W. H. D. Rouse, and E. H. Warmington. 521 vols. Cambridge: Harvard University Press, 1911–.
LXX	Septuagint (the Greek translation of the Jewish scriptures)
OGIS	*Orientis Graeci inscriptiones selectae*. Edited by Wilhelm Dittenberger. 2 vols. Leipzig: S. Hirzel, 1903–1905.
OTP	*Old Testament Pseudepigrapha*. Edited by James H. Charlesworth. 2 vols. Garden City, N.Y.: Doubleday, 1983–1985.
P. Oxy.	Oxyrhynchus Papyrus. (These papyrus texts were found at Oxyrhynchus in Egypt; images of these texts are available online at http://www.papyrology.ox.ac.uk/POxy/)

Illustrations

Preface

You recently spotted an ancient text. Etched into stone, the text jumbled together letters and images: a pair of roughly-outlined fish swimming between lines of words, with a leaning anchor in their midst. (If this scene does not sound familiar, take another look at the cover of this book.) Unless you read Greek or Latin, the letters meant little to you. You probably did not know that the "D" and "M" inscribed at the top stand for the Latin phrase *DIS MANIBUS*. Commonly inscribed on Roman grave markers, this abbreviation served to recognize the *manes*, the spirits of the deceased.

Below this reminder of Roman reverence for the spirits of the dead, two Greek words appear: *ICHTHYS ZŌNTŌN*, meaning "fish of the living ones." These two words add to the enigma of this slab of marble. Some believe that this "fish" (*ICHTHYS*) might be another abbreviation. If read as an acronym, *ICHTHYS* becomes *Iēsous CHristos THeou Yios Sōtēr*, or "Jesus **Christ**, Son of God, Savior." This interpretation, coupled with the common Christian symbols of the fish and the anchor (see Heb 6:19), has led many to cite this late second-century or early third-century C.E. tombstone as one of the earliest examples of Christian art.

Not all agree. The tombstone, in its current state, preserves the memory of a Roman woman. Her **epitaph** reads, "To Licinia Amias, well-deserving, [who?] lived . . ." The Latin text ends abruptly, leaving us to wonder who Licinia Amias was and how she lived. We might guess that her family followed Roman ancestral customs, given the invocation of the *manes*. The *ICHTHYS* inscription might be a play on the name of Licinia Amias, to whom this grave belonged. In Greek, *amias* means "tuna."

A glossary at the end of the book offers concise definitions of words that are in **bold font** in the text.

How can we decide whether the "fish" is Jesus Christ or Licinia Amias? More clues further complicate the question. Close examination of the marble slab reveals evidence of erasure; the epitaph has apparently replaced an earlier text. The presence of two different languages has generated other hypotheses: some scholars wonder if the Greek text, fish, and anchor were added at a later date.

When you first spotted this text on the book cover, you saw an old rock with unintelligible words and unimpressive artwork. I have invited you into the world of this inscription, helping you to traverse the language barriers, to understand the cultural and religious contexts, and to grapple with some of the questions the text raises. In the following pages, I will undertake the same task—in much greater detail—with a different ancient text: the New Testament.

I am not the first to set my hand to this task, nor will I be the last. In the past five years alone, at least fifteen New Testament introductions have been published ... in English. The question naturally arises: Why another introduction to the New Testament? My response is threefold: this book is the product of a conviction, the result of a concession, and the attempt at a contribution.

My conviction is this: In a New Testament class, the New Testament should take center stage. Reading the New Testament should be the top priority. I think that most New Testament professors would agree with me on this point. Yet, imagine the following scenario: a professor assigns her students to read Mark 1–8, in addition to the relevant portion of the textbook that describes the authorship, dating, **literary forms**, and theological themes of Mark. Which reading will the student prioritize? (Hint: Which material is more likely to be on the test?) I am concerned that a conventional textbook can serve as a rival claimant to students' attention. As a result, I am disinclined to use a conventional textbook in my New Testament classes—I want my students to focus on the New Testament itself.

Ideally, I would like my students to explore the Greek text of the New Testament, keeping in mind the social, economic, and political contexts of these writings. Context profoundly shapes meaning, after all. But here, I must make a concession. Not all students read *koinē* Greek, most do not know the works of Josephus, and rare indeed is the student who possesses a good working knowledge of the Roman empire. Twenty-first-century readers who do not speak Greek can make good sense of much of the New Testament, but contextual background can serve both to further illuminate the New Testament and to ward off some common (and damaging) misunderstandings that can arise in the absence of context. A good textbook will include this information, and much more. Many textbooks, however, sequester treatments of Greco-Roman and Jewish background in the opening chapters; then, they switch to lengthy treatments of the individual books of the New Testament in the subsequent chapters.

I prefer that my students spend the bulk of their time with the New Testament or other ancient texts, rather than summaries of past scholarship. In this book, instead of reviewing what scholars currently think about **crucifixion**, you will read what ancient authors wrote about crucifixion. Instead of exploring various scholarly reconstructions of the dating of Paul's letters, you will be able to compare Paul's letters with other ancient letters, seeing how Paul both followed conventions and innovated in his writings. And instead of reading a summary of discipleship in the Greco-Roman world, you will read ancient descriptions of teachers and their students in the Greco-Roman world.

My proposed contribution, then, is not another conventional textbook, as helpful as a textbook can sometimes be. Nor is the present text an anthology of readings from the ancient world, as helpful as a reader can be. Rather, my goal is to provide a readings-heavy aid to be used *with* a good study **Bible**. (A good study Bible will summarize authorship, dating, and other issues in the span of one to five pages for each book of the Bible; you might say that the study Bible is the course "textbook.") I aim to supplement the reading of the New Testament, not to supplant it.

Unlike most textbooks, this book does not match its chapters to the books of the New Testament. I take a more thematic approach. The first chapter offers a broad introduction to the New Testament itself, and the next two chapters orient the reader to some major historical, military, political, religious, and social contexts (with the understanding that any effort to distinguish sharply between these different contexts would be as prudent as the effort to un-scramble the eggs in an omelette). If used in a New Testament class, these opening chapters could be read prior to beginning the New Testament—perhaps in the first week or two of the class. The remaining chapters are intended to supplement the reading of the New Testament itself; each chapter stands alone, and they can be read in any order. Courses that follow the canonical order of the New Testament can continue with Chapter Four. Courses that start with Paul's letters may want to skip ahead to Chapter Eight or Nine instead.

A few more words about the character of this book as a "readings-heavy aid": I have included dozens of quotations of ancient texts in the pages that follow. In each case, the translation is my own, unless otherwise noted; biblical translations are also my own. I have generally privileged longer quotations over brief snippets. This book is intended to introduce readers to the "Texts and Contexts" of the world of the New Testament, so I try to provide lengthier texts that give readers more than a fleeting glimpse of the ancient contexts. Like an anthology, this book does not exhaustively interpret these longer texts. Unlike an anthology, this book places texts within a larger explanatory narrative framework. I hope that this combination of ancient texts and scholarly contextualization will equip my audience to read more sensitively and profitably. Since I am not trying to do the work of a biblical commentary, I do not always link an ancient text with a specific biblical text. I generally avoid giving background on particular passages. (If you want to know about how ancient Near Eastern shepherds secured their sheepfolds at night in order to better understand John 10:1–17, you will need to look at a commentary on the Fourth **Gospel** or at a heftier tome on the background of the New Testament.) Longer, more comprehensive works are available for those who want to go even deeper. My purpose is to enrich and illuminate the reading of the New Testament by introducing readers to fascinating voices and artifacts from the world in which the New Testament was written, shaped, and read.

Bibliography and suggestions for further reading

C. K. Barrett, ed. *The New Testament Background: Writings from Ancient Greece and the Roman Empire That Illuminate Christian Origins*. Revised edition. San Francisco: HarperSanFrancisco, 1995. (The revised edition of this comprehensive anthology is organized according to the ancient sources, not according to the New Testament. Thus, there are chapters on the Roman empire, Papyri, Mystery Religions, Qumran, and much more. Barrett also adds detailed introductions to the material, as well as commentary on the primary sources that are cited.)

Alison E. Cooley. *The Cambridge Manual of Latin Epigraphy*. Cambridge: Cambridge University Press, 2012. (This helpful handbook discusses the Licinia Amias inscription on pp. 233–234.)

Walter A. Elwell and Robert W. Yarbrough, eds. *Readings from the First-Century World: Primary Sources for New Testament Study*. Grand Rapids: Baker, 1998. (This shorter anthology—223 pages long—offers a rich trove of primary sources that will be of interest to readers of the New Testament. There are introductory comments at the start of each section, but there is little commentary on individual readings. Many readings are linked to particular New Testament passages.)

Simon Hornblower and Anthony Spawforth, eds. *The Oxford Classical Dictionary*. Third revised edition. New York: Oxford University Press, 2003. (Most of the basic biographical information provided in the following pages is drawn from this valuable resource, which has articles on everything from Abdera to Zeus.)

1

What is the New Testament?

Guiding Questions

What is the New Testament, and why is it called the "New Testament"?

What barriers to comprehension do twenty-first-century readers face when approaching a first-century text?

How might ancient texts shape our contemporary interpretations of the New Testament?

. . . There was an Ethiopian eunuch, an important official of Candace, queen of the Ethiopians; he was in charge of her entire treasury. He had come to Jerusalem to worship, and he was returning, seated in his chariot. He was reading the prophet Isaiah. The spirit said to Philip, "Go over and join this chariot." So Philip ran up and heard him reading the prophet Isaiah. Philip said, "Do you understand what you are reading?" And he replied, "How can I, unless someone guides me?" So he invited Philip to come up and sit with him.

(Acts 8:27-31)

"Do you understand what you are reading?"

Twenty-first-century readers who approach the New Testament for the first time can empathize with the Ethiopian **eunuch**. Reading an ancient text in translation can be challenging. Sometimes, the text is easy to understand:

"So he invited Philip to come up and sit with him." At other points, it is easy to understand *what* the text says, even if the text still leaves you with questions. The text may create a practical puzzle, leaving you to figure out *how* someone might do what the text says to do: "But I say to you, Love your enemies and pray for those who persecute you" (Matt 5:44). Other texts generate an interpretive puzzle, leaving you wondering *why* the text says what it does.

For example, if a twenty-first-century reader decides to start reading the New Testament, she might start with the Gospel of Matthew. If she perseveres through the rather daunting seventeen verses of **genealogy**, she will soon find a lively story about an engaged couple facing a deciding point in the relationship. The woman (Mary) finds herself pregnant prior to the wedding ceremony. The man (Joseph) contemplates a quiet divorce. Suddenly, an angel appears on the scene, speaking to Joseph in a dream: "Joseph, son of David, do not be afraid to take Mary as your wife ..." (Matt 1:20). Our attentive reader will remember that, just four verses earlier, the genealogy in Matt 1:16 identified Joseph as the son of a certain *Jacob*, not David! What is going on? Is the angel mistaken? Is the biblical text in error? Or did the translator make a mistake?

The translator is not mistaken; the **evangelist** has not erred. Rather, the identification of Joseph as "son of David" is not about biological fathers at all. The angel's words are a theological cue. The text is intentionally calling attention to Joseph's identity as a descendant of David, the ancient king of Israel. According to the Jewish **scriptures**, God promised that King David would have offspring, and this offspring of David would have an eternal throne. As God announced through the prophet Nathan, "I will establish the throne of his kingdom forever" (2 Sam 7:13). Thus, Matthew's genealogy is not designed to show that Joseph's father was a certain Jacob. Instead, Matthew's genealogy is designed to draw a line from David down through Jacob and Joseph to Jesus. Jesus comes from the line of David—a point that the **gospel**-writer first states in Matt 1:1 and then underscores in 1:20. A first-century Jewish reader could make these connections intuitively. Twenty-first-century readers can benefit, as the Ethiopian eunuch did, from someone to guide us.

Why do readers of the New Testament need guidance? First and foremost, the New Testament is an ancient text. We are not ancient people. Turn back the clock three hundred years, and you enter a world without telephone conversations, televised sporting events, air travel, microwave dinners, electric lights, and internet search capabilities. Continue backward another sixteen centuries, and you draw near to the world of the New Testament. We are separated from the ancient inhabitants of Galilee, Jerusalem, and Rome by time and (for most of us) space. The New Testament writings often imply a readership that is familiar with both the socio-economic world of the eastern Roman empire and the customs and beliefs of first-century Jewish culture, particularly with the collection of ancient texts that modern **Christians** call the "Old Testament," modern **Jews** call the **Tanakh**, and ancient Jews (such as Jesus and Paul) called "the scriptures" (see Matt 21:42; 22:29; Rom 1:2). First-century readers met those expectations. Twenty-first-century readers can fall short.

After all, the way we live has changed dramatically. We still eat, drink, work, and sleep. But other things have changed. Nowadays, many of us spend most of our time inside buildings. Many of us do not end up working in the same occupation that our parents did. Many of us have traveled more than ten miles away from the place where we were born. Many of us live in democracies. Many of us neither own other human beings as slaves nor are owned by other human beings as slaves. Many of us will live for more than fifty years—perhaps even for fifty more years after reading this sentence. And there is another example of cultural difference: all of us can read these words. Not only can we read, but many of us own books. Estimates of ancient literacy usually hover around or below ten percent of the population; production costs meant that even fewer people would own a book. Education and economics combine to generate yet another difference between then and now: we read books silently in the library or in our homes. First-century followers of Jesus, in contrast, would have typically encountered texts with their *ears*, not their *eyes*. We peruse an English translation visually; they heard Greek (or **Aramaic** or **Hebrew**) sentences read by a literate member of the **synagogue** or assembly. (You might consider reading the New Testament aloud as one small way to draw closer to the first readers of the New Testament.)

Second, the New Testament has been read and interpreted throughout the intervening centuries. Words and phrases like "our Lord Jesus **Christ**" and "**faith**" have been used and over-used to the point where the ways in which we use them may not relate well at all to the ways in which first-century authors used them. In their book *Made to Stick*, Chip and Dan Heath describe this phenomenon, which they call "semantic stretch." When certain words are used over and over again, they lose their potency and precision. Very few readers of the New Testament can give a sound definition of the word "faith," and even fewer accurately grasp the meaning of the word

"Christ." The meaning of these semantically-stretched words (and others) has been diluted. Part of this book's mission is to help modern readers understand how ancient writers used these words and phrases.

Third, we need to explore these words and phrases in both the original Greek and contemporary English. If you have studied a foreign language, you know that it is incredibly difficult, if not impossible, to say the exact same thing in two different languages. Even if you can find words that convey the same basic meanings, these words arrive already enmeshed in entire cultural networks of meaning. Even though teams of expert scholars have produced up-to-date translations of the New Testament that are based on the best Greek manuscripts, it is not always possible to convey the full range of meaning present in the Greek original. For example, see John 3:3, where Jesus tells a Jewish leader named Nicodemus that "unless someone is born *anōthen*, they cannot see the kingdom of God." The Greek word *anōthen* can mean "from above" or "again." Based on his response to Jesus' words, Nicodemus clearly thinks that Jesus means "born again," or "born a second time" (John 3:4). But the ambiguity of Jesus' words appears to be intentional—there is something about being born *anōthen* that involves both re-birth and belief in the **heaven**-sent Jesus (John 3:13). This ambiguity is shielded from the reader of an English translation of the New Testament—although many recent versions try to help by adding a translation note. Readers of the New Testament need to keep this linguistic barrier in mind; if a verse is unclear in one translation of the New Testament, consider looking at a few different translations for clarification.

> So, do you have to know ancient Greek to be a good reader of the New Testament? No. Would it help? Of course, but there is an abundance of resources available for an English-speaking audience that are written by scholars who know Greek. In addition to the present work, see the many resources given at the end of each chapter.

If this linguistic distance from the Greek original seems disheartening, keep in mind that many first-century Jews dealt with a similar problem. The Jewish scriptures were written in Hebrew, but many first-century Jews did not know Hebrew. Many Jews were scattered throughout the Mediterranean world, and they had grown more comfortable speaking

Aramaic and Greek. As a result, years before the New Testament was written, the Jewish scriptures were translated. The rather free translations into Aramaic—often closer to paraphrase than translation—are called *targumim*, and the best-known Greek translations are known as the **Septuagint**. According to an early legend, the Hebrew version of the Jewish scriptures was translated into Greek by a team of seventy (or seventy-two) scholars. (The Latin word *septuaginta* means "seventy," and the Septuagint is thus often abbreviated as "LXX," which is 70, in Roman numerals). The so-called *Letter of Aristeas* offers one account, which describes the translation process as taking seventy-two days of work by seventy-two learned scholars in the Egyptian city of Alexandria. The author—probably a Jew writing in the late second century B.C.E.—makes clear the authoritative nature of this new translation:

> As the books were read, the priests stood up, with the elders from among the translators and from the representatives of the "Community," and with the leaders of the people, and said, "Since this version has been made rightly and reverently, and in every respect accurately, it is good that this should remain exactly so, and that there should be no revision."
>
> *(Letter of Aristeas* 310; *OTP* translation)

Evidently, this legend served to assure Greek-speaking Jews that the Greek translation of their sacred text was completely trustworthy, requiring "no revision" and no second-guessing. The existence of such a legend implies that some Jews were uncomfortable with the idea of using a translation of their sacred texts. Still, ancient Jews used the LXX widely, and many early Christians accepted this Greek translation as authoritative.

The New Testament is a library

One place to begin our efforts is with the title itself: "New Testament." Why do we call it "New," and what exactly is a "Testament"? If we are to understand what this text is, we must first keep in mind that it is not just one text; it is a collection, or library, of texts. Over the years some Christians have been known to call their **Bible** "The Good Book." But the English word "Bible" comes from the Greek *ta biblia*, which literally means "the books." Like the larger Christian Bible of which it forms a part, the New Testament is composed of "books." The New Testament is thus more akin to a library than to a history book or a personal letter.

In fact, *ta biblia* can mean either "the books" or "the scrolls." In the time of Jesus, lengthier texts were usually written on scrolls; think, for instance, of the **Dead Sea Scrolls**. Around the time that the writings of the New Testament were being written, edited, and assembled, a new technology was being developed: the **codex**, or "book." Christians quickly adopted this new technology, and most early New Testament manuscripts exist in codex form.

There are twenty-seven books in the Christian New Testament. Impressively, Protestant, Roman Catholic, and Eastern Orthodox Christians are all in full agreement about which twenty-seven books form the New Testament. This sort of official list of sacred books is known as a **canon**. The Greek word *kanōn* can mean "measuring stick," so think of a canon as a list of books that "measure up" to a certain standard. We will learn more about the process of determining which books measure up to which standard in the Post-Script at the end of this volume; at this point, let us examine one such list of books: the Muratorian Canon.

The Muratorian Canon—also known as the Muratorian fragment, since the opening lines are missing—catalogues various texts that belong to the Christian New Testament. It offers brief comments on their authorship and on their status: should they be read, or not? Some scholars believe that this Latin fragment is a translation of a Greek original that was composed in the late second century C.E. in Rome; if so, this list would be the earliest extant canon. Other scholars have dated the origin of the underlying Greek text to the fourth century C.E. in Syria or Palestine. Regardless of date, this ancient text offers a glimpse into one "measuring" of early Christian texts. The Muratorian fragment begins with a mention of the Gospel of Luke and goes on to list many writings that are found in (what we now call) the New Testament. But other writings are also mentioned:

... There is current also (a letter) to the Laodiceans, another to the Alexandrians, forged in Paul's name for the sect of Marcion, and several others, which cannot be received in the catholic church; for it will not do to mix gall with honey. Further, a letter of Jude and two with the title John are accepted in the catholic church, and the Wisdom written by friends of Solomon in his honor. Also, of the revelations, we accept only those of John and Peter, the latter of which some of our people do not want to have read in the church. But Hermas wrote the Shepherd quite recently in our time in the city of Rome, when the bishop Pius, his brother, was seated on the throne of

the church of the city of Rome. And therefore it ought indeed to be read, but it cannot be read publicly in the church to the people either among the prophets, whose number is settled, or among the apostles to the end of time.
(Muratorian Canon, lines 63-80; W. Schneemelcher and R. McL. Wilson translation [Westminster John Knox, 1991], modified)

Whenever this text was written, there was clearly not a settled canonical list of books. In other words, when Christians talked about "the scriptures," they did not always have the same group of texts in mind. Moreover, this fragment brings to light a variety of ancient categories for texts. On one hand, Paul's letters to Philemon, Titus, and Timothy are sacred and can be read in the **church**. On the other hand, the letters to the Laodiceans and Alexandrians should be blacklisted as forgeries. Yet, there is also middle ground. The *Shepherd of Hermas* can be read privately, but not publicly; it is neither sacrilege nor sacred text. (Interestingly, the book of Revelation occupies a similar place in the Byzantine tradition; Revelation is never read publicly in the **liturgy**.)

> Why is "catholic church" not capitalized in the quote from the Muratorian Canon? First, here, "catholic" simply means "universal" (from the Greek *katholikos*), not Roman Catholic (a later designation). Second, whether composed in the second century or the fourth century, the original text would not have employed capital and lower-case letters. Most Greek manuscripts of this time period—including our earliest New Testament manuscripts— did not employ capitalization, did not utilize punctuation marks, and didnotevenhavespacesbetweenwords. These reader aids only arrived later—hence, the translations in the present work aim to preserve something of the less-marked original texts. For the sake of clarity, I do still capitalize personal names, place names, and the names of writings.

So, we have a canon, a set of texts that "measure up," and a theologically-informed process of selection. That canonical process is interesting in its own right and will be discussed at a later point in this book. For now, we must examine the writings that emerged from these centuries of sifting. After controversies over different letters, assorted gospels, and diverse **apocalyptic** texts, the final contents of this contested library included representatives of each of these different genres.

The literary forms of the New Testament

We know the main character of the New Testament: Jesus. Beyond that, things get complicated. No simple summary will suffice. Who is this Jesus? Some writings of the New Testament narrate the life of Jesus the first-century Jew. Others describe the (future?) actions of Jesus the heavenly lamb of God. Still others invoke "our Lord Jesus Christ" in the midst of debates over how the followers of Jesus should comport themselves. To read the New Testament, one must figure out how to read the various writings of the New Testament.

At an early stage, the current order of books in the New Testament was agreed upon. There are no documents that reliably explain the historical process of determining the order; Augustine of Hippo explains the order of the four gospels as due to their order of composition, but this hypothesis seems highly doubtful. Scholars have, nonetheless, been able to draw some conclusions; for instance, the Pauline (= attributed to Paul) letters to churches are roughly arranged from longest (Romans) to shortest (2 Thessalonians)— although Galatians and Ephesians should be transposed. They are followed by the Pauline letters to individuals, which are also arranged from longest (1 Timothy) to shortest (Philemon). The last seven letters are also arranged from longest (Hebrews) to shortest (3 John), with the exception of 1 John, which belongs between Hebrews and James if length is the criterion.

The twenty-seven discrete writings that constitute the New Testament come in three varieties: narratives, letters, and revelatory or apocalyptic literature. There are five narrative works: four gospels about Jesus (often classified as "biographies"), and one book of the Acts of the Apostles (generally categorized as a "history"). The last book of the New Testament is the book of Revelation, which scholars describe as "apocalyptic literature" (for further discussion, see Chapter Twelve). Between Acts and Revelation are twenty-one texts that appear in the form of "letters" (sometimes called "epistles"). Studying the New Testament, then, is often an exercise in reading someone else's mail.

This analogy can be helpful for understanding the New Testament. Many letters in the New Testament were written by a man named Paul (the subject of Chapter Nine). The followers of Jesus formed "assemblies" (also called "churches") throughout the cities of the Mediterranean world, and Paul helped to found, maintain, and connect these assemblies. So, to read a letter of Paul is to hear one half of a conversation between Paul and an early Christian community. It is no wonder, then, that scholars encounter difficulty in trying to create a tidy summary of Paul's belief system. They are trying to flatten and categorize the many letters of Paul written in different times and places, in a variety of circumstances, to a host of diverse communities. Such efforts may be useful; still, attention to **literary form** is absolutely necessary. Paul addressed a letter "to the assemblies in Galatia" (Gal 1:2), not to "academic theologians in Western universities."

Second Temple Judaism is simply the Judaism that existed during the time of the Second Temple. As the following chapter will explain, the first Jerusalem **temple** was destroyed by the Babylonians in the early sixth century B.C.E. The Jews built a second temple that was dedicated in 515 B.C.E. and destroyed in 70 C.E. Thus, "Second Temple Judaism" lasts from approximately 515 B.C.E. to 70 C.E.

Attention to literary form profoundly influences interpretation. For example, the book of Revelation can be read as a first-century pre-cursor to twenty-first-century Christian thriller novels, or it can be read against the backdrop of Second Temple Jewish apocalypticism (see Chapter Twelve for a helpful exploration of ancient **apocalypses**). The gospel depictions of "Jews" can be read with the flat stereotypes of anti-Semitic bias, or they can be read with an understanding of the beliefs and practices of Jews in the Second Temple period (the latter option is advanced in Chapter Eight). To go a bit deeper, we might also consider how to read the speeches in the book of Acts. Contemporary journalists reporting on a presidential speech are expected to quote verbatim from the address. What about the world before tape recorders, before radio broadcasts, before social media? New Testament scholars are fond of quoting the words of the fifth-century B.C.E. Greek historian Thucydides, who explains his use of speeches in the *History of the Peloponnesian War* as follows:

> And as far as what each one said in a speech, either when they were about to do battle, or when they were already engaged in battle, it was difficult to record with precision the words that were spoken, both those that I heard and those that have been reported to me from some place or another. Just as it seemed to me that each one would have said the most necessary things concerning their state of affairs, considering that these things are nearest to the general sense of what was truly spoken, so I have written.
>
> (Thucydides, *History* 1.22.1)

On one hand, Thucydides certainly wants to report "with precision" the words that were "truly spoken." On the other hand, that is hard to do. So, the Athenian historian has to settle for giving his best reconstruction of what would most likely have been said. And the accuracy of this reconstruction will depend on the quality of Thucydides' sources. Given the influence of Thucydides on later historians, it is unlikely that ancient authors and audiences would expect verbatim reports of speeches within historical narratives.

It should be clearer now that reading the New Testament is complicated. Ancient authors work with different sets of expectations. Reading Paul's mail has its limits. The gospels emerge from a different cultural context. Aware of these constraints, we can offer a working definition of the New Testament: *The New Testament is a carefully-selected collection of twenty-seven texts that were written between ca. 50 C.E. and ca. 100 C.E. by a variety of people throughout the eastern Mediterranean world. Though written in at least three distinct genres, all twenty-seven books are clearly connected to the person, work, or later influence of a main character named Jesus.* But why is it called the "New Testament"?

Why "Testament"?

To understand why this library of texts was called the "New Testament," we must examine both words carefully. Our English word "testament" comes from the Latin word *testamentum* (a translation of the Greek *diathēkē*). Both *testamentum* and *diathēkē* can be translated as "testament" or as **"covenant."** Traditionally, the former translation has been more popular. But because "testament" is rarely used in contemporary English (except to refer to a "last will and testament"), it might be more helpful to translate the Latin *novum testamentum* (or Greek *kainē diathēkē*) as "New Covenant" rather than "New Testament." What might this new covenant be?

To begin, a covenant may be defined as a binding agreement between two or more parties. In the ancient Near Eastern world, this sort of binding agreement was often solemnized through blood **sacrifice**. These covenants could be used to affirm friendship between parties of relatively equal status (e.g., in Gen 21:27), or parties of drastically unequal status. In the Jewish scriptures (or Christian "Old Testament"), covenants typically include God as the superior party and human beings (e.g., Abram in Gen 15) as the inferior.

If the covenant under discussion is a "new" covenant, then there must be an "old" covenant. Paul refers to an "old covenant" in 2 Cor 3:14, where the expression clearly refers to the covenant between God and Israel that was mediated by Moses on Mount Sinai (see Exod 19-20). For readers of the present work who are unfamiliar with Moses, Sinai, and the Sinai covenant, it may be helpful to review the contents of the **Pentateuch**—the first five books of both the Christian Bible and the Jewish Tanakh.

> Readers who are unfamiliar with the story of the people of God in the (Christian) Old Testament may find it useful to read some of the biblical re-tellings of the story of Israel. The following passages review the history of God's people: e.g., Deut 6:20-24 (from Egypt to **promised land**); Deut 26:5-9 (from Abraham to promised land); Josh 24:2-13 (from Abraham to promised land); Ps 78:12-72 (from Egypt to Davidic monarchy); Wis 10:1-12:8 (from creation of Adam to conquest of promised land); Acts 7:2-53 (from Abraham to Solomon's temple); 13:16-41 (from Egypt to Davidic monarchy); Heb 11:3-40 (from creation to Second Temple period).

To summarize, the book of Genesis describes the creation of the world (Gen 1-2), the human **fall** into **sin** and suffering (Gen 3-11), the divine **election** (= choosing) and call of Abram (Gen 12), the establishment of God's covenant with Abram/Abraham (Gen 15 and 17), and God's promises to Abraham's younger son Isaac (Gen 25:11) and to Isaac's younger son Jacob (Gen 27:27-29). Jacob, who is renamed "Israel" (Gen 32:28; 35:10), has twelve sons; his eleventh son, Joseph, is sold into slavery in Egypt (Gen 37-50). The book of Exodus opens with the descendants of Jacob/Israel (= "Israelites") living in Egypt as slaves (Exod 1). God raises up a prophet and leader named Moses, who persuades Pharaoh to let the people go (Exod 2-12). Moses parts the Red Sea (technically, the "Sea of Reeds") and leads the people to freedom; then, in the wilderness region of Mount Sinai, God makes a covenant with Israel (for more details, see Chapter Eight). This covenant binds God and the descendants of Jacob (= Israel) together in relationship; God self-identifies as "the Lord your God, who brought you out of the land of Egypt" (Exod 20:2). Most of the remaining chapters of Exodus, as well as all of Leviticus and the beginning of Numbers, are devoted to explaining the covenantal requirements that God expects Israel to fulfill, also known as the **law**. Deuteronomy (from the Greek words for "second" and "law") is largely a re-telling of God's covenantal expectations. Hence, despite the importance of creation and the call of Abram, it is fair to conclude that the Sinai covenant, or "old covenant" according to 2 Cor 3:14, lies at the heart of the Pentateuch.

The New Testament also includes explicit mention of a corresponding "new covenant." An early Christian writer highlights the references to a "new covenant" in one of the books of the prophets (Heb 8:8-13, quoting Jer 31:31-34). According to other early followers of Jesus, the cup of wine that Jesus gave to his **disciples** at the Last Supper is (or symbolizes? or establishes?) the new covenant: "And in the same way [he took] the cup after supper, saying 'This cup is the new covenant in my blood; do this as often as you drink it, in remembrance of me'" (1 Cor 11:25; compare Luke 22:20). But even these explicit references to a "new covenant" do not spell out what that new covenant is or what requirements it might involve.

What is the new covenant? If you directed this question to any of the authors of the New Testament, the response would likely deal with a person (Jesus), not a set of books. (For an early Christian like Paul, the Bible was simply the Jewish scriptures, now called the "Old Testament" by Christians.) This response would have stayed constant for decades. In the writings of Irenaeus, bishop of Lyons (ca. 130 C.E. – 202 C.E.), for example, we find explicit, sustained theological reflection on "new covenant" in relation to "old covenant." However, when Irenaeus talks about "old covenant" and "new," he is probably not linking these terms with collections of sacred texts (e.g., *Against Heresies* 4.15.2). The earliest evidence we have of a connection between a new covenant and a set of texts is in the writings of the North African theologian Tertullian (ca. 200 C.E.). In his *Against Praxeas* 15, Tertullian announces that he will draw evidence from the "new covenant" (*novum testamentum*) to support his argument about the relationship between God the Father and God the Son. By the end of the second century C.E., instead of reading gospels and letters that describe the new covenant inaugurated by Jesus, we find these very gospels and letters described as the books of the new covenant, or simply as "the new covenant."

> Tertullian was probably not the first Christian theologian to apply the term "new covenant" to a collection of writings. We have two earlier references to writings associated with the "old covenant," both by Greek theologians in the late second century C.E. (Melito of Sardis, *Fragments* 3, and Clement of Alexandria, *Stromata* 3.6.54). However, Tertullian may have been the first theologian to use another important term: *trinitas*, the Latin word for the **Trinity**.

The New Testament as drama

From a Christian perspective, the coming of Jesus and the inauguration of a new covenant begin to resolve the dramatic tension created by human disobedience to the divine will (Gen 3). More than one New Testament scholar has argued that the overall storyline set forth in the Christian Bible resembles a five-act play. Samuel Wells offers his version as follows:

Act I: Creation (and Fall)
Act II: Israel (from the call of Abram to the Babylonian exile and beyond)
Act III: Jesus (from **incarnation** to **resurrection**)
Act IV: Church (= Christians)
Act V: End (or, to use the fancy Greek term, **eschaton**)

Act I sets the stage by introducing the setting (heaven and earth) and the main characters (God and humanity). This act also introduces the basic conflict that moves the entire narrative forward (God lovingly creates humans, but humans resist God). Act II introduces the first step toward resolution: God chooses a person (Abraham) and a people (Israel) to bring reconciliation between God and humanity. Act III offers the resolution to the basic conflict: Jesus offers forgiveness for sin and reconciliation between God and humanity. In Act IV, Christians receive the **Holy Spirit** and the charge to continue the work of reconciliation in the world. And Act V will bring the dramatic finale, bringing both tragedy for those who resist God and joy for those who remain faithful to the end.

Nowadays, "**sect**" can have a pejorative connotation, somewhat like the word "cult." When scholars use the word "sect," though, they are referring to an organized sub-group within a larger religious (or philosophical) group or school of thought. The closest modern term might be "denomination," which is typically more value-neutral. Likewise, the term "cult" is associated with fringe religious groups in popular culture; scholars use "cult" to describe any system of ritual worship, whether mainstream or extreme.

Viewed from within this theological framework, this book primarily treats the end of Act II (the situation of the Jewish people after the Babylonian conquest) and Act III (Jesus, the star—or "superstar"—of the show). Less attention is paid to Acts IV and V, even though the writing of the New Testament might be placed in the first scene of Act IV and the eschaton will receive some attention in Chapter Twelve. We will begin by exploring the military, political, and social contexts of Acts II and III (Part One: The Setting). We will continue by learning more about the main characters in Act III; in addition to studying Jesus, we will look at John the Baptist, Mary, King Herod, and Paul, as well as other Second Temple Jews and Jewish sects (Part Two: The Cast of Characters). Then, we will take a closer look at three important words that tend to fall victim to semantic stretch or other forms of misunderstanding: **crucifixion**, faith, and apocalypse (Part Three: Reading Old Words). Finally, a Post-Script will dip into Act IV, exploring further the development of the Christian canon.

This dramatic metaphor helps to explain how the New Testament fits within a Christian theological framework, but the way this framework compresses the Jewish scriptures into two preliminary acts may raise concerns. Similarly, the label "New Testament" can be off-putting. Why this language of "old" and "new"? In our consumerist world, "new" means "good." You want to buy the "new and improved" product, not last year's model (which is likely marked down in price, as a token of its lesser value). Some see the label "New Testament" as a Christian claim to superiority over the Jewish "Old Testament." And this down-grading of the status of Jewish scriptures aligns neatly with past Christian down-grading of the status of the Jewish people and their religion. Some scholars have argued that this language should be replaced with more value-neutral terminology, like "First Testament" instead of "Old Testament," or "Christian Scripture" in place of "New Testament."

The sentiments behind this proposal are praiseworthy, but there are many problems with the proposed solutions. First, keep in mind that Jews do not call their scriptures the "Old Testament." Jews call their scriptures by a variety of names: the "Bible," the "scriptures," or most commonly, "*Tanakh*" (a Hebrew acronym that stands for the major divisions of the Jewish Bible: **Torah** ["law"], *Nevi'im* ["prophets"], and *Ketuvim* ["writings"]). Second, calling the New Testament "Christian Scripture" implies that what Christians call the "Old Testament" is not part of "Christian Scripture," when it most certainly is! Third, as will be discussed in Chapter Eight, at least parts of the New Testament were written before "Christianity" became a "religion" separate from Judaism; hence, "Christian Scripture" runs the risk of anachronism. For these reasons, I retain the label "New Testament" for the twenty-seven writings under discussion. As stated above, though, the sentiments behind alternate proposals are laudable, and I hope that the material in the subsequent chapters will help to achieve the same ends (e.g., preventing anti-Jewish readings of sacred texts) through different means.

Voices from the New Testament world

Before beginning our tour, I would like you to meet some of our more notable guides from the world of the New Testament. I will quote a variety of Greek and Roman historians, novelists, and philosophers; these non-Jewish authors will be introduced in the subsequent chapters. Here, I provide background on Jewish authors of the late Second Temple period.

1-2 Maccabees (second century B.C.E.)

The Maccabean histories form part of the Roman Catholic and Eastern Orthodox canons of scripture, but they are not considered canonical by Protestants or Jews. Regardless of modern opinions as to their canonicity, these histories are invaluable sources for the **Maccabean revolt** and subsequent **Hasmonean** rule. Written in the late second century B.C.E., 1 Maccabees chronicles the tumultuous time period from the rise of Antiochus IV Epiphanes in 175 B.C.E. to the death of Simon son of Mattathias in 134 B.C.E. The focus is on the (Jewish) Maccabean revolt against the rule of the

(Greek) **Seleucids**. This revolt, caused by events of 167 B.C.E., will be discussed in more detail in Chapter Two.

2 Maccabees claims to be an abridgment of a longer five-volume work (2 Macc 2:23), and like 1 Maccabees, it also recounts the Maccabean revolt. Second Maccabees covers a shorter period of time (ca. 175 – 161 B.C.E.). One striking feature of 2 Maccabees is the importance of **martyrdom**; 2 Macc 6-7 describes multiple executions, including a famous account of the martyrdom of a mother and her seven sons (2 Macc 7). All eight martyrs face their deaths valiantly, believing that they will rise from the dead. Like 1 Maccabees, 2 Maccabees offers insight into the political, religious, and social world of Second Temple Judaism—the world into which Jesus was born.

The Qumran community (second century B.C.E. – first century C.E.)

Little was known about the community that lived at **Qumran**, near the Dead Sea, until the Dead Sea Scrolls were discovered there in the 1940s. This trove of documents includes letters (e.g., 4QMMT), biblical commentaries (e.g., a commentary on Habakkuk, 1QpHab), community regulations (e.g., 1QS, the "Community Rule"), collections of hymns (e.g., 1QH), the earliest extant manuscripts of the Jewish scriptures (including at least parts of every book but Esther), and much more. The Qumran community is now a focus of scholarly study, but it is hard to sort out all the particulars of this mysterious community. From archaeological discoveries at Khirbet Qumran and from documents like 1QS (The Community Rule), we can say quite a bit about the practices of this ascetic sect—their process of initiation for new members, their emphasis on washings to maintain ritual purity, and their communal meals. We also can read about their self-conception as the "sons of light" who have separated themselves from the "sons of darkness," as well as their messianic hopes and their expectations of an eschatological battle. However, it is notoriously difficult to describe the history of this group with any detail.

Readers are often puzzled by citations from Qumran, due in part to the fragmentary nature of our texts, and due in part to the strange abbreviations. What is 1QS 6.27, for example? 1QS: "1" stands for the first cave, "Q" signals that the cave was one of the eleven caves at Khirbet Qumran, and "S" is short for *Serekh*. 1QS 6.27, then, is line 27 of column 6 of the "*Serekh*" (or Community Rule) scroll found in the first cave at Khirbet Qumran. Other

Figure 1.1 Cave Four at Qumran
The fourth cave, discovered in 1952, can be seen from Khirbet Qumran; of all the caves, this one held the largest collection of writings.

documents associated with the Qumran community include the Damascus Document, which was actually found in a synagogue in Cairo (hence its abbreviation as "CD," "Cairo Damascus").

Philo of Alexandria (ca. 20 B.C.E. – ca. 50 C.E.)

Philo of Alexandria was a learned philosopher, biblical scholar, and political leader. He was also a prolific writer. He lived in one of the greatest cities of the ancient world, Alexandria (in Egypt); this highly cosmopolitan city was home to the largest library of its time. Whereas Josephus (see below) focused on historical writings, Philo's writings are generally more philosophical and exegetical. The only event in Philo's life that can be dated with certainty is 39/40 C.E., when Philo led a Jewish embassy from Egyptian Alexandria to Rome, in order to protest the policies of the emperor, Gaius Caligula.

Flavius Josephus
(ca. 37 C.E. – ca. 100 C.E.)

Josephus was an educated Jew who was a contemporary of the authors of the New Testament writings. As described below, Josephus played an active role in the Jewish revolt against Rome, working first for the Jewish cause before later serving the Romans. His familiarity with Second Temple Judaism and his access to Roman sources combine to make him an invaluable source for the first century C.E., and he will be quoted more frequently than any other ancient writer in this book.

Josephus was born into a priestly family in Jerusalem, a few years after the crucifixion of Jesus. He underwent a rabbinic education, and he later traveled to Rome, returning to his native land in the fateful year of 66 C.E. (the year that the Jewish revolt began). In his autobiographical *Life*, Josephus claims that he tried to convince his fellow Jews not to revolt, but was unsuccessful. Still, he was appointed as the commander of Galilee, where he led the rebel forces. He held this post until he was captured by the Romans in Jotapata, following a two-month siege.

Josephus prophesied that his captor (Vespasian) would shortly become the next Roman emperor, which is exactly what happened in 69 C.E. Impressed, Vespasian allowed Josephus to accompany the Roman forces, and Josephus was an eyewitness to the fall of Jerusalem in 70 C.E. Josephus was offered an estate outside of Jerusalem, but he declined. Presumably, he was aware that he was perceived as a traitor by his fellow Jews. Josephus instead went to Rome, where he was made a Roman citizen and given Vespasian's former home. There, he wrote his *History of the Jewish War* (describing the Jewish revolt), the *Jewish Antiquities* (composed of twenty books, tracing the history of the Jews from the creation of the world down to the first century C.E.), his *Life* (an autobiographical addendum to *Jewish Antiquities*), and *Against Apion* (a fascinating polemical work that defends Jewish culture and customs).

Bibliography and suggestions for further reading

François Bovon. "Beyond the Canonical and the Apocryphal Books, the Presence of a Third Category: The Books Useful for the Soul." *Harvard*

Theological Review 105 (2012): 125–137. (Bovon emphasizes that ancient Christian communities accepted some texts as canonical, rejected others as apocryphal, and preserved a third category of texts as "useful for the soul"—texts like the *Acts of Paul* that were read in private but not in a public liturgy.)

Joel B. Green and Lee Martin McDonald, eds. *The World of the New Testament: Cultural, Social, and Historical Contexts.* Grand Rapids: Baker Academic, 2013. (A team of expert contributors investigates the Greco-Roman and Jewish contexts of the New Testament in great detail—readers of the present work who want to go even deeper will want to consult Green and McDonald's 640-page volume.)

Chip Heath and Dan Heath. *Made to Stick: Why Some Ideas Survive and Others Die.* New York: Random House, 2008. (This brilliant little book is designed to explain why some ideas are "sticky" and others are not. They include a discussion of "semantic stretch" on pp. 170–177.)

Jason B. Hood and Matthew Y. Emerson. "Summaries of Israel's Story: Reviewing a Compositional Category." *Currents in Biblical Research* 11 (2013): 328–348. (Hood and Emerson survey scholarly literature on the retellings of Israel's story within biblical and extra-biblical materials. They include an extensive list of Jewish and Christian "summaries of Israel's story" at the end of the article.)

Larry W. Hurtado. "Oral Fixation and New Testament Studies? 'Orality', 'Performance' and Reading Texts in Early Christianity." *New Testament Studies* 60 (2014): 321–340. (In this critique of "performance criticism" among New Testament scholars, Hurtado sums up recent scholarship on Greco-Roman reading practices, literacy rates, and scribal techniques.)

Lee Martin McDonald. *The Formation of the Christian Biblical Canon.* Nashville: Abingdon, 1988. (This short overview explains the concept of canon and the development of the canon of the Christian Old and New Testaments. McDonald treats a wide array of helpful primary sources in detail.)

Wilhelm Schneemelcher, ed. *New Testament Apocrypha: Volume One: Gospels and Related Writings.* Translated by R. McL. Wilson. Louisville: Westminster John Knox, 1991. (In addition to a translation and discussion of the Muratorian fragment, this volume includes both other earlier canonical lists and translations of many "apocryphal" gospels that have not become part of the Christian New Testament.)

Samuel Wells. *Improvisation: The Drama of Christian Ethics.* Grand Rapids: Brazos, 2004. (In this book, Wells puts forth a new way to understand "the practice of Christian ethics," using the language of theatrical improvisation. The third chapter describes a revised version of N. T. Wright's five-act drama of scripture.)

N. T. Wright. *The New Testament and the People of God*. Minneapolis: Fortress, 1992. (This first volume introduces Wright's larger project, "Christian Origins and the Question of God." In addition to explaining his methodology and investigating the Jewish and Greco-Roman backgrounds of the New Testament, Wright also sets forth his five-act model of the biblical story on pp. 141–143.)

Part I

The Setting

2

The Kingdom of . . . God?

Guiding Questions

How might various first-century **Jews** understand the phrase "kingdom of God"?

How has geography influenced history in the ancient Near East?

Why might the kingdom of God be such a central feature of Jesus' (and his followers') preaching?

But [Jesus] said to them, "I must also preach the good news of the kingdom (*basileia*) of God to the other towns, because I was sent to do this!"

(Luke 4:43)

What is in a name?

"Repent, for the kingdom of **heaven** has come near!" (Matt 3:2). These are the first words off the tongue of the camel-hair-clad, locust-eating John the Baptist in the Gospel according to Matthew. After Jesus is baptized and tested, he too begins to preach with the same words: "Repent, for the kingdom of heaven has come near!" (Matt 4:17). In the New Testament, this preaching seems to summarize the message of both John the Baptist and Jesus. How might a first-century Palestinian Jew react to such a proclamation?

Some readers might be tempted to think that this is an easy question: "Clearly, the Gospel message is simple: say that you are sorry for your **sins**, and you get to go to heaven. Isn't that the whole point of Christianity?" (In short, no. The repentance preached by John and Jesus involves both turning away from sin and reorienting one's life toward the God of Israel; this total reorientation of life—and its implicit challenge to the "ticket to heaven" understanding of Christian **faith**—will be explored further in Chapter Eleven.) A twenty-first-century hearer might respond in this way to the proclamation of the "kingdom of heaven," but a first-century Palestinian Jew would react in a very different way, having heard a very different message. To understand this reaction to the "kingdom of heaven," we must grasp the first-century meanings of the words "kingdom" and "heaven."

Let us begin with "heaven." Before thoughts of clouds and harps fill your mind, you should first know that not all first-century Jews would identify "heaven" as "the place we go when we die." The **Hebrew** *shamayim* and Greek *ouranos* can both be translated into English as either "heaven" or "sky." And this lofty place was remembered more often as the dwelling place of God (see Ps 11:4; 80:14; Eccl 5:2), not the guaranteed destination for righteous humans (Dan 12:1-3 represents a noteworthy exception). Next, consider the textual evidence from the **gospels**. If we compare Mark's version of Jesus' first words, then we will find the same basic message of the coming kingdom: "But after John was handed over, Jesus came to Galilee, preaching the good news (*euangelion*) of God and saying, 'The time is fulfilled, and the kingdom of God has come near—repent, and believe in the good news (*euangelion*)'" (Mark 1:14-15). Matthew and Mark's summaries of Jesus' first preaching are nearly identical. Yet, they differ with regard to what precisely is coming near: is it the kingdom of heaven, or the kingdom of God?

> The Greek word *euangelion* literally means "good message." Many older **Bible** translations translate *euangelion* as "gospel," which comes from the Old English *godspel*, a combination of *god* ("good") and *spel* ("tidings"). In this book, I usually translate *euangelion* as "good news," unless it refers to a written text like the Gospel of Mark.

In fact, Mark's kingdom of God and Matthew's kingdom of heaven were referring to the same thing. When Matthew writes "kingdom of heaven," he is referring to the same kingdom that he elsewhere labels the "kingdom of God" (see Matt 19:23-24, where both phrases are used with no apparent distinction). Matthew wants to emphasize the distinction between heavenly things and earthly things, and examples of this distinction abound throughout the Sermon on the Mount (Matt 5-7; see esp. Matt 6:10), as well as the rest of Matthew's Gospel.

A first-century audience might also recognize the practice of substituting "heaven" in place of "God." For instance, 1 Maccabees sometimes refers to God as "heaven." Judas Maccabeus could call upon his followers to "cry out to heaven, if he will show favor toward us and remember the covenant with our ancestors" (1 Macc 4:10). Heaven did not make a **covenant** with Judas's ancestors, but the God of Israel did. While scholars have long thought that Matthew preserves evidence of attempts to avoid the name of God, substituting "heaven" in its place, this proposal seems dubious. At least, Matthew is not very consistent; Matt 12:28 and 19:24 both refer to the "kingdom of God," and Matthew repeatedly uses the Greek word for "God" (*theos*), starting in 1:23. Second, the evidence for Jews avoiding the name of God is generally later. For example, this rabbinic discussion was not put in writing until roughly 200 c.e.: ". . . in the Temple they pronounced the Name as it was written, but in the provinces by a substituted word . . ." (**Mishnah**, tractate *Sotah* 7.6; H. Danby translation [Oxford University Press, 1933]). Third, early evidence does not suggest that first-century Jews avoided any mention of the name of God. Rather, the evidence points to restrictions on the use of one particular name for God.

> Nowadays, many Jews prefer to avoid writing down or pronouncing any of the names of God. Hence, when writing in English, some Jewish theologians might type "G-d" instead of "God." These later practices echo ancient expressions of reverence for the tetragrammaton. Similarly, Christian Bibles often translate the tetragrammaton not as "Yahweh," but as "LORD" (often in small caps). Again, this measure is designed to show respect for the sacred name of God.

This particular name is the sacred four-letter name of God, also known as the **tetragrammaton** (*tetragrammaton* is a Greek word meaning "four letters"). This name, often transliterated as YHWH and pronounced as "Yahweh," was (and is) considered by Jews to be holy, and its usage was highly restricted. The first-century Jew Josephus testifies to the holiness of the tetragrammaton in his re-telling of the life of Moses (compare Exod 3:13–15): "And God (*theos*) made known to Moses his name, which had never before reached men's ears, and about which I am not permitted to speak" (Josephus, *Jewish Antiquities* 2.276). Josephus is explaining Jewish traditions to a Roman audience. He obviously feels comfortable using "God" (*theos*) in his treatise. However, he does not reveal the tetragrammaton, for he is "not permitted to speak" of it. This deep reverence for the sacred name is rooted in the Jewish **scriptures**, and the New Testament writings consistently use Greek words like *theos* ("God") and *kyrios* ("Lord") in place of it. As a result, we should not make too much of Matthew's phrase, "kingdom of heaven." Instead, we should hear Jesus making the same announcement in Matthew and Mark (and Luke): "The kingdom of God has come near!"

What "kingdom" comes near? To answer this question, we need to begin with the word itself, "kingdom" (*basileia*). How would first-century Greek-speakers hear this word? After exploring a range of meanings, we can turn to the political history of Israel-Palestine for further insight into how first-century Jews might hear Jesus' proclamation.

The Greek word *basileia* can be translated as "kingdom" or "kingship." Thus, the "kingdom of God" can mean "the geographic expanse over which God rules." Or, it can mean "the God-given authority to rule." We find a clear instance of *basileia* meaning "kingship" or "royal rule" in the book of Revelation. There, an angel explains to John of Patmos what his latest vision means: "And the ten horns that you saw are ten kings who have not yet received royal power (*basileia*), but they will receive authority as kings (*exousian hōs basileis*) for one hour, along with the beast" (Rev 17:12). Beasts and horns aside, this verse puts *basileia* (translated as "royal power") in parallel with another Greek phrase that literally means "authority as kings." No territory is mentioned here; *basileia* is clearly kingly power or royal authority.

When Jesus uses *basileia*, which meaning does he have in mind? Think about this question for a moment. Imagine you are driving a car, and you are wondering whether to turn right or left. You ask your friend, "Should I turn left?" The friend responds, "Right!" Does your friend mean to say, "Yes, correct, turn left," or do they mean that you should turn to the right? "Right" can mean "affirmative" or "the opposite of left." You must decide between the two meanings. Our discussion of *basileia*, on the other hand, does not require a choice between opposites. The various strands of meaning in the word *basileia* need not be pulled apart. The coming of the *basileia* of God might mean that God will rule over a specific area, or that God has sent someone who shares in divine kingship to the people of God, or that God is about to act decisively in royal fashion. Or, Jesus could have been announcing some combination of all of the above.

The coming of God's kingdom thus may or may not involve specific geographic areas. Other gospel passages suggest that Jesus is indeed granted kingship over the people of God. Or, Jesus could simply be emphasizing the timing, implying that God is about to demonstrate royal power. But how might God display this power? Twenty-first-century Christian theologians can read this announcement as foretelling God's defeat of death in the **crucifixion** and **resurrection** of Jesus. The canonical gospels, however, offer no evidence that the first-century crowds who flocked to Jesus were hoping that he would suffer, die, and rise again to new life (see John 6:15 for a more realistic example of crowd expectations). What might they have expected the "kingdom of God" to look like?

The land of Israel-Palestine and the kingdoms of the world

The answer to this question must take into account the various "kingdoms" that Jesus' first-century hearers (and their ancestors) had experienced. We find one possible answer in the ancient *Testament of Moses*, a work by an unknown author that was probably written during the lifetime of Jesus— scholars have dated the work to the first thirty years of the first century C.E. The one incomplete manuscript that has survived claims to report the final words of Moses to his successor Joshua. Early in his speech, Moses commands Joshua to "firmly establish a kingdom" for the people of Israel (*T. Mos.* 2.2; *OTP* translation). Moses goes on to describe the future history of Israel, including the Babylonian conquest (3.1-3), the return from exile (4.6), various episodes from the Maccabean times, and a probable reference to Herod the Great (6.2-7). Before Moses' closing exhortation to Joshua (10.11-15), there is a lengthy eschatological prophecy:

> Then his kingdom will appear throughout his whole creation.
> Then the devil will have an end.
> Yea, sorrow will be led away with him.
> Then will be filled the hands of the messenger,
>   who is in the highest place appointed.
> Yea, he will at once avenge them of their enemies.
> For the Heavenly One will arise from his kingly throne.

Yea, he will go forth from his holy habitation
　　with indignation and wrath on behalf of his sons.
And the earth will tremble, even to its ends shall it be shaken.
And the high mountains will be made low.
Yea, they will be shaken, as enclosed valleys will they fall.
The sun will not give light.
And in darkness the horns of the moon will flee.
Yea, they will be broken in pieces.
It will be turned wholly into blood.
Yea, even the circle of the stars will be thrown into disarray.
And the sea all the way to the abyss will retire,
　　to the sources of waters which fail.
Yea, the rivers will vanish away.
For God Most High will surge forth, the Eternal One alone.
In full view will he come to work vengeance on the nations.
Yea, all their idols will he destroy.
Then will you be happy, O Israel!
. . .
And God will raise you to the heights.
Yea, he will fix you firmly in the heaven of the stars,
　　in the place of their habitations.
And you will behold from on high.
Yea, you will see your enemies on the earth.
And recognizing them, you will rejoice.
And you will give thanks.
Yea, you will confess your creator.

　　　　　　　　　　　　　　(*T. Mos.* 10.1-10; *OTP* translation)

The author here announces the arrival of God's "kingdom" as a dominion that comprises all of creation (10.1). Using **apocalyptic** symbols also found in the book of Revelation, he describes the earth-shaking end of the current order, an end that includes the defeat of Israel's enemies. What is the kingdom of God? According to the *Testament of Moses*, it is the coming of God's royal authority over the geographic expanse of the whole world—an eschatological kingdom that will one day triumph over the kingdoms of Israel's enemies.

And enemies are a recurring feature of the history of Israel, from the time of Moses to the New Testament period. According to the book of Exodus, Israel was a people born out of conflict with Egypt. According to the book of Joshua, the people of Israel won their future homeland by wresting it from the Canaanites. And according to the rest of the historical books of the Hebrew Bible—and the history books of the intervening centuries—conflict

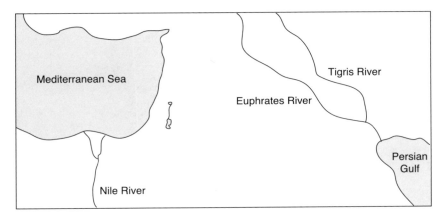

Figure 2.1 Map of ancient Near East

both plagued and continues to plague that small stretch of land between the Mediterranean Sea and the Jordan River. Why?

Here, a map helps more than a text (see Figure 2.1).

In the ancient world, rivers were givers of life. Rivers provided drinking water, water for crops and livestock, and routes for transportation, trade, and communication. Unsurprisingly, major civilizations took root and blossomed in the fertile earth watered by major rivers: the Yellow (or Huang He), the Indus, the Nile, the Tigris, and the Euphrates. The latter three rivers are most relevant to our discussion, for they gave rise to the two major centers of civilization that shaped much of Israel's early history: Egypt (around the Nile River) and Mesopotamia (literally, the land "in the middle of the rivers"— the Tigris and Euphrates Rivers). As they gained wealth and power, the Egyptian and Mesopotamian civilizations also looked to expand their boundaries through military means.

These aggressive tendencies spelled trouble for Israel. Around 1000 B.C.E., Israel was a respectable, second-rate military power with newly expanded boundaries and a divinely appointed king on the throne. It might appear that Israel would be well positioned for future prosperity. After all, if we look at Figure 2.2, we might think that warring Mesopotamian and Egyptian rulers would follow the route marked "A."

If the armies of the world powers followed route A—which was the most direct path, after all—Israel would not be on the itinerary. Unfortunately, route A leads directly through the Arabian Desert. In order to guarantee sufficient water and provisions for marching troops, the invading armies would follow route B, which led directly through Israel-Palestine.

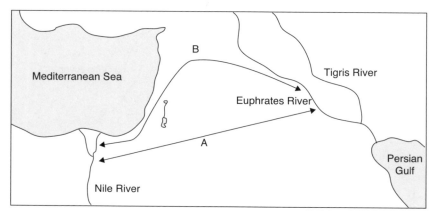

Figure 2.2 Map of ancient Near East, with alternate routes of conquest

This accident of geography proved tragic for the people of Israel. From the Assyrian conquest in the eighth century B.C.E. to the Bar Kokhba revolt in the second century C.E., Israel had as many enemies as there were empires in Mesopotamia, Egypt, and the rest of the eastern Mediterranean world. This military-political reality casts its shadow over the first-century writers, readers, and hearers of the New Testament.

Originating in northern Mesopotamia, the Assyrians were the first foreign power to trample through the kingdom of Israel, conquering the ten northern tribes in 722/721 B.C.E. The captive Israelites were forcibly relocated and brutally assimilated. References to the "ten lost tribes of Israel" do not refer to ten tribes who went hiking on a hot summer day and took a wrong turn at the crossroads. Rather, the Assyrian conquest meant that these Israelites lost their land, lost their freedom, and, to some degree, lost their identity.

More trouble for Israel soon followed from the East. In 587/586 B.C.E., King Nebuchadnezzar of Babylon sacked Jerusalem, destroyed the Jerusalem **temple**, and carried the Jerusalem elite off into exile. Thus, the Babylonian empire put an end to the hitherto unbroken line of Davidic kings. Because the two captured tribes comprised the southern kingdom of Judah, these captives became known not as "Israelites" but as "Judahites" or "**Jews**."

The Assyrian and Babylonian periods of dominance were followed by the Persian ascent to power. Cyrus II, also known as Cyrus the Great, conquered Babylon in 539 B.C.E., and he issued an edict in 538 that allowed the Jews to return to their homes. Moreover, he politically and financially supported the rebuilding of Jerusalem and the Jerusalem temple. This return from exile and rebuilding of the temple (finished and dedicated in 515 B.C.E.) marked the beginning of a period that has been labeled Second Temple Judaism, which lasted from the sixth century B.C.E. until the destruction of the **Second Temple** in 70 C.E.

Under Persian rule, many Jews were able to live in their ancestral homeland of Judah and to worship at the Jerusalem temple. This somewhat auspicious beginning of the Second Temple period lasted about two hundred years. Then, another invader arrived from a new quarter. Alexander the Great and his Macedonian army swept through the Mediterranean world in the late fourth-century, conquering the Persian forces at Issus in 333 B.C.E. and most of Palestine in 332 B.C.E.

Alexander the Great's conquest of the eastern Mediterranean world (and beyond) was not only military in nature. Where Alexander's troops conquered, the Greek language and Greek customs also took hold. This spread of Greek language and culture is known as Hellenization (literally, "Greek-ization"), and this widespread **Hellenism** (= "Greek-ism") explains both why Jews translated their scriptures into Greek (the **Septuagint**) and why the New Testament writings are all written in Greek—even centuries after Alexander's conquest.

Thus, in just over four hundred years, the people of Israel witnessed first-hand the dominance of three Mesopotamian empires (Assyrians, Babylonians, and Persians). They also experienced the power of Europe (the Macedonian conquest). Furthermore, they had to guard their southern flank. While never conquering the land of Palestine in this period, Egypt constituted a perennial threat—the Deuteronomistic history tells not only of political dissidents taking refuge in Egypt (e.g., 1 Kgs 11:17-18; 12:2), but also of Egyptian aggression (e.g., 1 Kgs 14:25; 2 Kgs 23:29).

The death of Alexander the Great spawned a new wave of conflict, as his empire was split up by his successors, the Diadochoi. (*Diadochoi* is the Greek word for "successors.") Positioned right between the holdings of two powerful Macedonian generals, the Jewish homeland suddenly became a bone of contention between these two Hellenistic (= Greek) kingdoms. To the north of Israel were the **Seleucids**, centered in Syria. The **Ptolemies** were based in Egypt, to the south. In the words of the author of 1 Maccabees, "Alexander ruled for twelve years and then died. His servants seized power, each in his own region. After his death they all put on diadems, and so did their sons after them for many years. They multiplied evils on the earth" (1 Macc 1:7-9).

> Some scholars question the portrait of Antiochus IV in the Maccabean histories. On the one hand, 1 and 2 Maccabees constitute our primary sources for knowledge of the Maccabean revolt. On the other hand, the Jewish authors of 1 and 2 Maccabees cannot reasonably be expected to provide an objective account of the arch-enemy of the Jews. The pro-Maccabean authors may down-play the extent of Jewish collaboration with the Seleucid ruler (alluded to in 1 Macc 1:11) and ignore other motives for the actions of Antiochus.

The greatest of these "evils" was brought on the Jews by the Seleucid ruler Antiochus IV Epiphanes, who became king in 175 B.C.E. In 167 B.C.E., Antiochus IV took steps to eradicate Jewish practices. In addition to desecrating the altar of the Second Temple, Antiochus IV prohibited the celebration of Jewish festivals, forbade sabbath observance and circumcision, and ordered the burning of **Torah** scrolls. These harsh actions set in motion a chain of events that would result in the **Maccabean revolt**. Against all odds, this revolt against Seleucid tyranny succeeded (under the leadership of the Judas Maccabeus mentioned earlier in this chapter), and in 164 B.C.E., the temple was re-dedicated. For the first time in over four hundred years, Jews in Judea were both able to worship in their own temple and free to govern themselves.

The descendants of the leaders of the Maccabean revolt formed the **Hasmonean** dynasty, which ruled Judea until 63 B.C.E. According to Josephus, some even took the title of "king," starting with Aristobulus I in 104–103 B.C.E. However, Hasmonean rule was significantly buoyed by an alliance with another foreign power: Rome. In 63 B.C.E., having been asked to intervene in a succession dispute, the Roman general Pompey arrived in Judea. While Pompey allowed a Hasmonean to retain the high priesthood, Judea was henceforth subject to Rome.

By the time of Jesus, then, Jews who knew their history knew that the "kingdoms" of the Assyrians, Babylonians, Persians, Ptolemies, Seleucids, and Romans had done more than just "come near." Each power had reigned over the Jews. But recent history and prophecy offered hope. After all, some of John the Baptist and Jesus' first hearers would have had parents and grandparents who lived under Hasmonean rule. Many Jews—such as the author of 1 Maccabees—saw the Hasmonean rulers as divinely appointed bearers of the kingship. Furthermore, there were ancient promises, like that found in the book of Daniel: "These four great beasts are four kings who will arise from the earth. But the holy ones of the Most High will receive the kingdom forever" (Dan 7:17-18). Such promises encouraged hope that the reigns of foreign kings would be succeeded by the reign of God.

Jesus' first hearers may have harbored hopes that Jesus would fulfill the words of Daniel the prophet: "In the days of those kings, the God of heaven will set up a kingdom that will never be destroyed, nor will his kingdom be given over to another people; it will shatter and destroy all these kingdoms, and it will endure forever" (Dan 2:44). The New Testament itself bears

Figure 2.3 Tenth Legion inscription at Abu Ghosh
Found at present-day Abu Ghosh (about nine miles west of Jerusalem), the inscription (VEXILLATIO LEG X FRE) signals the presence of the Tenth Legion, which played a major role in quelling the first Jewish revolt against Rome.

witness to this same hope. The book of Revelation describes a seventh trumpet blast that signals a heavenly announcement: "The kingdom (*basileia*) of the world has become [the kingdom] of our Lord and of his Messiah, and he will reign as king forever and ever!" (Rev 11:15). Was Jesus this **messiah-king**? And would his reign include military and political sovereignty? According to Luke, Jesus' **disciples** had hopes that the resurrected Jesus would immediately grant royal authority to the people of God: "Then, when they had come together, they asked him, 'Lord, now are you going to restore the kingship (*basileia*) to Israel?'" (Acts 1:6). If this question signaled a desire for immediate military or political sovereignty, then the answer was sure to disappoint.

According to the New Testament writings, Jesus does not rise from the dead in order to lead a revolution against Rome. In fact, the Maccabean revolt was the last successful military campaign waged by Jews for over two millennia. The armed Jewish revolt against Rome in 66 – 70 C.E. led to military defeat, the overthrow of Jerusalem, and the destruction of the Second Temple. And a second Jewish revolt (led by Shimon ben Kosiba, also known as "Bar Kokhba") in 132 – 135 C.E. was even more catastrophic, resulting in the deaths of thousands of Jews and the banishment of all Jews from Jerusalem.

Our ancient sources give conflicting accounts of the origins of the Bar Kokhba revolt. The rebellion may have originated as a reaction to two unpopular moves by Emperor Hadrian, who allegedly banned circumcision and renamed Jerusalem as the pagan city *Aelia Capitolina*. Either move would be sure to trigger widespread dissension.

Jesus, the kingdom, and the good news

So what does Jesus mean by his announcement of the imminence of the kingdom of God? According to some, this proclamation was just the wishful thinking of a failed prophet. According to others, the proximity of God's kingdom signaled the proximity of God's chosen king: Jesus, son of David (see Matt 1:1; 1:20; Mark 10:47; Luke 1:32; etc., as well as Chapter Six of the present volume). This message and this messenger could certainly prove perplexing, for a "kingdom" would typically require military might, and no "king" would be wandering through the villages of Galilee. A Greek papyrus from around the second century C.E. sums up one ancient view of kings and gods:

> What is a god? That which is strong.
> What is a king? One who is equal to a god.
>
> (Heidelberg Papyrus Collection, Inv. 1716 Verso)

This papyrus claims that gods and kings are defined by strength. Jesus' followers found themselves following a different sort of king. We have seen that the "kingdom of God" can mean a number of things: God's royal power, God's rule over a specific area, God's eschatological conquest over the kingdoms of the world, or even God's sending of someone who shares in divine kingship. These options are not mutually exclusive, but they all imply both divinity and power. Here, too, Jesus confuses. The words of Paul's letter to the Philippians describe Jesus as one "who, being in the form of God, did not consider being equal to God something to be grasped, but emptied himself, taking the form of a slave" (Phil 2:6-7). This rhetoric of self-emptying runs against the grain of Greco-Roman culture and its desire to gain honor and avoid shame.

So what exactly is the kingdom of God? Why is its coming identified as good news? And who is Jesus, the one announcing this coming kingdom? These were first-century puzzles, and they still challenge twenty-first-century minds. In a controversial passage in Mark, Jesus utters hard words that shed indirect light on our questions:

> Truly, I tell you that there is no one who has left house or brothers or sisters or mother or father or children or fields for my sake and for the sake of the good news (*euangelion*), who will not receive one hundredfold now in this time . . . and in the age to come, eternal life.
>
> (Mark 10:29)

Jesus here encourages his followers by telling them that their sacrifices will be rewarded, both with eternal life and this-worldly blessing. The "one hundredfold now" promise likely refers to the blessings of life in the family of God; note how Jesus' followers call each other "brother" and "sister" and share possessions (including "fields" in Acts 4:34-37). More importantly, observe that the sake of Jesus and the sake of the good news are in parallel— might they be the same thing? Is Jesus' arrival the good news? According to Matt 4:23, Jesus goes about "preaching the good news (*euangelion*) of the kingdom (*basileia*)." Is the good news that *Jesus* has come (Mark 10:29) or that the *kingdom* is near (Matt 4:23)? Or is the kingdom of God more bound up with the person and presence of Jesus than one might have thought?

Yes, according to the Gospel of Luke. Luke offers at least four perspectives on the kingdom of God: kingdom as royal authority, kingdom as geographic domain, kingdom as eschatological event (similar to the *Testament of Moses*, quoted above), and kingdom as personified in Jesus. In Luke 1, the angel Gabriel speaks to Mary as follows:

> And behold, you will conceive in your womb and will bear a son, and you will name him Jesus. He will be great and will be called Son of the Most High. The Lord will give him the throne of his father David, and he will reign over the house of Jacob forever. And of his kingdom (*basileia*) there will be no end.
>
> (Luke 1:31-33)

Here, Jesus is king, and his royal authority will endure for all time. Soon, though, we see the kingdom on the move. Jesus will not stay put to please the adoring crowds: "I must also preach the good news of the kingdom (*basileia*) of God to the other towns, because I was sent to do this!" (Luke 4:43). Jesus continues to spread the good news of the kingdom in Luke 8:1, and he sends more envoys out to herald the message in 9:1-5 (the twelve are sent) and in 10:1-11 (seventy more are sent). In the course of this geographic expansion, Jesus also teaches that people from all four corners of the earth will join Abraham, Isaac, Jacob, and the prophets at an eschatological banquet: "And they will come from the east and west, and from the north and south, and they will sit down to eat in the kingdom of God" (Luke 13:29; see also 14:15). The kingdom of God in Luke's Gospel appears as royal authority, as geographic expanse, and as eschatological promise.

As its eschatological character suggests, the kingdom of God is not yet fully present. Jesus warns against this assumption in Luke 17:20-21, noting that the kingdom's advance cannot be observed. Nevertheless, Jesus adds, "the kingdom of God is in your midst" (17:21). If the kingdom resides in the person of Jesus, this cryptic statement begins to make sense. In the final verse of Luke's second volume, we find additional evidence supporting the kingdom-as-Jesus interpretation. At the end of Acts, Paul seems to preach two things, but perhaps they are one and the same. Paul spends two years "proclaiming the kingdom of God and teaching about the Lord Jesus Christ, with all boldness, unrestrained" (Acts 28:31). Perhaps we need to ask a different set of questions: *What* is the kingdom of God in the New Testament? Royal authority, granted to Jesus and passed on to his followers (Luke 12:32; 22:28-30). *Where* is the kingdom of

God? Spread throughout Jerusalem, Judea and Samaria, and the ends of the earth (Acts 1:8), and "in your midst" (Luke 17:21). *When* is the kingdom of God? Inaugurated within human history, but only fulfilled at the **eschaton** (Luke 13:28-29). *Who* is the kingdom of God? Jesus, "Son of the Most High" (Luke 1:32) and "Son of David" (Luke 18:38-39). For more detail on how royal authority passes from divine father to divine son, we must look to Rome.

Summary timeline

722/721 B.C.E.	Assyrians conquer ten northern tribes of Israel
587/586 B.C.E.	King Nebuchadnezzar destroys Solomon's temple and carries two southern tribes of Judah to Babylon
539 B.C.E.	Cyrus II conquers Babylon (and in 538 permits Jews to return)
515 B.C.E.	Second Temple is dedicated in Jerusalem (under Persian rule)
332 B.C.E.	Alexander of Macedon conquers Palestine
167 B.C.E.	(Seleucid) King Antiochus IV Epiphanes desecrates Second Temple, triggering Maccabean revolt against Seleucids
164 B.C.E.	Second Temple re-dedicated
63 B.C.E.	Pompey the Great establishes Roman sovereignty (end of Hasmonean dynasty)
ca. 5 B.C.E.	Jesus born
ca. 30 C.E.	Jesus executed
50s – early 60s C.E.	Paul writes letters
66 – 70 C.E.	First Jewish revolt against Rome
70 C.E.	Destruction of Second Temple by Roman forces
132 – 135 C.E.	Second Jewish revolt (also known as the Bar Kokhba revolt)

Bibliography and suggestions for further reading

John J. Collins and Daniel C. Harlow, eds. *The Eerdmans Dictionary of Early Judaism*. Grand Rapids: Eerdmans, 2010. (This valuable resource includes a thorough essay on "Jewish History from Alexander to Hadrian" by Chris

Seeman and Adam Kolman Marshak, as well as a useful entry on "Kingdom of God" by Dale C. Allison, Jr.)

1-2 Maccabees. (These two books offer primary source accounts of the Maccabean revolt and the Hasmonean dynasty.)

Jonathan T. Pennington. *Heaven and Earth in the Gospel of Matthew*. Leiden: Brill, 2007. (This book demonstrates the weakness of the "circumlocution hypothesis"—that is, Pennington shows that Matthew's repeated use of "kingdom of heaven" is not simply an attempt to avoid using the divine name. He instead links the Matthean emphasis on "kingdom of heaven" to the book of Daniel, esp. Dan 2-7. He also comments helpfully on Matthew's use of the theme of heaven and earth.)

Wendell Willis, ed. *The Kingdom of God in 20th-Century Interpretation*. Peabody: Hendrickson, 1987. (See especially the essay by John J. Collins on "The Kingdom of God in the Apocrypha.")

3

When in Rome . . .

Guiding Questions

Which two "**gospels**" were circulating in the first-century Mediterranean world, and how do they compare?

What does it mean to be "son of god" in the Roman world?

How did various first-century Romans view the followers of Jesus?

How did various first-century followers of Jesus view the Roman empire?

And you, who were once estranged and were enemies in your minds in your wicked deeds, he has now reconciled in his body of flesh through death, so as to present you holy and blameless and beyond reproach before him, if indeed you persevere in the faith, established and firm, not shifting away from the hope of the gospel (*euangelion*) that you heard, which has been proclaimed in all creation under heaven, and of which I, Paul, became an agent (*diakonos*).

(Col 1:21-23)

Talking the talk

The New Testament sometimes seems like it was written not in Greek but in Christian-ese. Our English translations use all manner of churchy words like "gospel" and "savior" and "hope" and other religious language. The perception that these words are "churchy" or "religious" is one result of the deep influence of Christianity on Western culture. The influence of **Christians** runs so deep that we can forget the very humble beginnings of this movement, which started off as a very small group in a very big Roman empire. And this empire was using these words well before Christians did. For example, part of a famous inscription at Priene, dated to 9 B.C.E., reads as follows:

> Because Providence, which has arranged all aspects of our lives, lavishing attention and distinction on us, has set up the most perfect order for life by bringing forth Augustus, whom she filled with excellence for the benefit of humanity, having sent him—both for us and for those who will come after us—as a savior (*sōtēr*) who will cause war to cease and will order all things; and because Caesar [Augustus], by his appearance, [surpassed] the hopes (*elpis*) of those who received in past days, not only surpassing those who were benefactors before him, but not even leaving any hope (*elpis*) of surpassing him among those who are to come; and because the birthday of the god (*theos*) marked the beginning of good news (*euangelion* in plural) through him [. . .]
>
> (*OGIS* 458, lines 32-42)

Priene was a city in western Asia Minor, and this inscription was set up voluntarily by local subjects of Caesar Augustus, who ruled as emperor from 27 B.C.E. until his death in 14 C.E. (see Luke 2:1). Before Jesus was born, before the New Testament was written, and before anyone claimed to be a "Christian," the supporters of Augustus at Priene claimed that the emperor—here labeled as a "god"—was sent as a "savior" whose birth was "the beginning of the good news (= gospel) for the world."

Long before the Priene inscription, the title "savior" (*sōtēr*) was applied to rulers in the eastern Mediterranean world—both **Ptolemies** and **Seleucids**. Josephus identifies Ptolemy I (367/366 – 282 B.C.E.) as "Ptolemy the Savior" (*Jewish Antiquities* 12.11), and he also notes that Seleucus I (ca. 358 – 281 B.C.E.) was called "the Savior" (*Jewish Antiquities* 12.223). Even though "*sōtēr*" could be applied to the god Zeus, the title itself did not imply divinity. "Savior" was a functional title; a "savior" saved people from danger.

With this context in mind, the New Testament writings suddenly have a broader range of possible meanings. For instance, when Mark begins his Gospel by writing "Beginning of the good news (*euangelion*) of Jesus Christ [the Son of God]" (Mark 1:1), what is he saying? He could simply be beginning his narrative of the coming of Jesus **Christ**, which he evidently considers to be news worth sharing. Or, he might be borrowing his "good news" language from Isaiah—the prophet speaks of being "anointed to bring good news" in Isa 61:1. Or, Mark could be starting his story with a controversial claim that Jesus—*not* the Roman emperor—is the one who brings good news. This latter way of reading Mark 1:1 cannot be set aside lightly. The idea of the emperor as savior and bringer of good news was not restricted to one chiseled rock in Asia Minor. In his *Jewish War*, Josephus describes a very similar message several decades later:

> The people, freed at length from terrors, acclaimed Vespasian emperor, and celebrated with one common festival both his establishment in power and the overthrow of Vitellius. On reaching Alexandria Vespasian was greeted by the good news (*euangelion* in the plural) from Rome and by embassies of congratulation from every quarter of the world, now his own; and that city, though second only to Rome in magnitude, proved too confined for the throng. The whole empire being now secured and the Roman state saved (*sesōsmenon*, from the same root as *sōtēr*) beyond expectation, Vespasian turned his thoughts to what remained in Judaea.
> (Josephus, *Jewish War* 4.655-657; *LCL* translation [H. Thackeray])

Clearly, in the second half of the first century C.E., the language of salvation and good news was not confined to the **church**—although calling it "religious" language does not stray far from the mark.

Of gods and mortals

Roman emperors, after all, were no mere mortals. It started with the first emperor, Gaius Julius Caesar (100 – 44 B.C.E.), who was recognized by some as a deified being during his lifetime. (Ironically, these divine honors may have spurred on the successful plot to assassinate him.) The historian L. Cassius Dio (ca. 164 C.E. – after 229 C.E.) gives a detailed description of honors granted Julius Caesar, culminating with a bold conjunction of Caesar and Jupiter: "And finally they addressed him outright as Jupiter Julius and ordered a temple to be consecrated to him and to his Clemency" (44.6.4; *LCL* translation [E. Cary]). "Jupiter Julius"—*Iupiter* was the Latin equivalent of the Greek *Zeus*, ruler of the gods.

After Caesar's death, his divinization gained popularity. According to Pliny the Elder (23/24 C.E. – 79 C.E.), Julius Caesar was considered divine by the time of his successor, Caesar Augustus (63 B.C.E. – 14 C.E.). Pliny puts the following soliloquy into the mouth of Caesar Augustus:

> On the very days of my Games a comet was visible for seven days in the northern part of the sky. It was rising about an hour before sunset, and was a bright star, visible from all lands. The common people believed that this star signified the soul of Caesar received among the spirits of the immortal gods, and on this account the emblem of a star was added to the bust of Caesar that we shortly afterwards dedicated in the forum.
>
> (Pliny the Elder, *Natural History* 2.23.94; *LCL* translation [H. Rackham])

Whether or not the comet proved persuasive, the deceased Caesar could not rely on populist approval alone. Deification required a stronger consensus. The Roman historian Suetonius (ca. 70 C.E. – ca. 130 C.E.), writing in the early second century, confirmed that Julius Caesar was found worthy of divinity by all parties: "He died in his fifty-sixth year, and he was added to the number of the gods, not only by a formal resolution, but also in the conviction of the common people" (Suetonius, *Divus Julius* 88.1).

In the eastern Roman empire, Greek-speaking subjects sometimes referred to the emperor as a "god" (*theos* in Greek). There was a long history of divinized rulers in the East, so this usage was uncontroversial. In the western Roman empire, it was less common to refer to a living emperor as "god" (*deus* in Latin). There were exceptions: Gaius Caligula tried to persuade the **Jews** to call him "god" (*theos* in Josephus, *Jewish Antiquities* 19.284), and Domitian appears to have been called a "god" (*deus*) by some. More commonly, an emperor would be declared "divine" (*divus* in Latin) after his death. In the first century B.C.E., it would have been hard to distinguish between *divus* and *deus*; the esteemed Latin grammarian Varro argued that *divus* was a more honorable word than *deus*—even if later Latin-speakers came to believe the exact opposite.

The idea of worshiping a living human being did not sit well with some Romans. Thus, deification generally followed the emperor's death—even if many of their subjects were already offering worship to them as gods during their lifetimes. Thus, while Augustus was willing to take on the title *divi filius* ("son of a god"), he was not declared to be deified (*divus*) until after his death in 14 C.E. At that time, he was succeeded as emperor by his step-son Tiberius. Suetonius describes the funeral of Caesar Augustus:

> But though a limit was set to the honors paid him, his eulogy was twice delivered: before the temple of the Deified (*divus*) Julius by Tiberius, and from the old rostra by Drusus, son of Tiberius; and he was carried on the shoulders of senators to the Campus Martius and there cremated. There was even an ex-praetor who took oath that he had seen the form of the Emperor, after he had been reduced to ashes, on its way to heaven. His remains were gathered up by the leading men of the equestrian order.
>
> (Suetonius, *Divus Augustus* 100.3-4; *LCL*
> translation [J. C. Rolfe])

Even though Caesar Augustus was obviously dead—his corpse, after all, was there to be picked up by the equestrians attending his funeral!—he was still considered to be in the company of the gods as a *divus*. An ex-praetor's oath was required as evidence to prove that Augustus really did ascend to **heaven**.

This mode of heavenly ascent and divinization is not as impressive as some others. For example, Dionysius of Halicarnassus, a Greek historian writing in the late first century B.C.E. and early first century C.E., describes how Romulus, the founder of Rome, ascended to heaven: "While he was addressing the camp, darkness fell from a clear sky and a great storm broke out, and [Romulus] disappeared" (*Roman Antiquities* 2.56.2). Yet Romulus later returned. The later Latin historian Livy (59 B.C.E. – 17 C.E.) narrates the experience of Proculus Julius, a Roman nobleman who claimed to have encountered Romulus after the founder's death. According to Livy, Proculus Julius addressed the Roman people as follows:

> Romulus, the father of our city, descended from heaven at dawn this morning and appeared to me. In awe and reverence I stood before him, praying for permission to look upon him face to face. "Go," he said, "and tell the Romans that by heaven's will my Rome shall be capital of the world. Let them learn to be soldiers. Let them know, and teach their children, that no power on earth can stand against Roman arms." Having spoken these words, he was taken up again into heaven.
>
> (*Ab urbe condita* 1.16; A. de Sélincourt translation
> [Penguin, 1960], modified)

According to these historians, Romulus did not die like Caesar Augustus. Instead, the founder of Rome was carried up to heaven, whence he returned to give instructions to his followers.

Another precursor to the emperors' ascents to heaven was the Greek hero Heracles (*Hercules* in Latin). According to the first-century B.C.E. Greek historian Diodorus Siculus, Heracles also ascended into the company of the gods (*Library of History* 4.38.5). The Latin poet Ovid also wrote that Heracles was taken up into heaven (*Metamorphoses* 9.268-272). Heracles' heavenly ascent is unique, for the hero was said to be the child of a human mother (Alcmene) and a god (Zeus). His mixed parentage separates him from others who ascended to heaven; his ascent to heaven sets him apart from others of half-human, half-divine descent.

These narratives of ascent to heaven are not restricted to Greeks and Romans. The righteous man Enoch seems to disappear in Genesis 5:24. The prophet Elijah is described as ascending directly to heaven in 2 Kings 2:1-14. Josephus, too, explains how Moses was taken straight to heaven:

> As he [Moses] was embracing Eleazar and Joshua, and while he was still speaking with them, a cloud suddenly stood over him, and he disappeared in a certain ravine. But he wrote in the holy books that he died, for he was afraid that they might venture to say that, on account of his surpassing virtue, he returned to the Divine itself.
>
> (Josephus, *Jewish Antiquities* 4.326)

Enoch, Moses, and Elijah are described as righteous followers of God, and their reward is a painless passage from this life into the presence of God. But none of them are described as gods.

The followers of Jesus had their own story about an individual ascending to heaven (see Luke 24 and Acts 1). The narratives of Jesus' death, **resurrection**, and ascension would read differently for first-century readers, depending on their background. For a Jewish reader, Jesus' resurrection alone would not imply his divinity; the Old and New Testament both describe multiple instances of mortals returning from death to life (e.g., 1 Kgs 17:22; John 11:43-44; Acts 20:9-10; etc.). Likewise, ascent to heaven would merely signal divine blessing, not deification (as in the cases of Enoch and Elijah). For a (non-Jewish) Roman reader, resurrection and ascension would certainly put Jesus in a select group—with Romulus, Heracles, Augustus, and other heroic figures. However, later emperors were typically declared *divus* ("divine" or "deified") by a vote of the Roman Senate after their death. Jesus received no such vote.

Jesus received no vote from a Roman Senate, but he is presented as the "son of God" (*uios theou* in Greek) in the New Testament. Thus, a Roman reader could suppose that Jesus is *divi filius* ("son of a god") just as Caesar Augustus was *divi filius*. For Augustus, being *divi filius* meant that he was both the legitimate heir to Julius Caesar and a divine figure. If read along these lines, Jesus' identity as "son of God" would affirm Jesus' divinity, his legitimacy, and his favor in the eyes of his divine father.

What led some first-century Jews and **gentiles** to believe that Jesus was divine was not solely the impression that he rose from the dead or ascended to heaven. Instead, what moved them was the perception that the seemingly outrageous claims made by this Galilean prophet appeared to be vindicated by the God who alone has power over life and death. As the New Testament authors declare time and again, "God raised him from the dead" (Acts 13:30; see also Matt 28:7; Mark 16:6; Luke 9:22; John 21:14; Acts 2:24, 32; 3:15; Rom 4:24; etc.). This belief that Jesus was raised by God from the dead and "exalted to the right hand of God" led early followers of Jesus to reflect on their experiences and their **scriptures** (Acts 2:33; 5:31).

This process of reflection on scripture is already at work in the earliest New Testament writings (e.g., 1 Cor 15:1-8), and these earliest texts display a very high view of the Galilean prophet named Jesus (see Phil 2:5-11). These sorts of theological developments are the sort of thing that might have led a first-century Jew (like "doubting" Thomas) to cry out to the resurrected Jesus, "My Lord and my God!" (John 20:28). It is terribly interesting to consider that Domitian, Roman emperor from 81 to 96 C.E., was being addressed as *dominus et deus* ("lord and god") around the same time that John may have been writing his Gospel. Scholars have debated whether early Christians consciously set Jesus in opposition to the Roman emperor. Whether they did or not, it is clear that at least two (rival) gospels were circulating in the first-century Mediterranean world. One, carved into stones and published empire-wide, proclaimed Caesar to be, in the words of the Priene inscription, the "savior" whose birth was "the beginning of good news" for the world. The other, written on scrolls and in books, proclaimed that the good news was instead the birth of "a savior who is Christ the Lord" (Luke 2:11).

Romans and Christians

Thus far, we have explored how perceptions of Jesus might have compared to perceptions of divinized emperors. Now, we turn to how outsiders' perceptions of Christians might have influenced interactions between imperial authorities and the early followers of Jesus. The evidence from contemporary non-Christian writings suggests that Christians did not receive a warm welcome. Even the name "Christian"—which appears only three times in the New Testament (Acts 11:26; 26:28; 1 Pet 4:16)—reveals a potentially hostile context. True, the author of Acts informs us that the "**disciples**" of Jesus were first called "Christians" in Antioch (Acts 11:26). The name appears to be harmless enough. But *Christianoi* may first have been a more derisive label for this new group; instead of translating "Christians," perhaps "little Christ-ies" would better capture the flavor of the term. The only place that "Christian" appears in the New Testament outside of Acts is in 1 Pet 4:16, in the middle of a discussion of suffering. Someone who suffers as a murderer may be ashamed, the writer argues, but "if someone [suffers] as a Christian, let them not be ashamed, but glorify God" (1 Pet 4:16).

Is there any evidence of Christians suffering? In a word, yes. While there is little evidence of an empire-wide campaign to stamp out Christianity, we do find evidence that the followers of Jesus lived under imperial suspicion. Still, due to their small numbers, they did not pose a large threat. Mostly, they remained unknown to the authorities. Suetonius suggests that some Romans may have had a hard time sorting out Jesus' followers from other Jews: "Since the Jews constantly made disturbances at the instigation of Chrestus, he expelled them from Rome" (Suetonius, *Divus Claudius*, 25.4; *LCL* translation [J. C. Rolfe]). Many scholars agree that *Chrestus* is most likely a misspelling of *Christus*, the Latin word for Christ. Interestingly, Emperor Claudius (10 B.C.E. – 54 C.E.) and his supporters may have been both unable to spell *Christus* properly and hard-pressed to weed out the *Christus*-followers from the larger Jewish population of the city. They had the same **Bible** after all—Roman Christians would have likely used a Greek translation of the Jewish scriptures—and they shared many customs and ethical positions. Still, Claudius was happy to dispose of them all (see Acts 18:1-2 for a probable reference to this same event, which took place in the 40s C.E.).

Subsequent emperors varied in their approach towards Christians. The historian Tacitus (56 C.E. – after 118 C.E.) tells us how Nero, who was suspected of causing a destructive fire in Rome, tried to deflect blame onto the Christians:

To suppress this rumor, Nero fabricated scapegoats – and punished with every refinement the notoriously depraved Christians (as they were popularly called). Their originator, Christ, had been executed in Tiberius' reign by the governor of Judaea, Pontius Pilatus. But in spite of this temporary setback, the deadly superstition had broken out afresh, not only in Judaea (where the mischief had started) but even in Rome. All degraded and shameful practices collect and flourish in the capital.

(Tacitus, *Annals* 15.44; M. Grant translation [Penguin, 1989], modified)

The historian Tacitus is evidently no Christian apologist. Thus, his account of the execution of "Christ" provides one of the strongest pieces of *historical* evidence for the **crucifixion** of Jesus by Pontius Pilate. His history both relates Nero's persecution of the followers of "Christ" and reveals the historian's own bias against these "notoriously depraved" individuals.

The historian's bias pales in comparison with Nero's cruelty. Tacitus continues his account, recording the fate of the Christians as follows:

First, Nero had self-acknowledged Christians arrested. Then, on their information, large numbers of others were condemned—not so much for arson as for their anti-social tendencies. Their deaths were made into a mockery. Dressed in wild animals' skins, they were torn to pieces by dogs, or crucified, or made into torches to be ignited after dark as substitutes for daylight. Nero provided his gardens for the spectacle ...

Despite their guilt as Christians, and the ruthless punishment it deserved, the victims were pitied. For it was felt that they were being sacrificed to one man's brutality rather than to the national interest.

(Tacitus, *Annals* 15.44; M. Grant translation [Penguin, 1989], modified)

Although Tacitus seems to approve of capital punishment for the offense of being a Christian, he cannot condone the emperor's wanton and inhumane treatment of the Christians. In the end, neither Tacitus nor Nero shows any interest in the practices of this group. Nero is in the market for a convenient scapegoat; the "anti-social" Christians fit the bill. And Tacitus recounts this incident to mark (and condemn) yet another example of Nero's extravagant violence.

For a more nuanced description of Christians from an elite Roman perspective, we can look at the correspondence between Pliny the Younger (ca. 61 C.E. – ca. 112 C.E.) and Emperor Trajan (53 C.E. – 117 C.E.). Pliny was the governor of Bithynia-Pontus from approximately 110 C.E. to 112 C.E., and during his time in office, he encountered a peculiar group of people known as *Christiani* (Latin *Christiani* = Greek *Christianoi*). The existence of a group that met in private concerned Pliny, as his correspondence reveals. For example, we have a letter from Pliny that notifies the emperor of a major, destructive fire in the city of Nicomedia. Pliny writes seeking permission to establish a guild or association (*collegium*) of firefighters (Pliny, *Letters* 10.33). The emperor responds by denying the governor's request. Though Trajan acknowledges the validity of the idea, he warns Pliny of the dangers of such associations: "Whatever title we give them, and whatever our object in giving it, men who are banded together for a common end will all the same become political associations (*hetaeriae*) before long" (Pliny, *Letters* 10.34; *LCL* translation [W. Melmoth and W. M. L. Hutchinson], modified). Trajan had no interest whatsoever in encouraging independent political associations; freedom of speech and freedom to assemble were not high priorities on the imperial agenda.

> In *Jewish Antiquities* 14.215-216, Josephus claims that Julius Caesar—more than a hundred years before Trajan—forbade other cultic gatherings (*thiasoi*), yet granted a special exception to the Jews to meet together, eat together, and collect funds. The Jews were renowned for their antiquity and—as Josephus makes clear—for their political engagement with local authorities, and they thus had access to privileges that the upstart *Christiani* did not.

If the emperor is not willing to support even an association of firefighters, surely he will be even more suspicious about a relatively unknown group that meets outside of the public eye. Aware of Trajan's misgivings, Pliny brought his concerns before the emperor. I reproduce the letter here in its entirety:

It is a rule, my lord, which I inviolably observe, to refer myself to you in all my doubts; for who is more capable of guiding my uncertainty or informing my ignorance? Having never been present at any trials of the Christians, I am unacquainted with the method and limits to be observed either in examining or punishing them. Whether any difference is to be made on account of age, or no distinction allowed between the youngest and the adult; whether repentance admits to a pardon, or if a man has been once a Christian it avails him nothing to recant; whether the mere profession of Christianity, albeit without crimes, or only the crimes associated therewith are punishable—in all these points I am greatly doubtful.

In the meanwhile, the method I have observed towards those who have been denounced to me as Christians is this: I asked them whether they were "Christians." If they confessed it I repeated the question twice again, adding the threat of capital punishment; if they still persevered, I ordered them to be executed. For whatever the nature of their creed might be, I could at least feel no doubt that stubbornness and inflexible obstinacy deserved punishment. There were others also possessed with the same infatuation, but being citizens of Rome, I directed them to be sent to that city.

These accusations spread (as is usually the case) from the mere fact of the matter being investigated. Several forms of the mischief came to light. A placard was put up, without any signature, accusing a large number of persons by name. Those who denied they were, or had ever been, Christians, who repeated after me an invocation to the gods, and offered worship, with wine and incense, to your image, which I had ordered to be brought for that purpose, together with those of the gods, and who finally cursed Christ—none of which acts, it is said, those who are really Christians can be forced into performing—these I thought it proper to release. Others who were named by that informer at first confessed themselves Christians, and then denied it; true, they had been of that persuasion but they had quit—some three years ago, others several years ago, and a few as long as twenty-five years ago. They all worshipped your statue and the images of the gods, and they cursed Christ.

They affirmed, however, that the whole of their guilt, or their error, was this: they were in the habit of meeting on a certain fixed day before it was light, when they sang in alternate verses a hymn to Christ, as to a god, and bound themselves by solemn oath (*sacramentum*), not to any wicked deeds, but never to commit any fraud, theft, or adultery, never to falsify their word, nor to refuse to return a deposit when asked for its return; after which it was their custom to separate, and then re-assemble to partake of food—but food of an ordinary and innocent kind. Even this practice, however, they had abandoned after the publication of my edict, by which, according to your orders, I had forbidden political associations (*hetaeriae*). Therefore, I judged it even more necessary to extract the real truth, with the assistance of torture, from two female slaves who were called "deaconesses" (*ministrae*). But I could discover nothing more than depraved and excessive superstition (*superstitio*).

I therefore adjourned the proceedings, and hastened to your counsel. For the matter seemed to me well worth referring to you—especially considering the numbers endangered. Persons of all ranks and ages, and of both sexes are, and will be, involved in the prosecution. For this contagious superstition (*superstitio*) is not confined to the cities only, but has spread through the villages and rural districts. It seems possible, however, to check and cure it. It is certain at least that the temples, which had been almost deserted, begin now to be frequented, and the sacred festivals, after a long intermission, are again revived—while there is a general demand for sacrificial animals, which for some time now have met with very few purchasers. From this point on, it is easy to imagine what multitudes may be reclaimed from this error, if there is opportunity for repentance.

(Pliny, *Letters* 10.96; *LCL* translation [W. Melmoth and W. M. L. Hutchinson], modified)

In this letter, Pliny outlines his methods for dealing with ex-Christians and faithful Christians, offers his outsider's view of the practices and beliefs of Christians, and announces his hope that these Christians might show remorse for their "superstition." This letter reveals much about the early second-century Christian communities in Asia Minor, including the wide range in age and status among Christians. It also reveals that the Christians were not always welcomed by imperial authorities.

Is what Pliny describes a "religious persecution"? Yes, and no. On one hand, Christians are certainly suffering for what we would call their "religion"—but what Pliny dismisses as "superstition." On the other hand, Pliny shows only a passing interest in the Christians' theological beliefs; he is much more concerned with maintaining law and order. Torturing a slave to extract reliable information is part of normal judicial procedure; it is not a special punishment for "religious" minorities. Pliny outlawed political associations. This group is continuing to meet in violation of the law of the land. While these Christians may be no more harmful than firefighters, Pliny is determined to stamp out any possible opportunity for conspiracy to take root. The emperor approves of Pliny's actions; below is the imperial reply:

The method you have pursued, my dear Pliny, in sifting the cases of those denounced to you as Christians is extremely proper. It is not possible to lay down any general rule which can be applied as the fixed standard in all cases of this nature. No search should be made for these people; when they are denounced and found guilty they must be punished; with the restriction, however, that when they deny being a Christian, and shall give proof that they are not (that is, by worshipping our gods), they shall be pardoned on the basis of repentance, even though they may have formerly incurred suspicion. Information without the accuser's name should not be admitted as evidence against anyone, as it is introducing a very dangerous precedent, and by no means agreeable to the spirit of the age.

(Pliny, *Letters* 10.97; *LCL* translation [W. Melmoth and W. M. L. Hutchinson], modified)

Again, we see that Christians are being executed, but Trajan is by no means announcing a witch hunt. Rather, Pliny and Trajan are interested in maintaining proper procedures and minimizing threats to the empire.

Two centuries later, under the Christian emperor Constantine, Christians will find themselves in a very different relationship vis-à-vis Rome. But in the early years, some Christians found themselves at odds with the imperial authorities—even as they used Roman roads, drank water carried by Roman aqueducts, and lived in Rome and other Roman cities. The book of Revelation reveals some of this anti-Roman animus. For instance, Rome was renowned throughout antiquity as the city on "seven hills" (*montes septem*; see Pliny the Elder, *Natural History* 3.66). Revelation 17 describes a "great prostitute" (17:2), who is "drunk from the blood of the holy ones and the blood of the martyrs of Jesus" (17:6; compare Dan 8:24). Who is she? She rides on a beast with seven heads (17:7), and "the seven heads are seven mountains, on which the woman is seated" (17:9). The book of Revelation thus identifies the Christian-killing prostitute with a certain set of seven "mountains," or "hills." Other clues in the book of Revelation confirm that the blood-drunk prostitute is to be identified with Rome.

The New Testament, therefore, offers various portraits of Rome. In Revelation, Rome is depicted as the enemy, in most unflattering terms. This enmity does not sum up early Christian views of Rome, however. Paul, for example, encourages submission to governing authorities (see Rom 13:1-7). According to all three Synoptic Gospels, Jesus famously tells his opponents that they should "give to Caesar that which is Caesar's, and to God that which is God's" (Mark 12:17; compare Matt 22:21 and Luke 20:25). This ambiguous statement can be taken in different ways. Jesus might be seen as affirming the status quo and endorsing submission to Rome. Or, he might offer an implicit critique of an overreaching Caesar's claims—Jesus' followers were not the only first-century Jews who believed that God "made the heaven, the earth, and the sea, and everything in them" (Acts 4:24).

In the ancient Greco-Roman world (as in many other times and places), years were tracked by the reign of emperors, or by the tribunates, or by the list of archons (= rulers) of Athens. The Gregorian calendar currently used by most Western nations follows this tradition, dating the years by the reign of Jesus—A.D. stands for *anno domini* = "in the year of the Lord [Jesus]." (Due to an error in the calculations underlying this calendar—see Chapter Five for details—Jesus was actually born a few years "before Christ," but no one is seriously proposing a re-calibration of the calendars of the Western world.) The Jewish religious calendar, on the other hand, is dated from the creation of the world. So, if it is "the year of the Lord" 2015 for Christians, many Jews will instead identify the date as "the year of the world" 5775.

More often, the empire simply remains in the background. For instance, the empire provides the backdrop in Luke 3:

> In the fifteenth year of the rule of Tiberius Caesar, when Pontius Pilate was ruling over Judea, and Herod was the **tetrarch** of Galilee, and Philip his brother was the tetrarch of Iturea and the region of Trachonitis, and Lysanias was the tetrarch of Abilene, during the high priesthood of Annas and Caiaphas, the word of God came to John son of Zechariah in the desert.
>
> (Luke 3:1-2)

When did John the Baptist receive the word of God? Luke provides the year: the fifteenth year of Emperor Tiberius's reign, which started around 14 C.E. He then adds other contextual details that allow the reader to locate the setting more thoroughly. Having fixed the date of John's ministry, Luke proceeds to tell of the words and deeds of John, a peculiar prophet who preaches good news in an eastern province of the Roman empire.

Nowadays, we commonly refer to "Roman emperors," but the Latin title *imperator* (originally meaning "commander") was not used as an official title with the meaning of "emperor" until it was assumed by Vespasian. Earlier, Caesar Augustus established *princeps* ("leading man") as his preferred title for himself, and it was used by his successors. A more official title was *pater patriae* ("father of the fatherland"). In the New Testament, the emperor is typically referred to as "Caesar" (Greek *kaisar* in Mark 12:14; etc.). Ironically, even though "Caesar" would become a title for the emperor, Julius Caesar was only an *imperator* in the sense of "successful military commander."

Before we begin our investigation of this peculiar prophet in the following chapter, let us summarize our findings. In the world of Jesus and his followers, "good news" about an imperial "savior" arrived years before the Christian **gospel**. Given the popularity of emperor worship in the eastern empire, talking about Jesus as the savior and son of God charted a collision course with the Roman emperor and his supporters. Jesus and his followers rarely spoke out directly against the emperor—Revelation stands out as an exception to the norm. Still, the man who condemned John the Baptist to death was appointed by Caesar Augustus, and a Roman governor crucified Jesus. Another Roman governor, Pliny, has provided us with a fascinating account of how early Christians worshiped. Yet, he also tortured and executed many of these intransigent worshippers, who sang songs of praise not to the emperor, but to Christ, "as to a god."

Roman emperors

[Julius Caesar (Gaius Iulius Caesar, 100 – 44 B.C.E.)]
Augustus (Gaius Iulius Caesar Octavianus, 63 B.C.E. – 14 C.E., reigned ca. 27 B.C.E. – 14 C.E.)
Tiberius (Tiberius Iulius Caesar Augustus, 42 B.C.E. – 37 C.E., reigned 14 – 37 C.E.)
Caligula (Gaius Iulius Caesar Germanicus, 12 C.E. – 41 C.E., reigned 37 – 41 C.E.)
Claudius (Tiberius Claudius Nero Germanicus, 10 B.C.E. – 54 C.E., reigned 41 – 54 C.E.)
Nero (Nero Claudius Caesar, 37 C.E. – 68 C.E., reigned 54 – 68 C.E.)
Galba (Servius Sulpicius Galba, 3 B.C.E. – 69 C.E., reigned 68 – 69 C.E.)
Otho (Marcus Salvius Otho, 32 C.E. – 69 C.E., reigned 69 C.E.)
Vitellius (Aulus Vitellius, 15 C.E. – 69 C.E., reigned 69 C.E.)
Vespasian (Titus Flavius Vespasianus, 9 C.E. – 79 C.E., reigned 69 – 79 C.E.)
Titus (Titus Flavius Vespasianus, 39 C.E. – 81 C.E., reigned 79 – 81 C.E.)
Domitian (Titus Flavius Domitianus, 51 C.E. – 96 C.E., reigned 81 – 96 C.E.)
Nerva (Marcus Cocceius Nerva, ca. 35 C.E. – 98 C.E., reigned 96 – 98 C.E.)
Trajan (Marcus Ulpius Traianus, 53 C.E. – 117 C.E., reigned 98 – 117 C.E.)
Hadrian (Publius Aelius Hadrianus, 76 C.E. – 138 C.E., reigned 117 – 138 C.E.)

Bibliography and suggestions for further reading

Flavius Josephus. The Jewish War. Translated by G. A. Williamson. Revised by E. Mary Smallwood. New York: Penguin, 1981. (Josephus offers an eyewitness account of the first Jewish revolt—and of Jewish beliefs and practices in first-century Palestine.)

Scot McKnight and Joseph B. Modica, eds. *Jesus Is Lord, Caesar Is Not: Evaluating Empire in New Testament Studies*. Downers Grove: InterVarsity, 2013. (This collection of essays evaluates recent scholarship on the Roman empire and the New Testament.)

Michael Peppard. *The Son of God in the Roman World: Divine Sonship in Its Social and Political Context*. Oxford: Oxford University Press, 2011. (Peppard argues that the Nicene description of Jesus as "begotten, not made" has obscured our view of sonship in the time of Jesus. He explores the meaning of sonship in the socio-political context of early Christianity, suggesting that Mark's account of the baptism of Jesus has one set of connotations for Jewish readers, but a very different set of connotations for listeners aware of Roman imperial ideology. See also his helpful discussion of "Emperor Worship: Perspectives Old and New" on pp. 37–44.)

S. R. F. Price. "Gods and Emperors: The Greek Language of the Roman Imperial Cult." *The Journal of Hellenic Studies* 104 (1984): 79–95. (Price guides his readers through the linguistic issues that arise when comparing Latin and Greek descriptions of the imperial cult. His linguistic insights also illuminate our understanding of "gods" in the Greco-Roman world; see Peppard, however, for an updated discussion.)

C. Kavin Rowe. *World Upside Down: Reading Acts in the Graeco-Roman Age*. Oxford: Oxford University Press, 2009. (Rowe argues that Acts portrays the early Christian movement neither as hostile to Rome nor as seeking Roman approval; rather, he argues that the Christian confession of Jesus Christ as Lord requires seeing Caesar as a rival claimant to God's throne.)

Menahem Stern. *Greek and Latin Authors on Jews and Judaism*. 3 vols. Jerusalem: The Israel Academy of Sciences and Humanities, 1976–1984. (Stern has amassed an impressive collection of outsiders' descriptions of Jews and Judaism in antiquity, from the fifth-century B.C.E. historian Herodotus to the sixth-century C.E. philosopher Simplicius.)

N. T. Wright. *The Resurrection of the Son of God*. Minneapolis: Fortress, 2003. (Wright's massive volume provides the most thorough treatment of Jesus' resurrection that I am aware of; he covers both ancient conceptions of "life beyound death" and the subsequent theological significance of the risen Jesus.)

Part II

The Cast of Characters

4

John the Baptist and Other Movers and Shakers

Guiding Questions

Who was John the Baptist?
How did the story of Israel influence the thoughts and actions of **Second Temple** Jews, particularly with regard to the wilderness?

John appeared, baptizing in the desert (*erēmos*) and preaching a baptism of repentance for the forgiveness of sins. All the country of Judea and all the people of Jerusalem went out to him, and they were baptized by him in the Jordan River, confessing their sins. And John was clothed with camel hair and a leather belt around his loins, and he ate locusts and wild honey.

(Mark 1:4-6)

A man named John

Thus Mark introduces the popular prophet, John the Baptist. John lives in the *erēmos*, a Greek word that literally means "desolate or lonely"—it is usually translated as "desert" or "wilderness." John the Baptist thus lives in a strange place, he wears strange clothing, and he eats strange food. He also says strange things: John announces the coming of a "stronger one" (Mark 1:7). And he does strange things: John plunges people into water. Jesus is one of these people (Mark 1:9). Having said his words and done his deeds, John's purpose is fulfilled. Mark has John quickly exit stage left, arrested by Herod: "After John was handed over, Jesus came into Galilee preaching the good news (*euangelion*) of God" (Mark 1:14). In a later flashback, Mark will add more details about John's execution by Herod Antipas (Mark 6:17-29). But John plays no further role in Mark's account of the ministry of Jesus.

> In *Jewish Antiquities* 18.116, Josephus describes John as a man "who was called the Baptist." While John is commonly known as "the Baptist," readers must keep in mind that the Greek word *baptistēs* simply means "one who baptizes." John was not a member of any of the twenty-first-century Protestant denominations that include "Baptist" in the title.

All four canonical **gospels** describe John as an individual who baptizes in the Jordan River and who preaches about a coming figure who will be superior to John—so superior that John considers himself unworthy to handle this figure's dusty sandals (Matt 3:11 // Mark 1:7 // Luke 3:16 // John 1:27). There is full agreement that John is an important forerunner to Jesus, but he is also kept in his place: "Truly, I say to you, among those born of women there has not arisen one greater than John the Baptist; but the one who is least in the kingdom of heaven is greater than him" (Matt 11:11). No worse than the best, and worse than the least? What are we to make of John?

To understand John, it may be helpful to allow a fifth voice to join the canonical chorus. Josephus again sheds light on the New Testament as he analyzes a disastrous defeat of the army of Herod Antipas. We will discuss Herod the Great in the following chapter; this Herod Antipas was son of Herod the Great, and he ruled as **tetrarch** over Galilee and Perea for some forty years after his father's death (see Map 2). It was Herod Antipas, not Herod the Great, who killed John the Baptist. And Josephus believes that this execution had divinely ordained consequences for Herod Antipas:

> Some of the Jews believed that Herod's army was destroyed by God, who was most justly punishing Herod on account of what he had done to John, who was called the Baptist. For Herod killed this man, although he was a good man, who exhorted the Jews—if they were practicing virtue and living in righteousness toward each other and reverence toward God—to come together to baptism. For in this manner, it seemed to him, baptism was acceptable to God, when they used it not as a pardon for certain sins, but rather as a purification of the body, seeing that their soul was already purified by righteousness.

But when others gathered around John—for they were extremely delighted to hear his words—Herod feared that John's powers of human persuasion might lead to a revolt, for these people seemed ready to do whatever John advised. So, Herod thought it much better to seize the initiative and kill John, before he caused a rebellion, rather than to risk a future turn of events that would bring only trouble and regret.

As a result of Herod's suspicions, John was sent as a prisoner to Machaerus, the above-mentioned fortress, where he was killed. But the Jews thought that the destruction of Herod's army was an act of divine vengeance on John's behalf, as God wished to inflict harm on Herod.

(Josephus, Jewish Antiquities 18.116-119)

For Josephus, John the Baptist is only of passing interest. Josephus is much more interested in the failed military campaign of Herod Antipas. Even though Josephus places the death of John in a context different from the New Testament accounts, there is agreement on several points: (1) John baptized many people; (2) John's baptism was in some way linked with right or righteous living; (3) Herod Antipas felt threatened by John; and (4) Herod Antipas killed John.

The main difference between the New Testament and Josephus is in the characterization of John's ministry. For Mark and the other gospel-writers, John is preparing the "way of the Lord" (Jesus) and announcing an imminent "stronger one." His baptism is "for the forgiveness of sins," a sign of true repentance. For Josephus, however, John is simply concerned with water baptism as a sign of righteousness. Baptism is not for sinners, but for saints: "they were practicing virtue and living in righteousness toward each other and reverence toward God" (18.117). This water ritual does not seem terribly threatening. So why would this symbolic action in the middle of the wilderness raise concerns about a possible revolt? Is Herod Antipas simply paranoid, or might he have reason to be concerned?

Wilderness renegades

The Judean wilderness was inhospitable to human settlement, but as a symbolic place, it throbbed with meaning. For first-century **Jews**, the mention of wilderness might conjure up the ancient wilderness wanderings of their forebears (see the second half of the book of Exodus). Wilderness meant isolation and desolation, but it was also the place where God appeared to Israel and gave his **covenant** (Exod 19-24). The wilderness was an untamed place of fierce beasts (Deut 8:15), and yet the wilderness was the place where Israel had experienced intimacy with God (Hos 2:14-23, or 2:16-25 in some versions).

> When we think of "desert" or "wilderness," our mental images are often composed of miles of sand, dunes, and rock. But the "wilderness" of Judea is not a vast desert of sand. The **Hebrew** word *midbar* can be translated as "wilderness" or as "pastureland." Thus, it is a place that is too barren to sustain long-term human settlement, yet that can support nomadic peoples and herds.

As a place associated with divine action and deliverance, the wilderness was also fertile ground for subversive movements. According to 1 Maccabees, the **Maccabean revolt** began with a flight to the wilderness. Here is how it happened. An officer of King Antiochus IV arrived in the town of Modein, with orders to make the Jewish residents offer pagan **sacrifice**. Mattathias, a leading citizen, refused to sacrifice. When another Jew did offer sacrifice, Mattathias killed both the Jew and the officer. The revolt had begun:

> Mattathias cried out in the town with a loud voice, saying: "Let everyone who is zealous for the law and who supports the covenant come out after me!" And he and his sons fled to the hills and abandoned all they had in the town. Then, many who were seeking righteousness and justice went down to the wilderness to dwell there—they, their children, their wives, and their animals, for they were hard-pressed by evils. It was announced to the king's men and to the forces in Jerusalem, the city of David, that the men who rejected the king's command had gone down to the hiding places in the wilderness.
>
> (1 Macc 2:27-31)

As the revolt progresses, the Maccabean forces repeatedly withdraw to the wilderness to organize and regroup (see 1 Macc 5:24-25; 9:33, 62). The king's forces are centered in cities; the rebels concentrate their forces in the wilderness.

Josephus also describes how other rebel groups rallied their forces in the wilderness:

> Deceivers and cheats, who employed divine inspiration as a pretext for their incitement of revolutionary changes, persuaded the multitude to madness and led them into the desert, as if God would there show them the signs of liberation. Felix considered these things to be the groundwork for a rebellion,

so he sent cavalry and heavily-armed infantry and slaughtered a great many of them.

(Josephus, Jewish War 2.259-260)

The desert is the place where God will give "signs of liberation." The "deceivers and cheats" play on this popular understanding, but in this case, the Roman procurator Felix quickly disperses the wilderness revolutionaries. Still, this movement was one of many.

Josephus goes on to tell of another even bloodier clash in the wilderness between the Romans and would-be rebels. These rebels were led by a certain Egyptian prophet—quite possibly the same Egyptian that Paul was mistaken for in Acts 21:38. As Josephus makes clear, this Egyptian was on Rome's "Most Wanted" list for good reason:

> Around this time, a man came from Egypt to Jerusalem, claiming that he was a prophet. He advised the common people to go with him to the hill called the Mount of Olives, which lay opposite the city [of Jerusalem], at a distance of about half a mile. He said that he wanted to show them from there how the walls of Jerusalem would fall when he gave the command, and he promised to gain them entrance through the fallen walls.
>
> But when Felix learned of these things, he ordered his soldiers to pick up their weapons and, after mobilizing a large force of cavalry and infantry from Jerusalem, attacked those who were with the Egyptian. He killed four hundred of them, and he took two hundred alive. But the Egyptian himself escaped from the battle and disappeared. Again, the bandits incited the people to war against the Romans, saying that the people should not obey them at all. These bandits plundered those who refused to cooperate and burned their villages.
>
> (Josephus, Jewish Antiquities 20.169-172)

In another account of this same event, Josephus notes that the Egyptian led his multitude of followers "around from the desert to the hill called the Mount of Olives" (*Jewish War* 2.262). Thus, this revolt too had desert connections. But, more importantly, the idea of marching around a walled city in order to bring about its collapse was not exactly original. The famous story of Joshua and the battle of Jericho appears to have been the inspiration behind the Egyptian's plans (see Joshua 6 for the full account). Unless Josephus is taking great liberties with his sources, the Egyptian's plot was intentionally patterned after God's ancient act of deliverance at Jericho; only now, the holy city of Jerusalem stood in for the Canaanite city of Jericho. In spite of this subversive twist, the implication was obvious: as God acted then, so God was expected to act anew.

Josephus elsewhere provides an even better example of symbolic action intended to call upon God to deliver the people of God. The scene of action is once more the wilderness. This time, the protagonist is a man named Theudas, and he appears to be—like the Egyptian—imitating the famous biblical hero Joshua. Instead of re-enacting the battle of Jericho, Theudas wants to re-enact the crossing of the Jordan River (see Joshua 3, which is connected to the earlier Red Sea crossing of Exod 14):

> While Fadus was governor of Judea, a certain impostor by the name of Theudas persuaded a large crowd to take up their possessions and follow him to the river Jordan, for he was telling them that he was a prophet. He said that, by his command, he would divide the river so that he could provide them an easy crossing. When he said these things, he deceived many. However, Fadus did not allow them to take advantage of this ill-advised venture. Rather, he sent out a band of cavalry against them, which fell upon them by surprise, killing many and taking many alive. They captured Theudas alive, then cut off his head and carried it home to Jerusalem. These events took place among the Jews during the time of Cuspius Fadus the governor.
> (Josephus, *Jewish Antiquities* 20.97-99)

As Joshua led the Israelites through the parted waters of the Jordan River, so Theudas promises to lead his followers through the same river on dry ground. He persuades many followers, but Fadus quickly extinguishes their hope.

This unfortunate Theudas fits the description in Acts 5:36 of a failed rebel by the same name. When his story is viewed alongside the stories of the Egyptian, the unnamed "deceivers and cheats," and John the Baptist, we can see several similarities. In each case, the wilderness is the scene of action. In each case, there is some attempt to persuade God to intervene on behalf of the people of God. The "deceivers and cheats" (or "**sign prophets**," to use a more charitable term) lead the people out "into the desert, as if God would there show them the signs of liberation"—there, in the desert, God will act.

Cuspius Fadus ruled Judea as procurator from 44 C.E. to ca. 46 C.E. The Theudas who was beheaded by Fadus's troops bears close resemblance to the Theudas mentioned in Acts 5:36. However, Gamaliel's speech in Acts 5 is set at least a decade before the rule of Fadus. Unless there were two rebellions led by individuals named Theudas, Luke is liable to charges of anachronism.

A wide swath of Second Temple Jews expected God to act in the desert. Yet, at least one Second Temple Jew sounded a different note. In the lengthy discourse of Matthew 24-25, Jesus discusses the "end of the age" (Matt 24:3). Early in the discourse, there is a warning against prophetic figures that appear in the wilderness:

> Then if someone says to you, "Look, here is the messiah," or "Here!" do not believe them. For false messiahs and false prophets will arise and will offer great signs and wonders, so that they might deceive—if possible—even the chosen ones. Look, I have told you beforehand. So, if they say to you, "Look, he is in the wilderness," do not go out. Or, "Look, he is in the inner rooms," do not believe it.
>
> (Matt 24:23-26)

Just as in Josephus, we hear of messianic prophets who promise **signs** and wonders and who appear, among other places, in the wilderness. Of course, Jesus did not condemn all prophetic activity in the wilderness; according to the Gospel of Matthew, Jesus had high praise for John the Baptist (Matt 11:7-14).

In Matt 11:14, Jesus identifies John as the "Elijah who is to come." Herod Antipas, on the other hand, is more wary of John than impressed. In light of our discussion of "sign prophets" above, we can begin to understand how Herod may have viewed John. John lived in the wilderness and baptized people in the Jordan. Might John's contemporaries have associated the site of John's baptismal activity with the site of Joshua's crossing of the Jordan River? If so, John's baptism would be charged with extra meaning in this context. Even if John had no grander aspirations, Herod Antipas would be justly suspicious of a wilderness prophet in that locale—especially a popular wilderness prophet to whom "all the country of Judea and all the people of Jerusalem" were gathered.

Desert dwellers

At the same time, the wilderness was more than a hotbed for revolutionary activity. It was also a haven for people who wanted to break away from the social fabric. Josephus describes his encounter with one such individual in his autobiographical *Life*. Josephus has completed his education and sampled various Jewish **sects**. But he finds himself unsatisfied:

> ... Having decided that those experiences were not enough for me, I learned of a certain man by the name of Bannus. He lived in the wilderness, wearing

clothing made from trees, eating whatever grew in the wild, and washing himself many times, both day and night, with cold water for the sake of purity. I became his zealous follower (*zēlōtēs*). I spent three years with him . . .

(Josephus, *Life* 11-12)

Josephus then returns to Jerusalem after his time with Bannus. His account of Bannus has striking parallels with the New Testament descriptions of John the Baptist. Like John, Bannus lived a life of **asceticism** in the wilderness. Like John, Bannus wore unusual clothing. And like John, Bannus also practiced ceremonial washing with water. The gospel accounts, however, would distinguish John's baptism as a baptism of repentance.

John the Baptist, the **Qumran** community, and Bannus can all be described as practitioners of asceticism. The Greek word *askēsis* means "exercise," "practice," or "training," and it could be used for military training, athletic exercises, or any other sort of rigorous discipline. Typically, ascetic discipline involves sexual abstinence, **fasting**, and other acts of self-denial. Asceticism has been practiced by Jews (e.g., Bannus or John the Baptist), **Christians** (e.g., Anthony and other Egyptian Christians in the third and fourth centuries), philosophers (e.g., Diogenes the Cynic), and many others (e.g., Gandhi). For insight into the logic of asceticism, see 1 Cor 9:24-27.

Bannus and John were not the only first-century Jews to use water for ritual purposes, as the popularity of John's baptism attests. Ritual washing was widespread among Second Temple Jews, as we know from the hundreds of ritual bathing sites (singular, **miqveh**; plural, *miqva'ot*) that have been discovered by archaeologists. The *miqva'ot*, typically situated near places of worship, were used by Jews to restore a state of ritual purity.

One group that both practiced ceremonial washing and lived in the desert was the Qumran community. Qumran is best known as the site where many of the **Dead Sea Scrolls** were discovered. But some of these scrolls also tell of a sectarian community that lived at Qumran in the Second Temple period. Archaeologists have discovered some ten ritual baths at Qumran, and documents from this community shed some light on the importance of washing. Here is an excerpt from the "Community Rule" of the Qumran group:

For it is by the spirit of the true counsel of God that are atoned the paths of man, all his iniquities, so that he can look at the light of life. And it is by the holy spirit of the community, in its truth, that he is cleansed of all his iniquities. And by the spirit of uprightness and of humility his sin is atoned. And by the compliance of his soul with all the laws of God his flesh is cleansed by being sprinkled with cleansing waters and being made holy with the waters of repentance. May he, then, steady his steps in order to walk with perfection on all the paths of God, as he has decreed concerning the appointed times of his assemblies and not turn aside, either right or left, nor infringe even one of all his words. In this way he will be admitted by means of atonement pleasing to God, and for him it will be the covenant of an everlasting Community.

(1QS 3.6-12; García Martínez-Tigchelaar translation,
Dead Sea Scrolls Study Edition 1:75)

The close parallels to the preaching of John the Baptist—"waters of repentance"—have led some scholars to claim that John was actually a member of this "everlasting Community" at Qumran. After all, Khirbet

Figure 4.1 *Miqveh* near Gamla synagogue
Located near the synagogue at Gamla, this *miqveh* would have held hundreds of gallons of water for ritual bathing.

Figure 4.2 *Miqveh* south of Jerusalem temple
This *miqveh*, conveniently located south of the Jerusalem temple, also
dates from the Second Temple period.

Qumran is only a few hours' walk from where the Jordan River empties into
the Dead Sea.

While some connection is indeed possible, John's preaching and its
widespread appeal diverges rather sharply from the rigorous isolationist
stance of the Qumran community. This group sought to separate itself from
other Jews, as one of its key documents makes clear:

> . . . When these have become a community in Israel in accordance with these
> arrangements, they are to be separated from within the dwelling of the men of
> sin to walk to the wilderness in order to open there His path. As it is written,

"In the wilderness prepare the way of ****; make straight in the desert a pathway for our God." This is the study of Torah, which he commanded by the hand of Moses, in order to act in accordance with all that has been revealed from age to age, and according to what the prophets revealed by his holy spirit.

(1QS 8.12-16)

The Qumran community moved to the wilderness both to avoid the "dwelling of the men of sin" and to obey the words of the prophet Isaiah: "In the wilderness prepare the way of the Lord" (Isa 40:3). The Qumran community considered themselves the intended audience of Isa 40:3; they themselves were being called to the desert to prepare the way of the Lord. But how would they prepare the Lord's way? According to this group, the study of Torah is the way of the Lord. Consequently, the Qumran community studied **Torah** in the wilderness, fulfilling Isaiah's command as they interpreted it.

> Why the four dots in 1QS 8:14? As mentioned above, the sacred name of God was treated with great reverence. In this line, the Hebrew letters of *elohenu* ("our God") are spelled out, but the holy **tetragrammaton** is represented by four dots instead of its four Hebrew consonants. This respect for the divine name aligns well with another line from the Community Rule, which appears to forbid pronouncing the tetragrammaton (1QS 6.27).

The significance of Isa 40:3 to this group is all the more striking for us, because each of the four canonical gospels likewise presents Isa 40:3 as a prophecy applying to their contemporary time period. Instead of a call to study Torah in the desert, the gospels each introduce Isa 40:3 as a prophecy fulfilled by John the Baptist. John is the voice in the desert, John is charged with preparing the way of the Lord, and that Lord is none other than Jesus of Nazareth. The Qumran sectarians and the early Christian **evangelists** all read Isaiah as a prophetic word spoken directly to them, but their subsequent interpretations of that word diverge radically.

Salvation in the wilderness

The Maccabean rebels, the Egyptian, Theudas, Bannus, and the Qumran community either searched for, or offered, some form of salvation in the wilderness. There, also, John proclaimed a baptism for the forgiveness of sins. This wilderness location of John's activity was not a neutral site. In the lonely places of the Judean wilderness, there were echoing reminders of Israel's wilderness wandering, of the Maccabean revolt, and of other insurgent movements. The New Testament writings show ample awareness of the symbolic value of wilderness, from beginning (Matthew) to end (Revelation). The wilderness is a place of testing (Matt 4:1-10), and the wilderness is a place where angels minister to Jesus' needs (Matt 4:11). This view of wilderness as both testing ground and source of solace arises again in Revelation. In the Hollywood-worthy action sequence of Revelation 12, a star-crowned and sun-clothed woman flees with her newborn son to the wilderness, there taking refuge from a devouring dragon. When war breaks out in **heaven**, the dragon again pursues her. She again flees to the wilderness, where she survives a ferocious onslaught against herself and her child.

The woman of Revelation 12 and the Maccabean rebels both take refuge from their enemies in the wilderness. If the wilderness served them as a means of escape, it served John the Baptist, Bannus, and the Qumran group as more of a destination. This latter group did not flee violent persecution, but they did seek to separate themselves from the distractions and snares of the surrounding society (the "men of sin" of 1QS 8.13). Jesus may have felt a similar need for withdrawal (e.g., Mark 1:35). Jesus did not, like the sign prophets, withdraw to the wilderness to launch a military campaign. Nevertheless, the gospels claim that he did, like the woman and her son of Revelation 12, face down Satan in the wilderness (compare Mark 1:13 with Rev 12:9, 13).

In Revelation 12, the child is regularly identified as the **messiah**. Commentators dispute the identity of the mother; some say she is the **church**, others suggest she is the persecuted people of God. Over the centuries, the most popular proposal has linked this woman with Mary, the mother of Jesus. Before introducing her son, let us first set the stage by presenting five minor characters who nevertheless play significant roles in the New Testament narratives: a betrothed young woman, a ruthless king, a high priest, a Roman governor, and a Jewish teacher.

Bibliography and suggestions for further reading

Rebecca Gray. *Prophetic Figures in Late Second Temple Jewish Palestine: The Evidence from Josephus.* Oxford: Oxford University Press, 1993. (Gray

analyzes and provides further background for the accounts of various
prophetic figures in Josephus.)

Richard A. Horsley and John S. Hanson. *Bandits, Prophets, and Messiahs:
Popular Movements in the Time of Jesus*. Minneapolis: Winston, 1988.
(Horsley and Hanson have been criticized for their Marxist reconstruction
of first-century history, but they have created an accessible and extensive
overview of the sorts of prophetic movements described in this chapter.)

Flavius Josephus. *The Jewish War, Jewish Antiquities*, and *Life*. (All three texts
offer insight into Second Temple Judaism, sign prophets, and the
significance of wilderness. While a Penguin edition of *The Jewish War* is
widely available, the most accessible English translations of *Jewish
Antiquities* and *Life* are in the *LCL* series.)

John P. Meier. *Mentor, Message, and Miracles*. Vol. 2 of *A Marginal Jew:
Rethinking the Historical Jesus*. New York: Doubleday, 1994. [Now published
by Yale University Press.] (The first part of this volume discusses John the
Baptist and his relationship with Jesus.)

Hindy Najman. "Towards a Study of the Uses of the Concept of Wilderness in
Ancient Judaism." *Dead Sea Discoveries* 13 (2006): 99–113. (Najman surveys
the concept of wilderness as it is used in Second Temple Jewish literature;
she identifies three different uses: wilderness as suffering, wilderness as
purification, and wilderness as a locus for revelation.)

James VanderKam and Peter Flint. *The Meaning of the Dead Sea Scrolls: Their
Significance for Understanding the Bible, Judaism, Jesus, and Christianity*.
New York: HarperCollins, 2002. (Two leading scholars of the Dead Sea
Scrolls offer an accessible introduction to their importance for students of
Second Temple Judaism and the New Testament.)

5

A Virgin, a King, a High Priest, a Governor, and a Rabbi

Guiding Questions

In what ways did gender, ethnicity, and social status shape the lives of ancient **Jews** and gentiles?

What was Herod the Great's reputation in the ancient world?

What types of interactions did Pontius Pilate have with first-century Jews?

What roles did Jewish high priests and rabbis play in first-century Judea?

He has shown strength with his arm,
He has scattered the arrogant in the understanding of their hearts.
He has thrown down the powerful from their thrones,
And has lifted up the humble.
He has filled the hungry with good things,
And sent away the rich empty-handed.

(Luke 1:51-53)

The Virgin Mary

According to the Gospel of Luke, the woman who sings this song is Mary, and her lyrics strike against the very bedrock of her social setting. In her song of upheaval and revolution, this young Jewish woman blesses the Lord who judges the mighty, the powerful, and the rich, and who cares for the humble and hungry. Yet, in her eastern Mediterranean world, the powerful sat on thrones, and the hungry stayed hungry. While some merchants and freedpersons could hope for a comfortable but not luxurious life, a stable, middle-class life eluded most people. Nor could those living on the margins of life count on an extensive social "safety net," in case of hard times. Rather, in this world, kings, priests, and other authorities enjoyed good things, and the oppressed and marginalized all too often found themselves empty-handed.

> According to one study, almost 70 percent of the population of the Roman empire lived at or below subsistence levels as day laborers, small-shop owners, prisoners, slaves, or marginalized groups. Another 20 percent of the population likely maintained a stable lifestyle as merchants, traders, artisans, large-shop owners, or freedpersons. A smaller percentage lived in a position of moderate surplus (perhaps as military veterans or successful merchants), and an even smaller percentage (2 to 3 percent) belonged to the elite of society.

With this social setting in mind, let us examine five portraits of people who might be considered supporting actors to the "superstar" of the **gospels**. Before turning to Jesus (Chapter Six) and his **disciples** (Chapter Seven), we must familiarize ourselves with five other individuals: one woman from a humble background and four men from places of power and influence in first-century Palestine. The fates of these five individuals largely mirror the predictions of the verses quoted above: the humble woman has been lifted up—even venerated for centuries by **Christians**—and the four men are remembered primarily for their involvement in the lives of her son and his followers, not for their political, military, or religious achievements.

The woman, Mary, lived in the Greco-Roman world, a man's world. Our word "virtue"—which we would consider gender-neutral—comes from the Latin word *virtus*, which literally means "manliness." Men tended to hold positions of authority, especially in the public sphere, and children generally acquired status from their fathers, not their mothers. While women might wield power in the home, their public contributions were limited, due to their household responsibilities and to widespread misogyny. Josephus gives a clear example of how women were devalued, when he cites the judicial prohibition against convicting someone on the testimony of a single witness. This legal requirement of at least two or three witnesses comes from **Torah** (see Deut 19:15 for the general prohibition; in Num 35:30, multiple witnesses are only required for capital punishment). Josephus then adds another line that exists nowhere in the Jewish **scriptures**: "But let there be no testimony from women, on account of their frivolity and insolence" (*Jewish Antiquities* 4.219).

You may have read that the ancient world was patriarchal and that the Roman *paterfamilias* ("head of the household") had absolute power over the life and death of his household members (compare Gen 38:24, where Judah appears to be the ancient Israelite equivalent of the Roman *paterfamilias*). However, the term "patriarchy" has remained rather ill-defined, and the legendary powers of ancient fathers are now being questioned (some scholars think that the life-and-death power over children may in fact be merely legendary, suggesting that Gen 38:24 is an aberration). Hence, I focus less on "patriarchy" in this section and more on "patrilineality," the tracing of descent through the paternal line.

Josephus elsewhere exemplifies such misogynist attitudes. In his biography (written towards the end of the first century C.E.), he mentions three wives but names none of them. He does name his three sons (*Life* 5, 426). Of great interest to our present discussion, when Josephus traces his ancestry down from his paternal great-great-great-grandfather, he mentions only fathers, sons, and brothers, with one exception: Matthias, Josephus' great-great-grandfather, "married the daughter of Jonathan the high priest, who was the first member of the Hasmonean family to serve as high priest" (*Life* 4). Josephus thus excludes all women from his **genealogy**, except for the one who enables him to claim royal and priestly blood; even then, he does not name this "daughter of Jonathan" and wife of Matthias.

Seen in this light, the opening sixteen verses of the Gospel according to Matthew would have appeared—at first glance—rather ordinary. Matthew begins his Gospel by tracing Jesus' ancestry from Abraham down through David, all the way down to "Jacob, father of Joseph, the husband of Mary, who gave birth to Jesus, who is called Christ" (Matt 1:16). Initially, the genealogy appears to be a typical artifact from a patrilineal society. But some oddities soon come to light. For instance, look again at this ending verse 16—why does it not simply say "Jacob, father of Joseph, father of Jesus"? Why mention Mary? Here, Matthew's insertion of Mary has a theological rationale: according to Matthew, Joseph was *not* Jesus' father. Joseph was Mary's husband, and Jesus was Mary's child, but the baby Jesus was born "from the Holy Spirit" (Matt 1:20). So, Joseph was Jesus' legal father, not Jesus' biological father. To clarify that Jesus was only "son of Joseph" by adoption, Matthew had to include Mary in the genealogy.

But Mary is not the only woman to interrupt the parade of men from Abraham to Jesus. Tamar shows up in verse 3, Rahab and Ruth appear in verse 5, and the unnamed "wife of Uriah" is mentioned in verse 6. Are these women chaste paragons of virtue like Mary? Do they serve to enhance the royal or priestly lineage of Jesus, like the "daughter of Jonathan" did for Josephus?

Far from it. According to Genesis 38, Tamar, who was recently widowed (twice), seduced her father-in-law Judah in order to have a son. According to Joshua 2, Rahab was a prostitute. Ruth was married, widowed, and re-married. And while the wife of Uriah was a married woman, King David abused his royal power to bring her—better known as Bathsheba—into the royal bedroom. So, Matthew is not holding these women up as virtuous virgins.

The women of Matthew's genealogy were chosen to signal something else. Their sexuality is not as important to Matthew as their ethnicity. Tamar and Rahab were Canaanite women. Ruth was from Moab. And Bathsheba was the wife of Uriah *the Hittite*. None of these four women were Israelites. Each was a **gentile** (= non-Israelite). Jesus, the one promised to "save his people from their **sins**" (Matt 1:21), was born of Mary, a faithful member of "his people" Israel. But his genealogy included gentiles. Matthew appears to be signaling that not only Jesus' past ancestry, but also his future mission, would extend beyond the Jewish people to encompass many nations.

In addition to highlighting women in Jesus' genealogy, the Gospel of Matthew and the other gospels also depict women following Jesus and supporting his ministry (e.g., Luke 8:1-3). Women are shown to be present at Jesus' **crucifixion** (Mark 15:40-41), and all four gospels agree that women were the first to reach the empty tomb on Easter morning. The first individuals to proclaim that Jesus rose from the dead are, according to these sources, not male but female.

The gentile women in Jesus' genealogy appear in sharp contrast to Mary. No one doubted her identity as an Israelite. As early Christians pondered the key role played by Mary in the gospel stories, they became more and more interested in her origins. How did God come to lift up such a humble figure? A second-century text called the *Protevangelium of James* elaborates on the canonical gospel accounts, creating a whole narrative about the birth and upbringing of Mary. According to this later, legendary account, Mary was born into a priestly family. Sent to live in the Jerusalem **temple** at age three, a priest received her:

> And he placed her on the third step of the altar, and the Lord God put grace upon the child, and she danced for joy with her feet, and the whole house of Israel loved her. And her parents went down wondering, praising and glorifying the almighty God because the child did not turn back to them. And Mary was in the Temple, nurtured like a dove, and she received food from the hand of an angel.
>
> (*Protevangelium of James* 7.3-8.1; O. Cullmann and R. McL. Wilson
> translation [Westminster John Knox, 1991], modified)

In the *Protevangelium*, Mary happily stays behind in the temple; in Luke 2:41-51, Jesus is similarly nonplussed by his parents' departure without him. The abundance of such parallels suggests that the *Protevangelium*'s narrative of Mary's birth and early years is modeled on Luke's narrative of her son's birth and early years. Through such a comparison, the *Protevangelium* appears to be answering this question: How can this Jewish girl be considered worthy to give birth to the Son of God?

However implausible this later story of Mary's priestly origins and temple-dwelling may be, John Meier, a leading Catholic biblical scholar, points to convincing evidence that Mary and her family members may have been especially interested in their Jewish identity. Meier has highlighted the importance of the names of Jesus and his parents. While we might think of "Mary," "Joseph," and "Jesus" as simply the names of the "Holy Family," we only think so because we are reading and thinking in English. Our impressions will change if we take into account that we are reading English translations of Greek transliterations of **Hebrew** names. We translate the Greek *Maria* as "Mary," ignoring the fact that the Greek *Maria* comes from the Hebrew *Miryam,* or "Miriam." Likewise, when we read the Greek *Iēsous* as "Jesus" in the canonical gospels, we do not realize that the same Greek word *Iēsous* in Heb 4:8 is translated as "Joshua" in all the English versions. Why? Because Heb 4:8 clearly refers to the Joshua who brought the Israelites into the **promised land**. The Hebrew *Yehoshua* (or *Yeshua*) came into Greek as *Iēsous*. For whatever reason, "Joshua Christ" never caught on in English.

With all this in mind, we find that Matt 1:16 reads as follows: "Jacob, the father of Joseph, the husband of Miriam, who gave birth to Joshua." If you know the Old Testament, then you have heard of the **patriarch** Jacob, his well-clothed son Joseph, Moses' sister Miriam, and Joshua, the successor to Moses. These great figures from Israel's past were still inspiring the members of Jesus' family centuries later. In spite of the Roman conquest, hope remained alive—hope that God would intervene once more in the history of Israel. Did this new Joseph and Miriam ever dream that their young Joshua/Jesus would choose a new Twelve to restore Israel? In the next chapter, we will explore the expectations that various first-century Jews had for messianic figures.

King Herod

> Then, when he saw that he had been tricked by the magi, Herod became enraged, and he had all the children in Bethlehem and in all the surrounding region who were two years old or younger, according to the time that he learned from the magi, killed.
>
> (Matt 2:16)

Baby-killer and tyrant. King Herod does not receive great press in Matthew's Gospel. When he hears word that a "king of the Jews" has been born, Herod immediately begins his search for this usurper (Matt 2:2-4). When he fails to identify this upstart king, Herod is said to kill all the (male) children, ages two and under, in and around Bethlehem. Is such a bloodthirsty act even possible?

According to the Gospel of Matthew, Jesus was born during Herod the Great's reign. Herod died in 4 B.C.E. So, Jesus likely was born at least four years "before the Common Era" or "before Christ" (B.C.). This oddity of chronology can be blamed neither on Herod nor on Jesus nor on Matthew, but on the sixth-century monk Dionysius Exiguus, who devised the first calendar to count years from the birth of Jesus. Unfortunately, Dionysius erred in his calculations; however, before his mistake was discovered, his calendar caught on. Hence, we still use it today.

Many things were possible for Herod. Archaeological and literary sources yield a complex portrait of this man. A scarred-but-victorious general, a visionary builder, and a homicidal family man, Herod nursed grand ambitions. In the end, he founded a Herodian dynasty that ruled for decades; many of his building projects have stood for two millennia.

Josephus again serves as our primary source, telling the tale of this builder-king. From the historian we learn that, having served Rome on the battlefield, King Herod the Great (ca. 74 B.C.E. – 4 B.C.E.) was appointed by Rome to rule Judea. The reign of this renowned warrior lasted from 37 B.C.E. until his death. A masterful builder, Herod devoted much attention to the renovation of the Jerusalem temple, as Josephus describes:

> Thus, in the fifteenth year of his reign, he restored the Temple and, by erecting new foundation-walls, enlarged the surrounding area to double its former extent. The expenditure devoted to this work was incalculable, its magnificence never surpassed; as evidence one would have pointed to the great colonnades around the Temple courts and to the fortress which dominated it on the north. The colonnades Herod reconstructed from the foundations; the fortress he restored at a lavish cost in a style no way inferior to that of a palace, and called it Antonia in honor of [Marc] Antony.
> (Josephus, *Jewish War* 1.401; *LCL* translation [H. Thackeray])

Begun around 20 B.C.E., the renovation of the **Second Temple** would not be finished until 64 C.E., long after Herod's death. Herod's handiwork has certainly stood the test of time—the massive walls supporting the Temple Mount are still standing in the twenty-first century. It is no wonder that Luke speaks of first-century Jews admiring the stones (Luke 21:5).

In Luke's second volume, the fortress Antonia serves as the setting for a major speech of Paul (Acts 22:1-21). In Acts 21:34, a Roman tribune orders Paul to be arrested and brought inside, but Paul is soon granted permission to address his rioting audience from the steps of the fortress Antonia (21:40).

In addition to his temple renovation, Herod also built an artificial harbor along the Mediterranean coast (Caesarea Maritima). He designed an impressive fortress-palace on a hill (Herodium)—which was only constructed after his workers first built the hill on which it was to stand. He also fortified a nearly invincible stronghold on top of a steep plateau

Figure 5.1 Stones at the base of the Temple Mount
At the southern base of the Temple Mount's western wall, archaeologists
uncovered these stones, which once stood on top of the Temple Mount.
They were toppled by Roman legions in 70 C.E.

(Masada); he then added a tiered palace that hangs off of the edge of the
cliffs. The fortress at Masada had been first prepared by Jonathan, the brother
and successor of Judas Maccabeus (see Chapter Two). More than a century
later, Herod added further fortifications:

> On this plateau the high priest Jonathan first erected a fortress and called it
> Masada; the subsequent planning of the place engaged the serious attention
> of King Herod. For first he enclosed the entire summit, a circuit measuring
> seven furlongs, with a wall of white stone, twelve cubits high and eight broad;
> on it stood thirty-seven towers, fifty cubits high, from which access was
> obtained to apartments constructed round the whole interior of the wall.
> (Josephus, *Jewish War* 7.285-286; *LCL* translation [H. Thackeray])

A furlong is approximately 200 yards, and a cubit is approximately 18 inches.
Thus, the wall around the summit of Masada would be approximately 1,400
yards long (nearly a mile), approximately eighteen feet tall, and twelve feet
thick. The remains of these massive fortifications of a rugged, isolated plateau
are still standing today. Their ruin dates to 73 C.E. Even though the Jewish

Figure 5.2 Herodian harbor at Caesarea Maritima
In Caesarea Maritima, visitors can still see remnants of the massive artificial harbor built by Herod the Great.

revolt of 66 – 70 C.E. was effectively brought to an end with the capture of Jerusalem and destruction of the temple in 70 C.E., pockets of resistance remained. And the rebels who held out in Masada were able to endure for three more years, due to the strength of Herod's fortifications; only in 73 C.E. did they finally succumb to the Roman siege.

Herod's building projects won empire-wide acclaim. Strabo (ca. 64 B.C.E. – after 21 C.E.), a Roman contemporary of Herod, claimed that Herod was "so superior to his predecessors, particularly in his intercourse with the Romans and in his administration of affairs of state, that he received the title of king" (*Geography* 16.2.46; *LCL* translation [H. L. Jones]). His architectural prowess and savvy statecraft were truly exceptional.

But Herod went beyond buildings and alliances. In order to secure his throne, he took drastic measures, killing his own brother-in-law Aristobulus and his grandfather-in-law John Hyrcanus II. Also his wife Mariamne. And his mother-in-law Alexandra. And his son Alexander. And his son Aristobulus. And his son Antipater. Herod obviously ignored the "Thou shalt not kill" part of the Torah. Still, he did hold to at least some parts of the

Figure 5.3 Herodium
At this site, Herod the Great had his builders construct an artificial hill, an interior tunnel system, and a fortified palace on top. He was later buried here at the Herodium, where archaeologists claimed to locate his tomb in 2007.

dietary law (which forbade, for example, eating pork). Hence, Caesar Augustus was said to have once joked that "it is better to be Herod's pig than his son" (Macrobius, *Saturnalia* 2.4.1).

Herod I was appointed king of Judea by his Roman overlords. When he died, Caesar Augustus settled a succession dispute by dividing Herod's kingdom between three of his sons. Archelaus would rule Judea, Samaria, and Idumea. Herod Antipas would rule Galilee and Perea. And Herod Philip would rule Batanea, Trachonitis, Auranitis, and other regions. None of the three were granted the title of king. Rather, they would rule as "ethnarchs" (literally, "rulers of a nation") or "tetrarchs" (literally, "rulers of a fourth"). Ethnarchs and **tetrarchs** did not have the prestige of kings, but they still served as clients of Rome.

Figure 5.4 Herodian palace at Masada
At Masada, Herod the Great built this massive three-tiered palace, which seems to hang off the edge of the plateau. The Dead Sea is visible in the distance.

Still, not all of his family was killed; some survived to rule, once Herod had died. Thus, when reading the New Testament, we encounter *three* different Herods. In addition to Herod the Great, who plays a leading role in Matt 2 (see also Luke 1:5), we also find Herod Antipas and Herod Agrippa I. Herod Antipas (ca. 25 B.C.E. – after 39 C.E.), son of Herod the Great, was tetrarch of Galilee and Perea from around 4 B.C.E. to 39 C.E., when he was exiled to Gaul. It is Herod Antipas who is credited with arresting and executing John the Baptist (see Mark 6:14-29 and the discussion in the previous chapter), and it is Herod Antipas to whom Pontius Pilate sends

Figure 5.5 Roman encampment near Masada
Built in the first century C.E. as part of the siege of Masada, this large
Roman encampment still stands today.

Jesus in Luke 23:7 (see also Acts 4:27). Herod Agrippa I was the nephew of
Herod Antipas and the grandson of Herod the Great.

It is Herod Agrippa I who appears in Acts 12, furious with the people of Tyre
and Sidon (see Map 2). Luke's account of Herod's sudden and gruesome demise
in Acts 12 bears striking resemblance to the similar account in Josephus:

Acts 12:20-23	Josephus, *Jewish Antiquities* 19.344-346, 350
[Herod] was very angry with the Tyrians and Sidonians. But, with one accord they came to him, and after winning over Blastos, the king's chamberlain, they requested peace, because their land was supported by the king's land. On the appointed day, Herod, who was wearing royal vestments and sitting on the dais, delivered a public address to them. The people cried out, "The voice of	Now, on the second day of these shows, [Herod] put on a robe made entirely from silver ... and came into the theater in the early morning hours. Then, wondrously illuminated by the first glints of the sun's rays, the silver shone with frightful brilliance, inspiring those present to look on him with awe. Immediately, the flatterers began to shout out— and their cries were not beneficial to

a god, and not of a human!" Immediately, an angel (*angelos*) of the Lord struck him down, because he did not give the glory to God, and he died as worm-food.

Herod—from one place and another, hailing him as a god, then adding, "Show favor to us! If we have revered you only as a man until now, from this point on we will confess you as superior to mortal beings." The king neither rebuked these words nor declined their irreverent flattery. But then, after a little while, he looked up and saw an owl sitting over his head on a rope. He instantly realized that it was a herald (*angelos*) of evil, even as it had once been of good, and he felt heart-wrenching grief. Upon seeing it, pain began to take violent hold of his belly. [...] Thoroughly depleted after five straight days of pain in his stomach, his life came to an end, fifty-four years after his birth.

While Luke specifies that Herod Agrippa I is eaten by worms, Josephus simply speaks of a pain in the belly. Still, both authors agree in attributing the ruler's death to his flashy robe and subsequent hesitancy to correct the flattering crowd. His aspirations to divinity are dashed by his sudden and grotesque death, which is linked with the presence of a divinely-sent messenger (*angelos*). Herod Agrippa I has escaped the sword of his bloodthirsty grandfather, Herod the Great, only to fall from glorious heights to a shameful end.

Caiaphas the High Priest

Caiaphas, a **Sadducee**, served as high priest in Jerusalem from approximately 18 C.E. to 37 C.E., overlapping with the reign of Herod Antipas (son of Herod the Great). The high priesthood of Caiaphas also coincided with the ministry of a prophetic figure named John. Luke 3:2 introduces John the Baptist's public ministry as beginning "during the high priesthood of Annas and Caiaphas," and Acts 4:6 refers to "Annas the high priest and Caiaphas and John and Alexander and as many as were in the high-priestly family." Readers of the Old Testament expect to find one high priest in Jerusalem at a time. Readers of Luke-Acts, though, find multiple high priests. How can there be more than one high priest?

> Note the frequency of certain names among first-century Jews: not only was there more than one Jesus (Jesus of Nazareth, Jesus son of Gamaliel, and the Jesus son of Ananias that will be discussed in the next chapter), but there were many Josephs as well (Joseph the father of Jesus, Flavius Josephus, Joseph Caiaphas).

Josephus is helpful on this point; in his *Life*, he refers to another priestly pair: "the high priests Ananus and Jesus son of Gamaliel" (*Life* 193). Apparently, priestly customs changed over time. In the early period of the high priesthood, a high priest held the office until he died. Then, a new high priest would be anointed. However, from the time of **Hasmoneans** onward (see Chapter Two for a refresher on Hasmoneans), the high priesthood was a more political position, and the high priesthood was bestowed upon a political appointee, or sometimes simply to the highest bidder. Thus, high priests could be replaced before they died; Josephus records how Vitellius, the Roman governor of Syria, removed Caiaphas from office and installed Jonathan son of Ananus as high priest (*Jewish Antiquities* 18.95). A decade earlier, we find Annas, who was high priest from 6 to 15 C.E., alongside his son-in-law Caiaphas (see John 18:13). Both can be called "high priests," even if Annas might better be labeled "high priest emeritus."

Neither Josephus nor the New Testament writings shine the spotlight on Caiaphas. He makes headlines for his involvement in the trial of a notorious Nazarene, but he otherwise remains behind the scenes. Even if we do not learn much about the life of Caiaphas, we should keep in mind the important role of the high priest in Jewish life. On the most holy Day of Atonement (in **Hebrew**, *Yom Kippur*), the high priest offered **sacrifice** in the inner sanctuary to atone for the sins of the whole people of God. The redemptive significance of this high-priestly role would later inspire expectations of a priestly **messiah**, as we will discuss in the following chapter (for details on the Day of Atonement, see Lev 16; Josephus, *Jewish War* 5.236, also attests this practice).

The high priesthood of Caiaphas encompassed all of Pontius Pilate's tenure in Judea. Thus, as we explore Pilate's interactions with the Jews in the next section, keep in mind that Caiaphas was likely involved in several of the confrontations. Interestingly, though, the only texts that describe collaboration between Pilate and Caiaphas are in the New Testament, where Caiaphas is depicted as colluding with Rome in the execution of a Galilean teacher.

Pontius Pilate

Upon Herod the Great's death, his son Archelaus came to rule Judea, Samaria, and Idumea as ethnarch. His brutality drew the attention of Caesar Augustus, who banished Archelaus to Gaul (modern-day France) in 6 C.E. Henceforth, Judea would be ruled by Roman governors rather than Jewish client-kings. From 6 – 41 C.E., these rulers were called prefects (*praefecti*); from 44 – 66 C.E., they were known as procurators. Thus, the Roman governors who appear in Acts were procurators: Antonius Felix ruled from ca. 52 – 60 C.E. (see Acts 23-24), and Porcius Festus ruled from ca. 60 – 62 C.E. (see Acts 24-26).

Of all the Roman governors, the prefect named Pontius Pilatus (usually translated as "Pontius Pilate") had the largest impact on the New Testament writings. Every time Christians recite the **Nicene Creed**, they remember Pilate. In that statement of Christian belief, the only human beings to appear alongside Jesus are Mary, the mother of Jesus, and Pontius Pilate, the man who handed Jesus over to be crucified. Who was this Pilate?

We actually know more about Pilate than many of the other Roman governors. He is mentioned by Tacitus in his *Annals* (for the full quotation, see Chapter Three). The name "Pontius Pilatus" also appears in an inscription from Caesarea Maritima, the port city built by Herod the Great. But our best sources for information about Pontius Pilate are, again, the works of Josephus, where we learn that he ruled Judea for a decade (from 26 – 36 C.E.). In all of the following examples, Pilate shows himself rather unconcerned with his approval ratings. Over time, he won not only the enmity of his subjects, but the disapproval of his superiors. When reading the following example, it is important to keep in mind that the Ten Commandments include a prohibition against **idolatry**—that is, worship of any "idols" or "images." Given that Jerusalem was the site of God's temple, Jews strongly opposed the introduction of rival objects of worship:

> Sent to Judea as governor by Tiberius, Pilate secretly brought into Jerusalem the images of Caesar, which are called standards, by night. On the next day, this action created a great disturbance among the Jews. Those present were shocked at the sight of them, as their laws were being trampled, for they insist that no image be set up within the city. Besides the exasperation of those who lived in the city, those who lived in the country came along in crowds.
>
> Rushing off to Pilate in Caesarea, they began to implore him to carry the standards out of Jerusalem and to preserve their ancestral customs. When Pilate refused their request, they fell down prostrate around his house and continued lying down, immovable, for five days and as many nights.

On the following day, Pilate sat at his tribunal in the great stadium and summoned the multitude, as if he really wanted to answer them. He gave his soldiers an arranged signal to surround the Jews with their weapons. When three ranks of the phalanx of soldiers surrounded them, the Jews were mute with astonishment at this unexpected sight. Pilate said that he would slaughter them if they did not accept the images of Caesar, and he nodded to his soldiers to draw their swords.

But the Jews, just as if from a pre-arranged signal, fell down in crowds and bent their necks; they cried out that they were ready to be killed, rather than see the law violated. Utterly amazed by their intense superstition, Pilate ordered that the standards be removed from Jerusalem immediately.

(Josephus, *Jewish War* 2.169-174)

Risking life and limb, the Jews won the bloodless first round. Undeterred, Pilate continued to act without regard for the Jewish **laws**:

After these things, he sparked yet another commotion by spending the entire sacred treasure, which is called "*korbōnas*" [compare Matt 27:6, which uses the same word], on the building of an aqueduct. Thus he brought in water from a distance of four hundred stadia. This action exasperated the people, and when Pilate came to Jerusalem, they surrounded his tribunal and raised a tremendous clamor. Pilate, however, had expected them to make a commotion, and he secretly mingled throughout the crowd his soldiers—armed, but in civilian clothing. He had ordered them not to use their swords, but to strike the demonstrators with clubs. He gave the pre-arranged signal from his tribunal. Many of the Jews were killed, some beaten to death with the clubs, and others trampled to death by each other in the flight. Seeing the misfortune of those who perished, the terrified crowd stood silent.

(Josephus, *Jewish War* 2.175-177)

Pilate wants to build an aqueduct, so he confiscates the sacred treasury from the Jews and spends it on his construction project. This time, he meets the protesting Jews with force, pummeling them into silence.

Josephus presents Pontius Pilate as a brutally efficient ruler. This portrait is confirmed by another excerpt from Josephus. Apparently, Pilate's heavy-handed policies would eventually lead directly to his removal from office. The following anecdote details the aftermath of Pilate's suppression of an armed group of **Samaritans** who planned to meet on Mount Gerizim:

Pilate cut off their ascent, occupying the way in advance with a group of cavalry and infantry, who fought with those who had gathered in the village. When the two sides met, [Pilate's soldiers] killed some, turned others to flight, and captured many of them alive. Pilate killed the leading men among the captives, as well as the most powerful men among those who fled.

But when this uproar settled down, the council of the Samaritans sent a man of consular rank to Vitellius, governor of Syria, and accused Pilate of the murder of those killed; after all, those slain were not trying to revolt from Rome, but rather to escape from Pilate.

(Josephus, *Jewish Antiquities* 18.87-88)

Josephus goes on to describe how Pilate was forced to return to Rome to face the emperor. Fortunately for Pilate, the emperor Tiberius died before Pilate could go to Rome.

Rabbi Gamaliel

Perhaps Pilate would have been better off if he had adopted the laissez-faire strategy proposed by Rabbi Gamaliel in Acts 5:35-39. According to Luke, Rabbi Gamaliel proposed that the early followers of Jesus be left alone, for, "if this plan or this work is from human beings, it will be destroyed; but if they are from God, you will not be able to destroy them" (Acts 5:38-39). While Gamaliel plays a very small role in Acts, he is acknowledged as a member of the Jewish council, and he is even identified as the teacher of Paul in Acts 22:3. Who was this rabbi?

In rabbinic writings, one frequently finds debates between the disciples of Hillel and the followers of his contemporary Shammai. Even though Hillel and Shammai do not always appear to share the more relaxed or rigorous tendencies of their later followers, the rabbinic writings of the first few centuries C.E. do frequently feature debates between the more lenient House of Hillel and the stricter House of Shammai.

Gamaliel was the grandson of the great Rabbi Hillel, who was perhaps the most famous rabbi of Second Temple Judaism. Gamaliel was active in the first century C.E., and he belonged to the **sect** of the **Pharisees** (to be discussed later in Chapter Eight). While perhaps not as famous as his grandfather, we find evidence in the **Mishnah** that Gamaliel was nonetheless revered by later sages. In the tractate *Sotah*, the Mishnah includes a list of hyperbolic statements about great rabbis and students, including one such statement about Rabbi Gamaliel: "When Rabban Gamaliel the Elder died, the glory of the Law ceased and purity and abstinence died" (*Sotah* 9.15; H. Danby translation [Oxford University Press, 1933]). This respect for Rabbi Gamaliel is also conveyed by the respect shown for his legal decisions.

> The Mishnah is a written collection of early Jewish oral law, compiled around 200 C.E. The Mishnah also provides the basis for the centuries-later Talmud, which is set up as a commentary on the Mishnah.

According to the traditions compiled in the Mishnah, Rabbi Gamaliel was asked whether a woman could remarry, if only one witness could testify to her husband's death:

> Whereupon Rabban Gamaliel remembered that certain men were killed at Tel Arza and Rabban Gamaliel the Elder suffered their wives to marry again on the evidence of one witness. And the rule was established to suffer a woman to marry again on the evidence of one witness [who testifies what he has heard] from [another] witness, or from a slave or from a woman or from a bondwoman.
> (*Yebamot* 16.7; H. Danby translation [Oxford University Press, 1933])

The text goes on to offer the views of rabbis who dissented from Gamaliel's opinion, basing their arguments on other incidents. From this discussion, we can see that Jesus was not the only first-century rabbi to be asked about marriage (see Mark 10:2-12). But we also learn that the Gamaliel who is only briefly mentioned in Acts was a respected figure, whose views are preserved in one of the earliest post-biblical Jewish legal texts. He may, or may not, have encountered the rabbi from Galilee whose followers wrote the New Testament. To that Galilean teacher we now turn.

Bibliography and suggestions for further reading

Helen K. Bond. *Caiaphas: Friend of Rome and Judge of Jesus?* Louisville: Westminster John Knox, 2004. (This book tries to construct a biography of Joseph Caiaphas—at least, to the extent that is possible from our limited sources. Bond explores what we can know about Caiaphas himself; she then turns to a description of Caiaphas's role in each gospel.)

Steven J. Friesen. "Poverty in Pauline Studies: Beyond the So-called New Consensus." *Journal for the Study of the New Testament* 26.3 (2004): 323–361. (Friesen creates a "poverty scale" with seven categories, ranging from the wealthy imperial elites on one end, to the impoverished widows, orphans, and beggars on the other. He estimates the percentage of the population that might have belonged in each category during the Roman empire, and he also provides an approximate "economic profile" of the members of Paul's churches.)

John P. Meier. *The Roots of the Problem and the Person*. Vol. 1 of *A Marginal Jew: Rethinking the Historical Jesus*. New York: Doubleday, 1991. [Now published by Yale University Press.] (Meier is a leading scholar of the "historical Jesus." That is, his work attempts to draw historical conclusions about Jesus—conclusions based on criteria that Jews, Christians, agnostics, and others could all agree upon.)

Carol L. Meyers. "Was Ancient Israel a Patriarchal Society?" *Journal of Biblical Literature* 133 (2014): 8–27. (Meyers gives a negative answer to this question, mustering a wide array of arguments. She argues that studies of "patriarchy" have paid too much attention to legal texts and too little to archaeological findings and literary texts. Meyers concludes that women in Israelite society often had significant managerial responsibilities within households, not to mention their occasional roles as judges, sages, prophets, and poets; thus, scholars need to develop the concept of *heterarchy* to describe a variety of hierarchies in the ancient world.)

Peter Richardson. *Herod: King of the Jews and Friend of the Romans*. Columbia: University of South Carolina Press, 1996. (The Introduction to this book is composed of Richardson's fictional ancient newspaper reports about Herod. After this lighter reading, Richardson launches into a full-scale scholarly biography of Herod.)

Wilhelm Schneemelcher, ed. *New Testament Apocrypha*. 2 vols. Translated by R. McL. Wilson. Revised edition. Louisville: Westminster John Knox, 1991–1992. (This two-volume set includes translations of and commentary on various writings that are related to, but not included in, the New Testament writings. Of particular interest are the *Gospel of Thomas*, the *Gospel of Peter*, and the *Protevangelium of James*.)

H. L. Strack and G. Stemberger. *Introduction to the Talmud and Midrash*. Translated by Markus Bockmuehl. Minneapolis: Fortress, 1992. (This comprehensive resource is a widely-used reference guide for students of rabbinic writings. It includes a general introduction to rabbinic literature, as well as more detailed overviews of Mishnah, Talmud, the *midrashim*, and other ancient Jewish writings.)

6

Joshua the Carpenter's Son . . . or the Christ, the Son of God?

Guiding Questions

Who was Jesus, according to his contemporaries?

How does Jesus, son of Mary, compare and contrast with Jesus, son of Ananias?

What does it mean to label Jesus as "**Christ**"?

What sorts of messianic expectations were held by different first-century **Jews**?

And on the Sabbath he began to teach in the synagogue, and many who heard him were amazed, saying, "Where did he get these things? What is the wisdom that has been given to him? And such mighty deeds done by his hands!? Is this [guy] not the carpenter, the son of Mary and the brother of James and Joses and Judas and Simon? And are not his sisters here with us?" And they took offense at him.

(Mark 6:3)

Herod the King heard the report, for Jesus' name was known, and he said, "John the Baptist has been raised from the dead, and that is why these powers are at work in him!"

(Mark 6:14)

And Jesus asked them, "But who do you say that I am?" Peter answered him, "You are the Messiah."

(Mark 8:29)

Who was Jesus of Nazareth?

In the beginning of the previous chapter, we talked about the meaning of the name Jesus/*Iēsous*. The vast majority of scholars and non-scholars agree that this Jesus was a first-century Jewish man who preached in Galilee and who was executed on a cross around 30 C.E. These are well-attested historical facts. What more can we say? It seems likely that Jesus of Nazareth was, prior to his public activities, a Galilean Jew who worked with his hands. Mark tells us that he was a "carpenter"—the Greek word can also mean "craftsman," "workman," or "sculptor." Matthew tells us that Jesus was thought to be the "son of a carpenter" (Matt 13:55).

Jesus has been called many other things. In the canonical **gospels**, Jesus is called "**messiah**," "son of David," "son of God," "lord," "teacher," "rabbi," "prophet," "John the Baptist" (see Mark 6:14, quoted above), "Elijah," and "king of the Jews." In the canonical gospels, he describes himself as "son of

Figure 6.1 Capernaum synagogue
The lighter-colored stones form the walls of a fourth-century synagogue in Capernaum, on the northern shores of the Sea of Galilee. The black basalt stone foundation is from the first-century synagogue, where Jesus would have taught.

man," "living bread," "light of the world," "gate," "good shepherd," "the **resurrection** and the life," "way," "truth," "life," and "true vine." Modern scholars have given Jesus other names: Morton Smith published *Jesus the Magician* in 1978; John Dominic Crossan has published a variety of books about Jesus the "peasant Jewish Cynic;" Reza Aslan made headlines in 2013 with a book on Jesus titled *Zealot*.

Who was Jesus? The earliest texts to mention Jesus are the letters of Paul, composed primarily in the 50s and early 60s C.E. Paul has little to say about the miracles and teachings of Jesus, but he is still a valuable source. Paul is familiar with traditions surrounding the Last Supper (1 Cor 11:23-26), Paul affirms that Jesus died on a cross (Phil 2:8), and Paul claims that Jesus both rose from the dead and appeared to his followers (1 Cor 15:3-8). In subsequent years, the four canonical gospels were composed, offering a fuller picture of the life and ministry of Jesus. These sources shed light on Jesus' life from the perspective of his followers.

We also have sources that shed light on Jesus' life from an external perspective. Back in Chapter Three, we discussed the brief mention of Jesus by Tacitus, as well as the treatment of Jesus' early followers by Pliny. For another outsider's view, we need to turn once more to Josephus, whose *Jewish Antiquities* include two very important passages about Jesus. These two passages will provide the foundation for our discussion of Jesus of Nazareth in this chapter.

> This chapter focuses on putting Jesus in his first-century Jewish context. Some readers will be more interested in learning what Jesus said and did, and less interested in learning about what Josephus said about Jesus or about the **Qumran** community's messianic expectations. Those readers will find a much richer treatment of Jesus himself elsewhere—for example, in the Gospels of Matthew, Mark, Luke, and John.

Jesus the "wise man"

The longer passage occurs in Book 18 of *Jewish Antiquities*, in the midst of a description of a certain Pontius Pilate, the Roman prefect of Judea. This famous passage, sometimes called the *Testimonium Flavianum* (= Flavius Josephus' Testimony), is very controversial, and I have emphasized the most controversial portions:

There was around this time Jesus, a wise man, *if one can call him a man; for* he was a doer of wonderful deeds and a teacher of those who welcome the truth with pleasure. He won over both many Jews and many Greeks. *He was the Christ.* And when Pilate, at the behest of the leading men among us, condemned him to the cross, those who loved him in the beginning did not cease to do so. *For he appeared to them as one who again lived on the third day, since the divine prophets had announced these things and ten thousand other wonderful things about him.* To this present day, the tribe of the Christians, so named on his account, has not disappeared.

(Josephus, *Jewish Antiquities* 18.63-64)

Our Greek manuscripts include this passage in its entirety. Nevertheless, there is good reason to believe that the passages I have emphasized are later Christian editorial additions. If we remove those passages, we get a more neutral text—a text that a non-Christian Jew (like Josephus) might have written in the first-century:

There was around this time Jesus, a wise man; he was a doer of wonderful deeds and a teacher of those who welcome the truth with pleasure. He won over both many Jews and many Greeks. And when Pilate, at the behest of the leading men among us, condemned him to the cross, those who loved him in the beginning did not cease to do so. To this present day, the tribe of the Christians, so named on his account, has not disappeared.

(Josephus, *Jewish Antiquities* 18.63-64)

If we take this text—or something similar to it—as closer to what Josephus may have written, then we find Jesus described as a wise man and miracle worker who gathered a large following of Jews and **gentiles** before being executed by Pilate. Few who have read the canonical gospels will dispute that there is wisdom in the words of Jesus, and the fact that he acquired Jewish and gentile followers is well attested. This version of the account seems like something that an educated first-century Jew might write about a popular prophetic figure. The only real contention that might be raised is the mention of "wonderful deeds"—would Josephus the Jew really say that this Jesus performed miracles? Is this not another probable insertion by a later Christian author? Josephus is educated, after all—surely he would believe that miracles cannot happen!

Jesus the miracle worker

The above questions spring into the mind of many twenty-first-century Western readers. Nowadays, we pride ourselves on our ability to observe, measure, and manipulate our world. Many believe that the intangible and supernatural can be explained scientifically. Demonic possession makes for a terrifying horror movie, but scientific advances have now convinced most Westerners that epilepsy and Tourette's syndrome should be treated as medical conditions, not spiritual forces. Taking this confidence in science a step further, some twenty-first-century scholars are willing to go so far as to say that the gospels must be fictional accounts, because no eyewitness could honestly claim to have observed a miraculous event.

This last claim points to a real problem for twenty-first-century readers who are trying to assess the reliability of first-century texts. Some readers may be quite skeptical that Josephus would make a claim that a human being performed miraculous works. Many educated Western readers have never witnessed a miracle nor heard an eyewitness account of a miracle. However, this inexperience may simply result from a sort of elite parochialism—after all, there are many things that highly educated Westerners have not seen, heard, tasted, or touched.

In his recent two-volume work *Miracles*, Craig Keener notes that "today hundreds of millions of people claim to have witnessed miracles" (209). Keener provides enough examples of eyewitness claims to miraculous events to prove beyond reasonable doubt that many people can honestly claim to have witnessed inexplicable healings with their very own eyes. And this is nothing new.

> Many ancient people believed that miracles can happen, and many modern people believe that miracles can happen. Disbelief in miracles is not a recent development; some first-century elites (e.g., Cicero) disbelieved in miracles—but they would be less inclined to deny that other first-century individuals believed that miracles can happen.

For centuries, human beings have claimed to witness miraculous deeds. More to the point, Josephus himself both believed that inexplicable events could take place and that some of his Jewish contemporaries possessed abilities beyond those of most normal human beings. We find evidence in his *Jewish War*, where Josephus describes strange events taking place in the city of Jerusalem before and during the time of the first Jewish revolt (66 – 70 C.E.). Josephus first reveals his belief that "incredible" events can and do happen:

> What I am about to tell would, I suppose, sound like a fairy tale, if it were not told by eyewitnesses, and if not for the ensuing misfortunes that were worthy of such signs. Before sunset, chariots and armed phalanxes appeared high in the air, all around the country, darting across the clouds and surrounding the cities. And, at the feast that we call "Pentecost," the priests who were entering the inner temple courts at nighttime—as was their custom for sacred duties—said that they first perceived movement and a crash, and then the voice of a crowd: "We are going away from here."
>
> (Josephus, *Jewish War* 6.297-300)

Fully aware that many would dismiss his account as unbelievable, Josephus puts his trust in the eyewitnesses who reported the visions of heavenly armies and the voices of invisible multitudes. Writing with the benefit of hindsight, he confidently interprets these paranormal phenomena as accurate **signs** of the impending destruction of the Second Temple.

Josephus continues his discussion of this series of strange and wondrous events with an account of a first-century Jew named Jesus: Jesus, son of Ananias. I include the whole story here. Following the above-discussed portents, Jesus, son of Ananias, comes onto the scene, announcing woe to the city of Jerusalem. Like most prophets of doom, he is not appreciated by the ruling authorities, yet he perseveres in delivering the bad news:

> Even more terrifying than these things was the arrival of a certain Jesus, the son of Ananias, a common peasant. Four years prior to the war, when the city was at the peak of peace and prosperity, he came to the feast at which it is customary to set up tents before God. Suddenly, he began to cry out in the temple, "A voice from the east, a voice from the west, a voice from the four winds, a voice against Jerusalem and the temple, a voice against the bridegrooms and brides, a voice against all the people!"
>
> Day and night, he went around all the lanes and alleys, crying out these words. Some distinguished citizens were aggravated at his ominous speech and arrested the man; they beat him with many blows. But Jesus, saying nothing on his own behalf and nothing specifically to those who beat him, continued with the same loud cries as before.
>
> The officials assumed—as was true—that there was a rather miraculous force in the man, so they brought him to the Roman governor. There, he was whipped down to the bone, but he neither pleaded with them nor wept. Instead, changing his voice into the most plaintive tone he could muster, he answered each stroke with "Woe to Jerusalem!" When Albinus—this man

was our governor—asked him who he was, and where he came from, and why he said such things, Jesus answered none of these questions at all. He did not cease to cry out his dirge for the city, until Albinus declared him a madman and released him.

(Josephus, *Jewish War* 6.300-305)

The plaintive prophet of doom has a one-track mind. Jesus, son of Ananias, will not be turned from his mission by blows or scourging; his silence in the face of his accusers reminds New Testament readers of another bloodied Jesus who kept silence when questioned. Jesus, son of Ananias, also stayed true to his mission until the end:

Up until the time of the war, Jesus (son of Ananias) never approached any of those who lived in the city, nor was he seen speaking to anyone. Rather, every day, like a well-rehearsed prayer, he would lament, "Woe to Jerusalem!" He did not curse any of those who beat him every day, nor did he bless those who shared food with him. His reply, that gloomy invocation, was the same for all.

He cried out loudest at the festivals. For seven years and five months, he said the same thing, his voice never wavering nor wearing out, until the time came when he saw in the siege the fruit of his invocation; then, he ceased. While going around on the wall, he was yelling loudly, "Woe again to the city, and to the people, and to the temple!" And as he added a final word—"Woe also to me!"—a rock launched from the stone-thrower struck him dead immediately, and he lost his life while still uttering those invocations.

(Josephus, *Jewish War* 6.306-309)

For Josephus, at least one first-century Jew named Jesus plainly had preternatural abilities. The prophet's campaign is proven valid by the subsequent destruction of Jerusalem. Moreover, his prophetic status is instantly and ironically confirmed by the rock that lethally interrupts his prediction of his own demise.

Jesus, son of Ananias, is accepted by Josephus as a prophet with extraordinary abilities. It is plausible, then, that Jesus, son of Mary, was accepted as (at least) a wonder-working wise man. While some twenty-first-century readers might find it impossible to believe that a human being can walk on water or raise the dead, we should not forget the difference between believing in miracles and believing that others believe in miracles. Whether or not you believe in a thoroughly materialist world, it is quite likely—from a historical perspective—that certain first-century Jews did believe that Jesus healed the sick, exorcized demons, and raised the dead.

The account of Vespasian's healing of a blind man by spittle is remarkably paralleled by John 9:6-7, where Jesus heals a blind man with spittle. Is John's Gospel responding to the imperial healing narratives? While possible, I think it is unlikely, given that the earlier Gospel of Mark also includes an account of Jesus healing a blind man with spittle (see Mark 8:22-25). If Mark's account, with its two-stage healing, was intended to be a response to Vespasian, then it was not a very compelling one—both Matthew and Luke omit this material from their Gospels.

First-century belief in miracles was not, however, limited to Jews. Writing in the early second century C.E., Suetonius describes the healing of a blind man and a lame man by none other than the Emperor Vespasian:

Vespasian as yet lacked prestige and a certain majesty, so to speak, since he was an unexpected and still new-made emperor; but these also were given him. A man of the people who was blind, and another who was lame, came to him together as he sat on the tribunal, begging for the help for their disorders which [the Egyptian god] Serapis had promised in a dream. For the god declared that Vespasian would restore the eyes, if he would spit upon them, and give strength to the leg, if he would deign to touch it with his heel. Though he had hardly any faith (*fides*) that this could possibly succeed, and therefore shrank even from making the attempt, he was at last prevailed upon by his friends and tried both things in public before a large crowd; and with success . . .

(Suetonius, *Divus Vespasianus* 7.2-3; *LCL*
translation [J. C. Rolfe], modified)

Historians have questioned the veracity of this account; the need for Vespasian to establish his nascent rule may have led to a staged healing. Still, such a charade would be senseless apart from a widespread belief that miracles could and did happen.

Jesus the Messiah

The second reference to Jesus of Nazareth in the works of Josephus is less descriptive and less controversial than the first. It occurs near the end of the *Jewish Antiquities*, as the historian describes the high priest Ananus the Younger. According to Josephus—who shows little love for **Sadducees** like

Ananus—Ananus has a hot temper and a mean streak. He also has a sense of timing:

> Given that Ananus was so disposed, he believed that he now had a suitable opportunity: Festus was dead, and Albinus was still on the road. So, he gathered the council (*sunedrion*) of judges and brought before them the brother of Jesus, who was called Christ. His name was James (*Iakōbos*). He brought some others as well. Ananus made an accusation against them as law-breakers, and he handed them over to be stoned.
>
> (Josephus, *Jewish Antiquities* 20.200)

Here, Josephus is describing some of the outrageous actions of the high priest Ananus the Younger. To give a particular example, Josephus identifies a man named James (*Iakōbos*). *Iakōbos* was a very common name at the time, so Josephus identifies this James as "the brother of Jesus, who was called Christ." This passing reference to Jesus appears very unlikely to be a Christian addition, and most scholars are in agreement about its authenticity.

Some **Christians** hold that Mary was perpetually a virgin – before and after the birth of Jesus. Josephus is not concerned to preserve this belief; he freely refers to a "brother of Jesus." In doing so, Josephus aligns with many New Testament writings that mention Jesus' siblings (Matt 13:55; Mark 6:3; John 7:3-5, 10; Acts 1:14; 1 Cor 9:5). Later theologians have suggested that these "brothers" of Jesus may be "half-brothers" from a previous marriage between Joseph and another woman, even though the New Testament does not offer any evidence for this conjecture.

What does this tell us about Jesus? First, for those inclined to be skeptical, this reference is another piece of strong evidence from a non-Christian ancient source that Jesus of Nazareth did indeed exist. Second, it tells us that at least one first-century Jew who did not follow Jesus was nonetheless aware that some other Jews considered Jesus to be Christ, or Messiah.

From Josephus' account, it might appear that "Christ" is simply the last name of Jesus. But "Christ" is not a name. "Christ" is a title. "Jesus Christ" is the name given to the man "Jesus" who was believed to be "the Christ." Now, what is a "Christ"? To answer this question, we must begin with some linguistic calisthenics: "Christ" is our English version of the Greek *christos*, and the Greek *christos* is simply a translation of the **Hebrew** word *mashiach* (=Messiah).

These two words, *christos* and *mashiach* both mean "Anointed One." (Thus, in John 1:41, Andrew tells his brother Simon that he has found the "*mashiach*"—transliterated in Greek as "*messias*"—which the narrator then translates as "*christos*.") Whether we call Jesus the "Christ," the "Messiah," or the "Anointed One" simply depends on whether we want to use the Greek root word, the Hebrew root word, or an actual English word. All three are references to someone who has been "anointed"—that is, someone who has had oil dabbed, smeared, or poured onto their head or another part of the body. To review, "Christ" (from Greek *christos*) = "Messiah" (from Hebrew *mashiach*) = "Anointed One" (the meaning of both *christos* and *mashiach*). So, what does it mean to be the "Anointed One"? Some historical background is necessary.

> In addition to kings and priests, it appears that prophets were sometimes anointed. In 1 Kings 19:16, God commands the prophet Elijah to anoint Elisha as his prophetic successor. However, in 19:19, Elijah apparently designates Elisha as successor by casting his cloak over the shoulders of Elisha. (See also Sirach 48:8 for a possible reference to Elijah's anointing of Elisha.) While prophets are not often anointed, they often anointed others.

In the Jewish **scriptures**, kings and priests were regularly anointed. Moses receives instruction to anoint Aaron and Aaron's sons as priests (Exod 28:41; 30:30). The prophet Samuel anoints Saul as the first King of Israel (1 Sam 15:1), and he later anoints Saul's successor David (1 Sam 16:13). The priest Zadok anoints Solomon as king (1 Kgs 1:39). Priests and kings are marked out as God's chosen leaders through this anointing.

> Perhaps the strangest messianic text in the **Bible** is Isaiah 45:1, which begins as follows: "Thus says the Lord to his anointed one, to Cyrus, whose right hand I have grasped to subdue nations (*goyim*) before him"—King Cyrus of Persia is here referred to as an "anointed one" (*mashiach*). According to the prophet, the gentile ruler Cyrus is chosen by the God of Israel.

Thus, the history of Israel included many anointed figures, and thus many messiahs. In the time of Jesus, there were hopes for a new anointed figure (or figures). But we must emphasize that there were *hopes*; we do not find a single, monochrome expectation that someone called the "Messiah" was coming. In Jesus' day, there was certainly no widespread expectation that a "Messiah" would come and die and save the people from their **sins**. It is quite obvious in the canonical gospels that Jesus' **disciples** were not expecting their leader to die on a Roman cross.

What were these hopes that lived in the hearts of **Second Temple** Jews? Mostly, there were hopes for a royal, Davidic messiah. For a few, there were hopes for a priestly, Aaronic messiah. And at least one community hoped for two messiahs.

The New Testament bears witness to hopes for a royal, Davidic messiah. As discussed in the previous chapter, Matthew seems to have arranged his **genealogy** in order to set up Jesus as a new Davidic king. These hopes for a new David figure were grounded in the Jewish scriptures. After all, God had promised as much to David himself: "Your house and your kingdom will be confirmed forever before you; your throne will be established forever" (2 Sam 7:16). Several decades before Jesus' time, an anonymous Jewish author had given voice to this hope:

> See, Lord, and raise up for them their king, the son of David, to rule over your servant Israel in the time known to you, O God.
>
> Undergird him with the strength to destroy the unrighteous rulers, to purge Jerusalem from gentiles who trample her to destruction ...
> (*Psalms of Solomon* 17.21-22; *OTP* translation)

Clearly, there was hope for a Davidic king to rise up and free Israel from gentile (Roman?) rule.

> For an even more detailed description of a Davidic king reigning over a restored and united kingdom of Israel, see the famous prophecy of Ezekiel 37 in the valley of dry bones. This passage is better known as the inspiration for a popular African-American spiritual.

Recalling that both kings and priests were regularly anointed, we find this hope doubled in the Qumran community. The community's "sons of light" were waiting for God to act decisively, for God to vanquish the "sons of darkness." According to their Community Rule, the **sect** needed to obey the teachings of the group "until the prophet comes, and the messiahs of Aaron and Israel" (1QS 9.11). The Qumran community is apparently the only ancient Jewish community to articulate a hope for *two* messiahs: one priestly figure ("of Aaron"), and one royal figure ("of Israel"). (Although Zechariah 4:14 does not use the word *mashiach*, it may also bear witness to an expectation of two "anointed ones.")

Might Jesus be considered a priestly messiah? Based on a comparison of the structure of Leviticus 16 and John 17, many scholars agree that Jesus' prayer in the latter passage can be labeled a "high-priestly prayer." More explicitly, the Letter to the Hebrews describes Jesus as a high priest:

> When Christ came as a high priest of the good things that have come, then through the greater and perfect tent not made with hands—that is, not of this creation—he entered once and for all into the holy places, not by the blood of goats and young bulls but by his own blood, so obtaining an eternal redemption. For if the blood of goats and bulls, and the sprinkling of defiled people with the ashes of a young cow, sanctify for the purification of flesh, how much more will the blood of Christ, who through the eternal Spirit offered himself unblemished to God, purify our conscience from dead works to worship the living God! For this reason, he is the mediator of a new covenant, so that those who are called might receive the promised eternal inheritance, since a death has come about for their redemption from the transgressions under the first covenant.
>
> (Heb 9:11-15)

Jesus the Christ is clearly envisioned as a priestly figure by his followers. As a new high priest, he offers a worthy **sacrifice** and mediates a new **covenant**—combining the roles of Aaron and Moses.

It is even possible that Jesus thought of himself in priestly terms. Jesus quotes Ps 110:1 as an apparent self-reference in Matt 22:44 // Mark 12:36 // Luke 20:42-43. This same psalm identifies a figure as a "priest forever in the order of Melchizedek" (Ps 110:4).

Yet, as Matthew's genealogy suggests, Jesus is more than a "Messiah of Aaron." When Christians think about Jesus' death on a cross, there is a tendency to think about the theological meaning of Jesus' death, to ponder the suffering of Jesus, or to give thanks for sins forgiven. Too often, the placard above Jesus' head is forgotten, the sign reading "King of the Jews" (Matt 27:37 // Mark 15:26 // Luke 23:38 // John 19:19). According to all four canonical gospels, Jesus of Nazareth was executed by the authorities as a royal pretender, as a political threat. The authorities may have equated messianic claims with claims to royal power; in Luke 23:2, Jesus is accused of "saying that he himself is *christos* (= "messiah"), a king."

> John's Gospel describes a wide array of messianic expectations, suggesting that the coming messiah would "announce all things to us" (John 4:25), conceal his identity (7:27), work many **signs** (7:31), be born in Bethlehem (7:42), and "remain forever" (12:34).

In sum, Luke 3:15 may accurately reflect the amorphous but active expectations and wonderings of certain first-century Jews. According to the canonical gospels, Jesus' disciples were confounded by this messiah from Nazareth (see John 1:45-46). These disciples appear to have wanted their leader to take on a more active role—according to Acts, even after Jesus' resurrection, the disciples are eager for action: "Lord, now are you going to restore the kingdom to Israel?" (Acts 1:6). Was not the messiah supposed to be a mighty warrior like the original David, a shepherd-turned-king with a mighty sword and accurate sling (see 1 Sam 17; 21:11; etc.)?

Such messianic expectations might have been better served by a certain Athrongaeus, active during the rule of Herod the Great's son Archelaus. While Josephus never labels him as a "messiah," the historian shows us how Athrongaeus fits the Davidic model:

> Then, a certain shepherd dared to lay claim to kingship (*basileia*); he was called Athrongaeus. His bodily strength and death-despising soul recommended this hope to him—moreover, there were four brothers just like him. Athrongaeus placed an armed company under the command of each of his brothers, and he engaged them as generals and satraps for his raids. But he, like a king, handled more dignified matters. At that time, he put a diadem on his head, but he continued to ravage the countryside with his brothers for quite a while.
>
> (Josephus, *Jewish War* 2.60-62)

After a string of successes, the brothers began to fall to Archelaus and his Roman allies. Interestingly, Josephus does not describe the ultimate fate of Athrongaeus; still, his incomplete account supports a limited comparison between David and Athrongaeus. Like David, Athrongaeus rose from the lowly status of shepherd up to the lofty rank of king. And, like David,

Athrongaeus enjoyed military success against a variety of foes. Unlike David, whose cause is espoused by prophets and priests, Athrongaeus appears in more secular guise. Josephus depicts him as an eastern despot, wearing a diadem and deploying "satraps" to govern. Still, behind the historian's dismissive portrayal, we can see this self-styled king making a bid to free Judea from Roman rule—perhaps even attempting to restore the kingdom to Israel.

"Who do you say that I am?"

According to the canonical gospels, Jesus of Nazareth amazed crowds, thwarted opponents, perplexed authorities, and regularly baffled his disciples. There was something about Jesus that drew a crowd, something that kept his followers coming back, even after they fell away. Presumably, the signs and wonders that (the gospels claim that) he performed formed a large part of his appeal. His new teachings have also attracted many hearers, from the first century to the twenty-first century. According to the New Testament writings, the signs, wonders, and teachings functioned as important pointers to the significance of Jesus, but these words and deeds were not the source of Jesus' significance. According to the New Testament writings, the mystery of Jesus' true identity and purpose were not finally revealed by what Jesus said or did, but by what Jesus suffered. The passion (= suffering), death, and resurrection of Jesus revealed the nature of his messianic mission.

Yet, is it fair to call Jesus a "messiah" (= anointed one) at all, if he was never anointed? According to Mark, Jesus was anointed with costly ointment by a woman—but Jesus explains that she has anointed his "body for its burial" (Mark 14:8). While Jesus' death appears to have been part of his messianic mission, one suspects that he came to do more than die.

Luke, in his two volumes, makes clear that Jesus received a different sort of anointing for his mission. In Acts 10, Peter preaches that "God anointed him with holy spirit and with power" (10:38; see also 4:27). Much earlier, at the outset of Jesus' public ministry, Jesus identifies his anointing in the language of the book of Isaiah: "The spirit of the Lord is upon me, because he has anointed me to preach good news (*euangelisasthai*) to the poor; he has sent me to proclaim release to the captives and recovery of sight to the blind . . ." (Luke 4:18). After reading this passage from the Isaiah scroll, Jesus declares, "Today, this scripture has been fulfilled in your hearing" (Luke 4:21). According to Luke's narrative, the anointing took place before that particular day; in Luke 4:14, we find Jesus already manifesting "the power of the spirit." When exactly did Jesus receive this anointing? In Luke's Gospel, the anointing follows Jesus' baptism: "And the Holy Spirit descended on him in bodily form like a dove" (Luke 3:22).

Luke and the other **evangelists** portray Jesus as a spirit-anointed, spirit-filled messiah who has come to preach good news to all who will hear. Those who expected a royal messiah were disappointed to see their hero crucified as "King of the Jews." Those who expected a priestly messiah found a man who never set foot in the inner sanctuary of the Jerusalem temple. Instead, the gospel accounts describe Jesus as a suffering messiah who "was counted with the lawless; he took up the sins of many and was handed over on account of their sins" (Isa 53:12 LXX; see Luke 22:37). According to the New Testament authors, this messiah again confounded and exceeded expectations by rising again to new life—and promising this life to all who would follow him.

Bibliography and suggestions for further reading

John J. Collins. *The Scepter and the Star: Messianism in Light of the Dead Sea Scrolls*. Second edition. Grand Rapids: Eerdmans, 2010. (Collins draws on evidence from the Dead Sea Scrolls and other Second Temple Jewish texts to give a nuanced portrait of the varieties of messianic expectations in circulation around the time of Jesus.)

Zeba Crook. "On the Treatment of Miracles in New Testament Scholarship." *Studies in Religion/Sciences Religieuses* 40.4 (2011): 461–478. (Whereas Keener advocates for more careful attention to the miracles of the New Testament, Crook suggests that scholars of Christian origins should adopt a more naturalistic approach, eschewing "sui generis claims" and playing by the same rules as classicists and anthropologists.)

Richard A. Horsley and John S. Hanson. *Bandits, Prophets, and Messiahs: Popular Movements in the Time of Jesus*. Minneapolis: Winston Press, 1985. (Horsley and Hanson offer good historical background to various popular movements of the first century, with a focus on the role of what they call the "Jewish peasantry.")

Craig S. Keener. *Miracles: The Credibility of the New Testament Accounts*. 2 vols. Grand Rapids: Baker Academic, 2011. (Keener offers both a philosophical response to Hume's skepticism and a multitude of eyewitness accounts to miraculous events.)

John P. Meier. *A Marginal Jew: Rethinking the Historical Jesus*. 5 vols. New Haven: Yale University Press, 1991–present. (Currently, Meier is working on his fifth (and final?) volume of this major series, which offers some of the best in contemporary "historical Jesus" scholarship. The second half of Meier's second volume is devoted to the question of Jesus' miracles.)

7

The Twelve Learners

Guiding Questions

How do the followers of Jesus compare to the followers of Elijah, or to the followers of Socrates?

Why does Josephus present Jewish **sects** as "philosophies"?

What is the difference between a disciple and an apostle?

As Jesus passed by along the Sea of Galilee, he saw Simon and Simon's brother Andrew casting nets into the sea; for they were fishers. And Jesus said to them, "Come follow me, and I will make you into fishers of people." And immediately they left their nets and followed him.

He went on a little farther, and he saw James the son of Zebedee and his brother John, who were in the boat mending their nets. And immediately he called them. They left their father Zebedee in the boat with the hired hands and followed Jesus.

(Mark 1:16-20)

What are disciples?

While many people follow Jesus as he wanders through Galilee, Samaria, and Judea, these individuals are never simply called "followers." Simon, Andrew, James, John, and the other followers of Jesus are usually labeled "**disciples**." What does it mean to be a "disciple" of Jesus? To answer this question, we need to define the word "disciple." Our English word "disciple" is based on the Latin word *discipulus*, meaning "learner." When the word "disciple" appears in your English translation of the New Testament, it is typically translating the Greek word *mathētēs*, which means "learner." So the "twelve disciples" of Jesus are more literally the "twelve learners." Hence, it makes sense that their leader Jesus is often called "Teacher" (*didaskalos* in Greek), or "Rabbi" (which means "my master" in **Aramaic**, but as John 1:38 points out, usually is best translated as "teacher").

> Interestingly, in the **Gospel** of Matthew, only outsiders refer to Jesus as a "teacher." The disciples never call Jesus "teacher." For Matthew, Jesus is much more than a teacher.

Why would the earliest followers of Jesus be called "learners"? Why not "adherents," "supporters," "groupies," or "fans"? Was it normal to wander around the countryside listening to someone preach and teach? Were there not fish to catch, fields to plant, wares to sell? Is there any precedent for this sort of activity? How were Jesus' disciples similar to and different from other ancient disciples?

To answer these questions, we will begin with a review of the master-disciple relationships between prophetic figures within the Jewish **scriptures**; Elijah and Elisha are the premier exemplars. Jesus is cast as a new prophet like Elijah, and this Israelite background shaped New Testament depictions of Jesus. While Jewish readers of the New Testament would recognize the parallels between Jesus and Elijah, non-Jewish readers might find their view of Jesus and his disciples to be refracted through the lens of Greco-Roman philosophers. Accordingly, we will next take a look at Hellenistic philosophers and their followers. The influence of this philosophical milieu is evident in the presentation of Jewish sects as "philosophies" in the work of Josephus. Finally, we will zero in on what the New Testament writings reveal about disciples and discipleship in the first century C.E. Throughout the chapter, we will explore how different conceptions of discipleship might have influenced both outsider perceptions of early Christian discipleship and the self-understanding of Jesus' first followers.

Models for discipleship

The paradigmatic master-disciple relationship in the Jewish scriptures was between Elijah the prophet and his successor Elisha. As mentioned in the previous chapter, God orders Elijah to anoint Elisha as his successor (1 Kgs 19:16). Elijah sets out to obey the divine command immediately:

> He left that place and found Elisha, son of Shaphat, who was plowing. There were twelve yoke of oxen in front of him, and he was with the twelfth. Elijah went over to him and threw his cloak over him. Elisha left the oxen, ran after Elijah, and said, "Please let me kiss my father and my mother, and then I will follow you." Elijah said to him, "Go on back again, for what have I done to you?" So he turned away from following him, took the yoke of oxen, and slaughtered them; using the wooden yoke from the oxen, he boiled the flesh, and gave it to the people, and they ate. Then he arose and followed after Elijah, and he served as his attendant.
>
> (1 Kgs 19:19-21)

Surprisingly, Elijah does not anoint Elisha. Within this narrative, the placing of Elijah's cloak (or "mantle," to use the traditional term) over Elisha serves as the only sign that Elisha has been granted official status as prophetic successor to Elijah. And after this sudden beginning, nothing else is said about Elisha's role until the end of Elijah's ministry. In 2 Kings 2, Elisha makes clear his devotion to Elijah, and he is rewarded with the sight of his master Elijah ascending into **heaven** in a chariot of fire (2:11). Elisha then takes up the mantle of his predecessor, strikes the Jordan River, and—like his master Elijah—walks through the parted waters (compare 2:14 with 2:8). A group of prophets recognizes that Elisha has indeed received the spirit of Elijah, and when Elisha subsequently works two miracles, his status is fully legitimated.

To review, we have seen that Elisha is called away from his family to follow a charismatic leader. When his master departs to heaven, Elisha bears the (literal) mantle of authority. And his status is confirmed by working the same types of miracles that had been wrought by his master. Elisha is recognized as one who bears the word of God (2 Kgs 3:12), and he goes on to stand before kings (2 Kgs 3:13; 6:21; 7:1; etc.). If you have read the Gospel according to Luke and the Acts of the Apostles, then this general storyline may sound familiar. (And it appears that Luke would want you to pick up on the connections—see Luke 4:25-27.)

In the Jewish scriptures, then, Elijah and Elisha offer the premier example of the master-disciple relationship, as there are only a few other references to discipleship—in the book of Isaiah, for instance, the prophet refers to his "disciples" (Isa 8:16, *limmudim* in Hebrew). Later retellings of the Elijah and Elisha narratives explicitly recount the presence of additional disciples.

In his *Jewish Antiquities*, Josephus includes his version of the Elijah and Elisha narratives. According to Josephus, Elisha had disciples: "But Elisha was not unaware of the king's wrath; sitting in his own house with his disciples (*mathētai*), he warned them that Joram, the son of the murderer, had sent someone to take off his head." (Josephus, *Jewish Antiquities* 9.68; *LCL* translation [R. Marcus]). According to the parallel account in 2 Kings 6:32, Elisha is sitting with "the elders" while he awaits the attack of King Jehoram (= Joram). But, for Josephus, Elisha is a master with disciples. Elisha can order his disciples to protect him (as in *Jewish Antiquities* 9.68-69), and Elisha can send a disciple (*mathētēs*) to anoint Jehu as king of Israel (as in *Jewish Antiquities* 9.106; compare 2 Kgs 9:1-3).

Philosophers and disciples

Why does Josephus import this "disciple" (*mathētēs*) language into his retelling of the Jewish scriptures? In all likelihood, this language is informed by the historian's cultural context. In the first-century Mediterranean world, disciples (or "learners") were often associated with philosophy. In that culture, there were no public universities with land grants from the state, no small liberal arts colleges on perfectly groomed campuses. There were schools, in Athens and elsewhere. But, in many cases, teachers were itinerant—they were always on the move. Their students would literally follow them around to learn from them. For an example, consider the following story about Socrates:

> Xenophon, the son of Gryllus, was a citizen of Athens … He was a man of rare modesty and extremely handsome. The story goes that Socrates met him in a narrow passage, and that he stretched out his stick to bar the way, while he inquired where every kind of food was sold. Upon receiving a reply, he put another question, "And where do men become good and honorable?" Xenophon was fairly puzzled. "Then follow me," said Socrates, "and learn." From that time onward he was a student (*akroatēs*) of Socrates.
> (Diogenes Laertius 2.48; *LCL* translation [R. D. Hicks], modified)

"Follow me." Socrates does not hand Xenophon a business card or invite him to enroll in fall semester classes. Instead, Socrates demands his would-be student to follow. The parallel with this chapter's opening citation from Mark 1 is hard to miss.

Why is Xenophon called a "student" (*akroatēs*, a Greek word literally meaning "hearer"), instead of a disciple (*mathētēs*)? Diogenes Laertius may be preserving Socrates' supposed distaste for the term "disciple" (*mathētēs*)—he tends not to use the term for his own followers. Plato portrays Socrates as adamantly refusing to be cast as a teacher (*didaskalos*) of disciples (*mathētai*): "Indeed, I was never the teacher (*didaskalos*) of anyone!" (Plato, *Apology* 33A). Later philosophers did not maintain this aspect of the Socratic tradition.

Parallels between the philosophers and the disciples of Jesus abound. It is not entirely clear whether these parallels are purely coincidental or whether there is influence in one direction or the other. What is clear is that a reader who knew the philosophical tradition would certainly find their reading of the New Testament writings to be colored by this background knowledge. Thus, someone like Diogenes Laertius (who lived and wrote in the first half of the third century C.E.) may or may not have known the gospel traditions about Jesus and the disciples, but he would certainly see connections with the philosophical tradition if he did encounter the New Testament writings. For example, Diogenes Laertius writes about Diogenes the Cynic:

> He was the first, say some, to fold his cloak because he was obliged to sleep in it as well, and he carried a bag (*pēra*) to hold his food, and he used any place for any purpose, for breakfasting, sleeping, or conversing. And then he would say, pointing to the portico of Zeus and the Hall of Processions, that the Athenians had provided him with places to live in. He did not lean upon a staff until he grew infirm; but afterwards he would carry it everywhere, not indeed in the city, but when walking along the road with it and with his bag (*pēra*) ... He had written to someone to try and procure a cottage for him. When this man was a long time about it, he took for his abode the tub in the Metroon [a temple in Athens devoted to the mother goddess Cybele], as he himself explains in his letters.
>
> (Diogenes Laertius 6.22-23; *LCL* translation [R. D. Hicks], modified)

Diogenes carries a bag or sack (*pēra*) for his food. He eventually carries a staff. And, for a time, he famously lives in a tub. This description of Diogenes' minimalist lifestyle bears some interesting resemblances to Jesus' commands to his followers in Mark 6, where he orders the twelve to go on a journey with only a staff, but "no bread, no bag (*pēra*), no money for their belt" (Mark 6:8; compare Matt 10:9-10; Luke 9:3; 10:4). If Diogenes reduced his needs to the bare minimum, Jesus' disciples do not have even the minimum; they will necessarily be dependent on the hospitality of those whom they encounter on the way (Mark 6:10-11).

This austere lifestyle was prized by philosophers of many different stripes. For "wisdom-lovers" (the literal translation of the Greek *philosophos*), the pursuit of wisdom was to be prioritized above all other needs. For a reflection on the reward of philosophy, we can turn to Xenophon (ca. 430 B.C.E. – 350s B.C.E.), son of Gryllus, whose encounter with Socrates (as narrated by Diogenes Laertius) appeared earlier in this chapter. Xenophon's *Memorabilia* includes a scene where Antiphon the Sophist addresses Socrates and speaks critically of philosophy:

> Socrates, I supposed that philosophy must add to one's store of happiness. But the fruits you have reaped from philosophy are apparently very different. For example, you are living a life that would drive even a slave to desert his master. Your meat and drink are of the poorest. The cloak you wear is not only a poor thing, but is never changed summer or winter. And you never wear shoes or a tunic. Besides, you refuse to take money, the mere getting of which is a joy, while its possession makes one more independent and happier. Now, the teachers (*didaskaloi*) of other subjects try to make their students (*mathētai*) copy their teachers. If you intend to make your companions (*sunontas*) do that, you must consider yourself a teacher (*didaskalos*) of unhappiness.
>
> (Xenophon, *Memorabilia* 1.6.2-3; *LCL* translation [E. C. Marchant])

For Antiphon, the pursuit of philosophy is the pursuit of misery, at least when viewed from the perspective of physical needs (food, clothing, and money for other needs). Socrates neglects these bodily needs, and he inculcates this neglect in his "companions" (*sunontasi*), or followers. In response to Antiphon, Socrates will go on to point out the higher virtues that he is cultivating: "I am growing in goodness and I am making better friends" (*Memorabilia* 1.6.8). Both Jesus and Socrates refuse to privilege comfort and convenience over the higher goods of life. For Socrates, these higher goods include growth in virtue and improved relationships. For Jesus, disciples should likewise seek higher (or "heavenly") things, and they should also try to win friends (see Matt 6:24-33 and Luke 16:9).

The Jewish philosophies

Further evidence of the similarities between the teachings of Hellenistic philosophers and Jewish teachers can be found in Josephus. Josephus wrote his *Jewish Antiquities* for a Roman audience, and his research was funded by a Roman emperor. To make his Jewish background more appealing to his audience, Josephus utilized philosophical language: "Since the most distant ancestral past, the **Jews** have had three philosophies: one of the Essenes, one of the Sadducees, and a third that went by the name of Pharisees" (Josephus, *Jewish Antiquities* 18.11). According to this presentation, the **Pharisees, Sadducees**, and **Essenes** are not simply **sects** of **Second Temple** Judaism; they are described as philosophical schools. (Interestingly, Josephus does not consider the **Samaritans** here—for the historian, they do not qualify as a Jewish sect.) If we turn to the second book of his *Jewish War*, we find his account of these three groups:

> Now there are three forms of philosophy among the Jews. The followers of the first are the Pharisees; then, the Sadducees; and the third, which claims to practice reverence, are called Essenes. This group is Jewish by birth, and they seem to love one another more than the others. These Essenes turn away from pleasures as from evil, but they consider self-control and mastery over one's passions to be virtue (*aretē*).
>
> (Josephus, *Jewish War* 2.119-120)

Josephus will devote the majority of his discussion to the **Essenes**. This sect prizes celibacy; to preserve their own existence, they recruit children from other non-Essene Jews. This way, they can avoid the dangers of sex . . . and women: "They do not oppose marriage or its perpetuation of the human race, but they are on guard against the dissolute nature of women, convinced that no woman preserves her fidelity (*pistis*) to one man" (Josephus, *Jewish War* 2.121).

The Essenes avoid all manner of worldly pleasures, eschewing sex, possession of private property, and normal hygiene of their time. In exchange, they gain all the advantages (and disadvantages) of communal living, plus an extensive network of hospitality:

> They are despisers of wealth, and their communal sharing of property is amazing. There is no one to be found among them who possesses more than the others. In fact, there is a rule that those who enter the sect (*hairesis*) must declare their private property to be for the public use of the order. As a result, among them all, there is no lowliness of poverty or superiority of wealth, but the possessions of each member are mixed together, just as if all were brothers with one shared fortune.
>
> They consider oil to be a defilement, and if someone is anointed unwillingly, they purge the oil from their body. They consider it noble to have dry skin and to be dressed in white at all times. They elect individuals to manage the

communal goods, and each of them gives their undivided attention to their duties, for the benefit of all.

They have no city of their own, but many take up residence in every city. They make available their resources to visiting members of the sect who come from a different place, to use as if they were their own. And they go into the homes of those they have never seen before as if they were the most familiar of friends. Therefore, when they make a journey, they bring nothing at all, apart from weapons in case of bandits. In every city, a guardian who cares for visitors is specially appointed for the order, so as to dispense clothing and other necessary provisions.

(Josephus, *Jewish War* 2.122-125)

This picture of the Essenes must be seen as, in part, a propaganda piece. Knowing that his elite Roman audience respects the **asceticism** of the philosophers, Josephus brings forth the Essenes as a parade example of the virtues of Judaism. Of course, to a twenty-first-century reader, the Essenes may seem to be a disturbed cult-like sect: a group of misogynists who brainwash children, shun the comforts of life, and live in some sort of 1970s commune (minus the "free love"). To a first-century reader, the Essenes presumably made a better impression, based on their manly virtue (recall the discussion in Chapter Five), unflinching asceticism, and utopian sharing of possessions (closely paralleled in Acts 2:44-45 and 4:32). Josephus goes on to underscore the parallels between Essenes and Hellenistic philosophers:

They (the Essenes) firmly believe that bodies are perishable and that their matter is not permanent, but that souls are immortal and live on forever. These souls come from the lightest air and are mingled into bodies as if into prisons, hauled down by some natural spell. But when they are released from the bonds of the flesh, then, as if delivered from a lengthy bondage, they rejoice and are borne off high above.

(Josephus, *Jewish War* 2.154-155)

Those familiar with Platonic ideas like the immortality of the soul and the materiality of the body will have no problem accepting the Jewish Essenes as fellow philosophers.

The **Dead Sea Scrolls** are thought to be written by a group of Essenes living at **Qumran**, a few miles west of the northeastern shores of the Dead Sea. No scroll contains the word "Essene" (which comes from a Greek word—the scrolls are mostly written

in **Hebrew** and Aramaic). But some of the initiation rituals
described in Josephus (not quoted here) resemble rituals described
in the Dead Sea Scrolls.

After his lengthy description of the Essenes, Josephus eventually gives
briefer descriptions of the other two sects, the Pharisees and the Sadducees:

> Of the other two mentioned earlier, the Pharisees are those considered to
> interpret the laws with strictness (*akribeia*). They bear the title of leading sect
> (*hairesis*), and they attribute all things to fate and to God. For them, acting
> rightly or not rests, for the most part, with humans, but fate assists each
> person. Every soul is imperishable, but only the souls of the good pass into
> another body; the souls of the wicked are condemned to eternal punishment.
>
> The Sadducees, who are the second order, completely reject fate and place
> God beyond the doing of some evil or the seeing of evil. They say that good
> and evil are left to the choice of human beings; according to the judgment of
> each person, one of these two is chosen. They reject the persistence of the
> soul, as well as the punishments and rewards of Hades.
>
> The Pharisees also are friendly with each other, and they work towards
> unity and the public good. But the Sadducees treat each other more savagely;
> their dealings with their companions are as rough as if they were dealing with
> strangers.
>
> (Josephus, *Jewish War* 2.162-166)

Can you tell which of these two sects is preferred by Josephus? The Pharisees
interpret **Torah** most skillfully, affirm divine providence, and believe in the
immortality of the soul. The Sadducees eliminate providence, affirm human
free will, and deny any sort of afterlife. Moreover, the Pharisees are friendly,
and the Sadducees are . . . not so friendly. Or so says Josephus.

Readers of the New Testament generally do not come away with a
high opinion of Pharisees. The Pharisees can seem like the "bad
guys," the "foil" for Jesus. But it would be a mistake to interpret
passages like Luke 11:38-44 as a blanket condemnation of all
things Pharisaic. Jesus and the Pharisees agreed on the importance
of Torah, the coming final judgment, the **resurrection** of the dead,
and many other theological convictions. Indeed, the extent of
agreement between Jesus and the Pharisees presumably intensified
the dispute over points at which Jesus and the Pharisees diverged.

> The canonical gospels, written at a time when the followers of Jesus were still competing with other Jewish sects, underscore the conflict between Jesus and Pharisees, allowing the many points of agreement to recede into the background.

What conclusions can we draw? For Josephus, an educated Greco-Roman audience should see Jews not as barbarians, but as philosophers. The differences between Jewish sects have a philosophical character, having to do with debates over the immortality of the soul or the interplay between fate and free will. Just as educated Romans might try out various philosophical schools, so Josephus could test-drive the various philosophies of the Jews, as he explains in his autobiography:

> Around the age of sixteen, I desired to gain personal experience of the sects (*haireseis*) that were among us. There are three of them. The sect of the Pharisees is first, the sect of the Sadducees second, and the third is that of the Essenes, as we have said many times. I thought that, in this way, I could choose the best, if I had examined them all closely.
>
> Undergoing hardship and suffering many things, I went through all three of them. [. . . *Josephus then describes his experience with Bannus, quoted above in Chapter Four* . . .] When I had accomplished my desire, I returned to the city. At the age of nineteen, I began to live my life as a member of the sect of the Pharisees, which is equivalent to what the Greeks call the Stoic sect.
>
> (Josephus, *Life* 10-12)

Like other elite scions, Josephus styles himself as one who has sampled the philosophies of his day. The teenage son of a priestly family casts himself as a philosopher, and his sect of choice is the (allegedly) Stoic-like Pharisees. Josephus' story thus testifies to the possibility of interpreting the lifestyle of a first-century Jew through a philosophical lens.

Disciples in the New Testament

But is that what the authors of the canonical gospels are trying to do—cast Jesus as a philosopher with his ring of earnest disciples? If so, they did a strikingly poor job of it. Jesus' disciples are hardly model philosophers. Jesus may sound like Socrates when he calls his followers to embrace poverty and value higher goods over bodily needs. But there is no sign that the disciples followed Jesus in order to burnish their philosophical credentials. Rather than discussing wisdom, the immortality of the soul, or human free will, we find Jesus' disciples more concerned with saving their earthly skin (Matt 8:25), locating their next meal (Mark 8:14-16), or securing positions of power (Mark 10:35-37). Socrates would not be impressed.

> Within the New Testament itself, Jesus does not have a monopoly on disciples. In the Gospels and Acts, we meet disciples of the Pharisees (Matt 22:15-16; Mark 2:18 // Luke 5:33), as well as disciples of John the Baptist (Matt 9:14 // Mark 2:18 // Luke 5:33; Matt 11:2 // Luke 7:18; Matt 14:12 // Mark 6:29; John 3:25; 4:1; and perhaps Acts 19:1-3). The Gospel of John also includes a Pharisaic claim to be "disciples of Moses" (9:28), and Saul of Tarsus has his own "disciples" in Acts 9:25.

Thus, educated first-century readers might have been ready to file Jesus and his motley band into their mental "Cynic" or "Socratic" folder. But those who read the four gospels would likely be discouraged by what they found; Jesus and friends did not fit neatly into any particular philosophical school. Moreover, as the New Testament writings attest, the behavior of Jesus' followers sometimes failed to impress. Back in Chapter Three, we discussed Tacitus's description of Nero's persecution of **Christians**. We did not dwell on the latter part of the quote, which testifies both to the early popularity of the Christian movement and to the impression it made on some Romans:

> But in spite of this temporary setback the deadly superstition had broken out afresh, not only in Judaea (where the mischief had started) but even in Rome. All degraded and shameful practices collect and flourish in the capital.
>
> (Tacitus, *Annals* 15.44; M. Grant translation [Penguin, 1989])

Tacitus here reveals that he considers Christianity—which was apparently flourishing in Rome—"degraded and shameful." The disciples of Jesus attracted the notice and the disgust of at least one elite Roman.

How should we view the disciples of Jesus? We have discussed various outsider perspectives; let us now turn our gaze from the philosophical parallels and look at the New Testament writings. To gain an insider's view of discipleship in the New Testament, we need to add two more ingredients to our discussion: the number 12, and the word "apostle."

A full explanation of the symbolism of "the twelve" in the canonical gospels would require at least an additional chapter. The expectation of a restoration of Israel as a united kingdom of twelve tribes can be traced throughout the prophetic writings of the Jewish scriptures. To see some representative examples, read Isa 11:12; Jer 31:1; Ezek 20:27-44; 37:15-28; Mic 2:12.

Obviously, Jesus had more than twelve disciples. But the gospel-writers do frequently refer to a select group that is known simply as "the twelve" (e.g., Matt 26:20; Mark 4:10; 6:7; Luke 8:1; John 6:67, 71; 20:24). Why would the twelve be singled out as a select group of disciples? Jesus' **election** of a new twelve appears to be a symbolic action, initiating the process of restoration that will culminate in the reconstitution of the twelve tribes of Israel. Jesus' words to the twelve are revealing: "Truly, I tell you, that you who have followed me—in the restoration (*palingenesia*), when the Son of Man will sit on his throne of glory—you also will sit on twelve thrones judging the twelve tribes of Israel" (Matt 19:28; compare Luke 22:30). Thus, while Jesus gathered many disciples, the choice of an inner circle of twelve was intended to link Jesus' ministry with the process of restoring the twelve tribes of Israel.

Sometimes, a disciple is labeled an "apostle" (*apostolos*, a Greek word meaning "one who is sent"). The singular "apostle" is never found in the Gospels or Acts or Revelation; it most commonly is used by Paul, referring to himself (e.g., Rom 1:1; 1 Cor 1:1; 2 Cor 1:1; Gal 1:1; but see also Heb 3:1 and 1 Pet 1:1). Much more frequently in New Testament narratives, we find references to "apostles" who are sent on missions by Jesus. When Jesus sends his disciples out, they are frequently called "apostles" (Matt 10:2; Mark 6:30; Luke 9:10; etc.). For a more detailed description of apostleship, we can look at a speech of Peter in the book of Acts; here, Peter is discussing how to replace a member of the twelve: "Therefore, it is necessary for one of these men who have accompanied us during the whole time that the Lord Jesus went in and out among us, beginning with the baptism of John, until the day when he was taken up from us, to become with us a witness to his resurrection" (Acts 1:21-22). A few verses later, the believers pray and ask God to reveal the divine choice for taking up "the apostleship" (*apostolē* in Acts 1:25). So, in Acts, we find apostles being defined as those who give "testimony to the resurrection of the Lord Jesus" (Acts 4:33).

In conclusion, then, we have observed earlier master-disciple relationships in the Jewish scriptures. We also noted the surface parallels between the followers of Jesus and the followers of Greco-Roman philosophers. Finally, we have looked at some of the ways in which the followers of Jesus are unique. Yet, even though we acknowledge their uniqueness, we cannot forget their Second Temple Jewish context. For instance, the post-Easter followers of Jesus powerfully emphasize resurrection. This emphasis aligns them with some Jewish sects (e.g., the Pharisees) and puts them at odds with others (e.g., the Sadducees—compare Luke 20:27 with Josephus, *Jewish War* 2.165). The expectation of a restoration of Israel constitutes a hope shared by the followers of Jesus and by other Jewish sects, such as the Qumran community (1QM 2:2-3 issues a call for twelve Levites to serve each of the twelve tribes in the **eschaton**). To further explore how the followers of Jesus converged with and diverged from other first-century Jewish groups, we will need to explore Second Temple Judaism, the topic of Chapter Eight.

Bibliography and suggestions for further reading

John Dominic Crossan. "Open Healing and Open Eating: Jesus as a Jewish Cynic?" *Biblical Research* 36 (1991): 6–18. (Crossan concedes that Cynics were "urban, individualistic, and unorganized," whereas Jesus' followers were "rural," "communal," and "organized around healing missions." Still, Crossan argues that Jesus can be viewed as a "Jewish Cynic.")

Paul Rhodes Eddy. "Jesus as Diogenes? Reflections on the Cynic Jesus Thesis." *Journal of Biblical Literature* 115 (1996): 449–469. (Eddy reviews the thesis that Jesus was a "thoroughly hellenized, noneschatological, contra-cultural" Cynic figure, and he finds that it falls short. At the heart of Eddy's critique is the way that Jesus-as-Cynic theories tend to de-emphasize the Jewishness of Jesus.)

Joel B. Green, Jeannine K. Brown, and Nicholas Perrin, eds. *Dictionary of Jesus and the Gospels*. Second edition. Downers Grove: IVP Academic, 2013. (This dictionary is a very useful resource for students of the New Testament; substantive articles include helpful bibliography for further research. Note, for example, the excellent article on "Disciples and Discipleship" by M. J. Wilkins.)

Justin Martyr. *First Apology*. (Justin, the author of this second-century C.E. defense of Christianity, saw no conflict between wearing the philosopher's cloak and taking up his cross to follow Jesus. His *Apology* is available in many English translations.)

John P. Meier. *Companions and Competitors.* Vol. 3 of *A Marginal Jew: Rethinking the Historical Jesus.* New Haven: Yale University Press, 2001. (Meier devotes two chapters to Jesus' disciples, as well as additional chapters on Pharisees and Sadducees. Of particular interest is his discussion of the evolution of descriptions of the Pharisees in the works of Josephus—see pp. 304–305.)

8

The Jews

Guiding Questions

What does it mean to be Jewish?
What varieties of Judaism existed in the **Second Temple** period?
How might a gentile become a Jew?

So, what advantage has the Jew? Or what is the benefit of circumcision? Much, in every way! First, they were entrusted with the words of God.

(Rom 3:1-2)

The man went off and announced to the Jews that Jesus was the one who healed him. For this reason, the Jews began to persecute Jesus, because he was doing these things on the sabbath. But Jesus answered them, "My Father is working until now, and I too am working." For this reason, then, the Jews were seeking all the more to kill him, because he was not only breaking the sabbath, but he was also saying that God was his own Father, making himself equal to God.

(John 5:15-18)

All the people answered, "His blood be upon us and upon our children!"

(Matt 27:25)

Pilate also wrote an inscription and put it on the cross; it read, "Jesus the Nazorean, the King of the Jews."

(John 19:19)

Jews, anti-Judaism, and the New Testament

The passages above give a sampling of how "the **Jews**" are portrayed in the New Testament. On the one hand, Paul's letter to the Romans argues that the Jews are indeed the chosen, blessed people of God, and the **Gospel** according to John affirms that "salvation is from the Jews" (John 4:22). On the other hand, the Gospel according to John describes a group of Jesus' opponents as "the Jews." Given the popularity of this Gospel through the centuries, it is no surprise that some have come to believe that *all* Jews opposed Jesus. Likewise, readers of Matthew's Gospel can all too easily (and erroneously) assume that the Jews as a whole should be blamed for the death of Jesus. Over the centuries, many Christian scholars, clerics, and laypeople have (mis-)used the New Testament to promote anti-Jewish attitudes and behaviors. In a tragic irony, the canonical gospels—these messages of "good news"—have served as fuel for hatred and violence. With only passing knowledge of Second Temple Judaism and the wider first-century context, it is easy to see the absurdity of harnessing the good news of Jesus of Nazareth for such purposes. One of the few things that New Testament scholarship agrees on is this fact: Jesus of Nazareth was a Jew.

Moreover, aside from Jesus, other Jews play almost all of the leading roles throughout the New Testament writings (which might also be considered "Jewish scripture"). Joseph and Mary were Jews. Simon Peter was a Jew. James and John the sons of Zebedee were Jews. The rest of the twelve **disciples** were Jews. Paul was a Jew. The vast majority of Jesus' earliest followers were Jews, as were most of his opponents. If we want to understand better the Jews who populate the pages of the New Testament, we need to learn a bit more about Second Temple Judaism.

Second Temple Jews

What does it mean to be a Second Temple Jew? To review a few lessons of Chapter Two, we can first recall that the **Second Temple** was dedicated in Jerusalem in 515 B.C.E. and destroyed by the Romans in 70 C.E. The Second Temple period thus begins in the late sixth century B.C.E. and ends around 70 C.E. (Some scholars will tack on another six decades and mark the end in the

Figure 8.1 Second Temple (scale model)
This scale model depicts the Temple Mount, as renovated by King Herod.
The Second Temple is in the center; to the left of the temple stands a
roofed structure, the "Royal Portico." To the right, just outside the Temple
Mount, is the fortress Antonia.
Model © Holyland Tourism 1992, Ltd.

130s C.E. with Bar Kokhba's failed revolt against Rome.) So, a Second Temple
Jew is simply a Jew who lived during this approximately six-hundred-year
time period.

> The English word "Jew" has an amazingly complex etymology.
> According to the *Oxford English Dictionary*, the modern English
> "Jew" is the successor of the Middle English form "Gyu" or "Giu,"
> which was derived from the Old French *giu*, which was earlier
> *juieu*. This French word came from the Latin *iūdaeus*, which was
> the equivalent of the Greek *ioudaios*. The Greek *ioudaios* came
> from the **Aramaic** *yehudai*, which came from the **Hebrew** *yehudi*,
> which was ultimately based on the Hebrew *Yehudah*.

And who is a Jew? The word "Jew" has its earliest roots in the Hebrew word *Yehudah*, which is usually translated as "Judah," a name with many possible referents. First, Judah was the fourth son of Jacob/Israel (Gen 29:35); second, the descendants of Judah were known as the tribe of Judah. According to the book of Joshua, the tribe of Judah was allotted a large portion of the **promised land** of Canaan. This large expanse in southern Canaan became known as Judah, a third use of the term (see Josh 15:1-12 for a description of the boundaries).

The fourth use of Judah requires a look at a later portion of the biblical narrative. The first three kings of Israel—Saul, David, and Solomon—ruled over a united kingdom. This kingdom was divided when Solomon's son Rehoboam ascended to the throne (see 1 Kings 12 for the details). Only two of the twelve tribes remained loyal to Rehoboam: Judah and Benjamin. Judah was the larger of these two tribes; consequently, the southern kingdom, with Jerusalem as its capital, was called "Judah." When the southern kingdom of Judah was conquered by the Babylonians in 587/586 B.C.E., the conquered people were known not as "Israelites" (= "sons of Israel/Jacob") or "**Hebrews**," but rather as the inhabitants of "Judah." These exiles from the land of *Yehudah* (in Hebrew) or *Yehud* (in Aramaic) came to be known as *Ioudaioi* (in Greek), and this word *Ioudaioi* (= plural; *Ioudaios* is the singular form) is almost always translated as "Jew" in the New Testament.

Some New Testament scholars prefer to translate *Ioudaios* as "Judean" instead of as "Jew." Why? Simply put, "Judean" is a good reminder of the strong geographical connection with the land of Judea/Judah. Also, "Judean" does not have any religious connotations; given the absence of any established concept of "world religions" in the first-century Mediterranean world, some scholars prefer this more neutral term.

Note, however, that this word "Jew" came from the word *Yehudah*, which could refer to either the *land* of Judah or the *tribe* of Judah or the *kingdom* of Judah—and it was not always easy to distinguish between these three possibilities. To be a Jew meant that you were part of an ethnic group that was associated with a particular geographic location. But when this people group was uprooted from that location and transported to Babylon, they retained this identity through various means. They married other Jews, preserving their ethnic identity. They continued to observe as much of the Torah as was possible—although, of course, offering required **sacrifices** in the Jerusalem **temple** was hindered by the destruction of the temple by the Babylonians—in order to preserve their customs and beliefs.

Thus, the Jews remained Jews, no matter where they lived. We call ancient Jews who lived in Jerusalem, Judea, and the surrounding areas "Palestinian Jews." Jews who were deported to Babylon or who emigrated to Egypt, Asia Minor, and beyond are known as "**Diaspora** Jews." The Greek word *diaspora* means "scattering," so Diaspora Jews are Jews who were scattered throughout the Mediterranean world.

Still, the question remains: Whether living in Palestine or in the Diaspora (= anywhere but Palestine), whether living in the Second Temple period or earlier or later, who is a Jew? In the discussion that follows, we need to try to step outside our twenty-first-century conceptions of identity. We think of our religious identity (Christian? Muslim? Agnostic?), our geographic identity (Midwesterner? New Englander? Southerner?), and our ethnic identity (Native American? Latin American? Creole?) as separate categories. It was not so in the ancient Mediterranean world.

"Jew" (*Ioudaios*) began as a geographical label for people from Judah. But the people living in Judah prior to the Babylonian conquest shared much more than a zip code. They served the same king, they worshiped in the same temple, they held to a common set of beliefs and practices, and they had a common ancestry. So, while the translation "Judean" is legitimate, it is misleading. If a **gentile** merchant's wife gave birth to a baby in Jerusalem, the child would not be considered a "Judean" by anybody.

Over time, the meaning of "Jew" shifted. The word came to have less geographical content and more (what we would call) religious or philosophical content. Coinciding with this shift in meaning was the arrival of a new word: *Ioudaismos*, or literally, "*Ioudaios*-ism." The first known use of this word is from 2 Maccabees, a history of the **Maccabean revolt** that was written in Greek during the second century B.C.E.:

> The exploits of Judas Maccabeus and his brothers, and the purification of the great temple, and the consecration of the altar, and further the wars against Antiochus Epiphanes and his son Eupator, and the epiphanies that came from heaven to those who fought bravely and honorably for "Judaism" (*Ioudaismos*), so that—though being few in number—they plundered the whole land and pursued the barbarian hordes, and reclaimed the temple that is renowned world-wide, and liberated the city, and restored the laws that were about to be abolished, with the Lord being merciful to them with all

kindness—this, which has been described by Jason of Cyrene in five volumes, we will attempt to condense into a single composition.

(2 Macc 2:19-23)

According to 2 Maccabees, the rebels fought for *Ioudaismos*, which appears to be linked not only with the land of Judah but also with temple worship and "laws." Thus, instead of being strictly an ethnic or geographical term, "Judaism" here carries more of a religious or cultic meaning.

This new word signals new opportunities for those who were not Jews. You cannot change your ancestry. But you can change your work schedule, your diet, and your religious practices. Suddenly, being Jewish was—theoretically, at least—possible for outsiders. In other words, *conversion* to Judaism was now possible in a way that was impossible before. Before we discuss conversion to Judaism, though, we should say more about what it meant to be *Ioudaios*, or Jewish.

I will use the words "Jew" and "Judaism" in the rest of the chapter, but I do not mean to imply that these are purely "religious" terms. A word similar to *Ioudaismos* is *Hellenismos*, which can be translated as "**Hellenism**" or "Greek-ism." But Hellenism brought with it Greek customs, Greek language, Greek thought; Hellenism was by no means a religion. Thus, in what follows, keep in mind that "Judaism" is not strictly a religious identification; then and now, it carries much more meaning than what would fit neatly into our modern compartments and categories.

Being Jewish

To be a Jew meant to be a member of the chosen people of God. In genealogical terms, a Jew was a descendant of Jacob (later re-named "Israel" by God in Gen 32:28). Jacob was the blessed son of Isaac, who was the promised son of Abraham, and Abraham was called by God to become the father the people of God. Yet, ancestry alone did not guarantee a permanent place in the people of God. To be part of the "holy nation" of God required obedience:

Moses went up to God. The Lord called to him from the mountain, saying, "Thus you shall say to the house of Jacob, and declare to the Israelites: You yourselves have seen what I did to the Egyptians, and how I carried you on eagles' wings and brought you to me. So, then, if you listen to my voice and keep my covenant, you will be my own treasure out of all the peoples. For all the earth is mine, but you will be for me a kingdom of priests and a holy nation. These are the words that you shall speak to the Israelites."

(Exod 19:3-6)

The sons and daughters of Israel who obey God's voice and keep God's **covenant** are promised membership in the people of God. What did this membership entail?

> The **Pentateuch** makes clear that ancestry alone did not ensure permanent blessing by God. In extreme cases, disobedience to Torah could result in being "cut off" from the people of God (see Exod 12:15, 19; 30:33, 38; 31:14; Lev 7:20-27; etc.; for a complete list, see the **Mishnah**, tractate *Keritot* 1.1).

According to the Pentateuch, when God gave Israel the covenant at Sinai, there were sets of obligations for each covenantal party. God promised to watch over Israel as the chosen people of God. Israel promised to keep the covenant. What does it mean to keep the covenant? Fundamentally, keeping God's covenant meant keeping God's law, the Torah (Torah literally means "teaching" or "instruction," but it is generally translated as "law"). The Torah was given as part of the Sinai covenant. Thus, for Israel, faithfulness to the covenant was bound up with observance of Torah, a comprehensive set of instructions for how to live in a God-pleasing manner. Torah covers everything from how to offer a correct sacrifice in the temple to how to treat foreigners to how to handle your pots and pans properly.

Certain aspects of the law functioned to set the Jews apart from the surrounding nations, as we can see in the following excerpt from 1 Maccabees. Here, King Antiochus IV Epiphanes issues the orders that led to the Maccabean revolt:

The king wrote to his whole kingdom that everyone should be one people and that each should abandon their own customs. And all the gentiles accepted the king's word. Even many from Israel were pleased with his rites of worship; they offered sacrifice to idols and profaned the sabbath. The king sent scrolls (*biblia*) by messengers to Jerusalem and the towns of Judah, commanding that they follow customs foreign to the land, forbid burnt offerings, sacrifices, and drink offerings in the sanctuary, profane the sabbaths and festivals, defile the sanctuary and the holy priests, build altars and shrines and temples, sacrifice pigs and other unclean animals, leave their sons uncircumcised, and make themselves abominable by every impure and profane thing, so that they might forget the law and change all the commandments.

(1 Macc 1:41-49)

This **Seleucid** king wants his kingdom to be more uniform, to consist of "one people" (1:41). However, the law (or Torah) is specifically designed to set apart or mark off the people of God. Parts of Jewish law observance stick out, and these are the "boundary markers" that show everyone that Jews are different. The laws of Antiochus are designed to impose Hellenism by erasing these boundary markers: sabbath observance, worship of the God of Israel alone, eating only "clean" animals, and circumcision.

For Jews, erasing the boundary markers is equivalent to erasing the people of God. If there are no boundary markers, the Jews are just one more of "the nations." The mid-second-century B.C.E. book of *Jubilees* creatively attributes the uniqueness of the Jewish nation to Abraham, who speaks the following lines:

And you also, my son, Jacob, remember my words, and keep the commandments of Abraham, your father. Separate yourself from the gentiles, and do not eat with them, and do not perform deeds like theirs. And do not become associates of theirs. Because their deeds are defiled, and all of their ways are contaminated, and despicable, and abominable.

(*Jubilees* 22.16; *OTP* translation)

The language of defilement and abomination calls to mind the earlier citation from 1 Maccabees, where King Antiochus IV Epiphanes is described as attacking the walls that separate the Jews from the rest of the people. This intentional separation from gentiles was achieved precisely by observance of Torah, as the second-century B.C.E. *Letter of Aristeas* makes clear:

In his wisdom the legislator . . . surrounded us with unbroken palisades and iron walls to prevent our mixing with any of the other peoples in any matter, being thus kept pure in body and soul, preserved from false beliefs, and worshiping the only God omnipotent over all creation . . . So, to prevent our being perverted by contact with others or by mixing with bad influences, he hedged us in on all sides with strict observances connected with meat and drink and touch and hearing and sight, after the manner of the Law.

(*Letter of Aristeas* 139, 142; *OTP* translation)

According to this author, Torah functions to separate Jews from the impurity and **idolatry** of the nations. The boundary markers keep Jews pure and set apart.

These marks of Judaism were well-known in the ancient world. Jews were known as a set-apart people. As we will discuss shortly, the uniqueness of the Jewish people attracted the respect of some outsiders. But for others, this uniqueness made them a target of distrust and fear. The Roman historian Tacitus offers an example:

> But the rest of the world they confront with the hatred reserved for enemies. They will not feed or intermarry with gentiles. Though a most lascivious people, the Jews avoid sexual intercourse with women of alien race. Among themselves nothing is barred. They have introduced the practice of circumcision to show that they are different from others. Proselytes adopt the same practices, and the very first lesson they learn is to despise the gods, shed all feelings of patriotism, and consider parents, children, and brothers as readily expendable. However, the Jews see to it that their numbers increase. It is a deadly sin to kill a born or unborn child, and they think that eternal life is granted to those who die in battle or execution – hence their eagerness to have children, and their contempt for death.
>
> (Tacitus, *Histories* 5.5; K. Wellesley translation [Penguin, 1995], modified)

Circumcision is again perceived as an identifying Jewish mark. Tacitus also notices—and condemns—Jewish worship of one God alone. For a polytheistic observer who offered regular worship to many gods, the Jews (and **Christians**) were exclusivist and intolerant. For all the rancor between Jews and Christians over many sad centuries, it is somewhat ironic that many ancient observers could not easily tell the two apart.

Second Temple Judaisms

For ancient observers and modern readers of the New Testament, it is easy to imagine Second Temple Judaism as a unified religion that is both monotheistic and monolithic. It is as easy to make that mistake as it is to imagine twenty-first-century Christianity as monolithic and unified. But try getting a room full of Southern Baptists, Episcopalians, Roman Catholics, Russian Orthodox, Pentecostals, and Methodists to agree about the meaning of the Lord's Supper ... or the propriety of infant baptism ... or the validity of women's ordination. This disparate group of

Christians sings different hymns (or praise songs), employs different worship styles, and uses different liturgical calendars—they even celebrate Easter (= the annual celebration of the **resurrection** of Jesus) on different days.

The same fragmentation and diversity characterizes Second Temple Judaism, or (as the above sub-title reads and as some scholars prefer) Second Temple *Judaisms*. Recall the characterization of **Pharisees, Sadducees**, and **Essenes** as competing "philosophical sects" in Josephus (see Chapter Seven). Josephus described how both Essenes and Pharisees believe in the immortality of the soul, as opposed to the Sadducee belief that souls can perish. Compare Luke 20:27 and Acts 23:8, which affirm that Sadducees do not believe in a resurrection or afterlife. Pharisees, Sadducees, and Essenes all worshiped the God of Israel, observed the sabbath, and practiced circumcision. But this unity was often hidden from view in the sharp disputes between the different **sects**.

To read the New Testament writings—and other sources that describe Second Temple Jews—we need to keep in mind that Jesus was not engaged in an inter-faith dispute between Jews and Christians. First, the label "Christian" did not yet exist in the time of Jesus (see Acts 11:26). Second, and more importantly, the canonical gospels portray Jesus as being involved in an intra-faith dispute *with his fellow Jews*. Jesus is not shown as someone who debates whether to keep Torah (see Matt 5:17). Rather, Jesus is engaged in debates over how to observe Torah (Matt 5:21-47), how to prioritize different commandments (Mark 12:28-34), and how to interpret the **scriptures** (Mark 12:35-37). He indeed brings new teachings and challenges traditional assumptions, but at no point does Jesus suggest that Jews should give up circumcision, or that Jews should abandon sabbath observance (despite his re-prioritizing of such observance in Mark 2:23-28).

During the events narrated in the canonical gospels and in Acts, the followers of Jesus were predominantly Jewish, and they were considered a "sect" (e.g., "the sect of the Nazarenes" in Acts 24:5), just like the Pharisees and Sadducees (compare Acts 5:17 and 15:5). Some individuals, like Josephus, moved from one sect to another. For instance, Acts 15:5 makes a fascinating reference to "some who had believed from the sect of the Pharisees." These believers in Jesus came from a Pharisaic background. The Greek is ambiguous, but the most probable reading is that these believers retained their Pharisaic interpretations of Torah—hence their interest in circumcising gentile believers in Jesus.

For an outstanding example of the complexity within Second Temple Judaism, see Luke's account of Paul's trial before the Sanhedrin in Acts 23. There, Paul takes advantage of the conflicting views of Pharisees and Sadducees, turning the adherents of the two sects against each other by raising the disputed topic of resurrection (Acts 23:6). If twenty-first-century readers doubt that Jews could have such strong disagreements with each other when they agree upon so much, it may help to consider the sharp divisions between different Baptist denominations, between liberal and conservative Catholics, or between Shiite and Sunni Muslims.

Yet, while Sadducees and especially Pharisees dominate the pages of the New Testament, there were many other Jewish groups in the Second Temple period. In the discussion below, I will briefly treat Essenes, **Samaritans**, and **Zealots**. Then, we will finally turn to the question of "conversion" to Judaism.

Essenes

Josephus has a lengthy description of the Essenes, cited in Chapter Seven. Modern scholars have attempted to connect the Essenes described by Josephus with the authors of the **Dead Sea Scrolls** discovered at **Qumran** in the 1940s. The Qumran texts make no mention of "Essenes," but similarities between the practices of the Qumran group and the Essenes described by Josephus are intriguing. What is even more compelling is the description of a Dead Sea sect by Pliny the Elder (23/24 C.E. – 79 C.E.) in his *Natural History*:

> On the west side of the Dead Sea, but out of range of the noxious exhalations of the coast, is the solitary tribe of the Essenes, which is remarkable beyond all the other tribes in the whole world, as it has no women and has renounced all sexual desire, has no money, and has only palm-trees for company. Day by day the throng of refugees is recruited to an equal number by numerous accessions of persons tired of life and driven thither by the waves of fortune to adopt their manners. Thus through thousands of ages (incredible to relate) a race in which no one is born lives on for ever: so prolific for their advantage is other men's weariness of life!
> (Pliny, *Natural History* 5.15.73; *LCL* translation [H. Rackham])

From the modern site of Khirbet Qumran (where most of the Dead Sea Scrolls were discovered), one can see the northwest coast of the Dead Sea. This passage further supports the Essene identification of the Qumran community, a strict ascetic group devoted to the study of Torah (see 1QS 8.12-16, quoted in Chapter Four). Like other Jews, the Qumran community worshiped the God of Israel and observed Torah. Unlike other Jewish groups, the Qumran community used a 364-day solar calendar rather than a 354-day lunar calendar, leading them to celebrate their festivals at different times from other Jews. Even more striking was the Qumran group's avoidance of the Jerusalem temple, a site that they considered to be "defiled" (CD 20.23). For the Qumran group, their community would be "an everlasting planting, a holy temple for Israel" (1QS 8.5; compare the striking parallels in 1 Cor 3:16-17 and Eph 2:19-22). The self-conception of the community-as-temple did not imply that there would be no further need for a physical temple; there are detailed blueprints for the construction of a new temple building in one of the scrolls (11Q19).

At some point between the eighth century and the sixth century B.C.E., a temple to Yahweh was built on Elephantine, an island in the Nile River. Scholars debate the rationale behind the construction of the Elephantine temple, which was destroyed in 410 B.C.E. It may have been built as a rival temple to the Jerusalem temple, perhaps out of protest against King Manasseh's introduction of idols into the courts of the Jerusalem temple (see 2 Chr 33:4-8). Or, it may have been built out of convenience, to save local Jews a trip to Jerusalem. Most of our knowledge of Elephantine derives from a collection of Aramaic papyri written between the sixth and fourth centuries B.C.E.

Samaritans

And the Qumran group was not the only Jewish sect with concerns about the Jerusalem temple. The Samaritans actually built a rival temple on Mount Gerizim in the north, as Josephus mentions:

> Now it happened that the Jews in Alexandria and the Samaritans who worshiped at the Gerizim temple from the time of Alexander [the Great] began to dispute with each other, arguing over their temples before Ptolemy himself. The Jews were saying that the temple was, according to the law of Moses, to be built in Jerusalem. But the Samaritans said it should be in Gerizim.
>
> (Josephus, *Jewish Antiquities* 13.74)

Note that the dispute is about *where* to worship the God of Israel, not about *whether* to worship the God of Israel. When Antiochus IV Epiphanes set out to erase the Jewish customs of his southern subjects, he desecrated both the Gerizim temple and the Jerusalem temple (2 Macc 6:2).

Who are the Samaritans? It depends on who you ask. Most twenty-first-century readers of the New Testament associate Samaritans with the famous parable of the Good Samaritan (Luke 10:30-37). The power of this parable lies in the identification of the "Good" Samaritan as a hated foreigner; as the Fourth Gospel explains, "For Jews do not associate with Samaritans" (John 4:9).

Josephus describes various incidents that illustrate the animosity between Samaritans and Jews (or Judeans). In 8 C.E., Samaritans defiled the Jerusalem temple during Passover by scattering human bones in the temple courts (Josephus, *Jewish Antiquities* 18.29-30). Another dispute during a Jewish festival involved bloodshed:

> It was the custom of the Galileans that, when they came to the holy city during the festivals, they would travel through the Samaritan region. At this time, there was a village by the name of Ginae, located on the border of Samaria and the great plain, on the way. Some Samaritans attacked the traveling Galileans and killed many of them.
>
> (Josephus, *Jewish Antiquities* 20.118)

Such incidents did not inspire trust between Jews and Samaritans. They do, however, help to explain why a Jewish audience might be surprised to see a Samaritan coming to the aid of an ambushed traveler.

Can Samaritans properly be labeled a "Jewish" sect if they are always described as conflicting with "Jews"? Keep in mind the geographical associations of "Jew" with the southern kingdom of Judah; the Samaritans are thus named because they live in Samaria, north of Judah/Judea. In fact, it might even be helpful to distinguish between the more value-neutral term "Samarians" (= those who live in the region of Samaria), versus the more sectarian term "Samaritans" (= those who believe that God should be worshiped at Gerizim, not Jerusalem). Unfortunately, though, this division is not made in the ancient texts; as we have discussed above, ancient peoples did not have a separate category for "religion." The scholarly consensus is that Samarians/Samaritans should be considered as one of many Jewish groups, until the second or first century B.C.E. Only then did Samaritans introduce variant readings into their version of the Pentateuch—readings supporting worship at Gerizim instead of Jerusalem. From this point onward, Samaritanism diverges from Judaism, eventually developing into a separate religion. If, however, you were to speak with a twenty-first-century Samaritan—today, Samaritans live in the Israeli city of Holon and in the Palestinian city of Nablus, near Mount Gerizim—you would hear a different story, according to which Samaritans are the true Jews and "Jews" are actually apostates from the true religion.

Zealots

The final Jewish sect to mention is the Zealots, a group that has generated much misunderstanding. Throughout the history of Israel, many figures are identified as "zealous for the Lord." The first was Phinehas, son of Eleazar and grandson of Aaron the priest. Phinehas won divine favor by summarily executing an Israelite man who was engaging in illicit sexual relations with a non-Israelite woman; for this action, Phinehas was praised as one who "was zealous for his God and made atonement for the sons of Israel" (Num 25:13). Zeal for God and for God's Torah was a praiseworthy character trait, and the praiseworthy action of Phinehas is echoed in the claims of the prophet Elijah (1 Kgs 19:10, 14) and in the call to arms of Mattathias, leader of the Maccabean revolt (1 Macc 2:27; note the reference to Phinehas in 1 Macc 2:54 and in Sir 45:23). Over the years, various individuals could claim the title "zealot"—including a follower of Jesus (Simon the "zealot," so called in Luke 6:15 and Acts 1:13).

But these zealots should be distinguished from "the Zealots," a later group that appears only in the works of Josephus. Josephus identifies the Zealots as a group that formed during the Jewish revolt against Rome; this group of rebels seized control in Jerusalem, appointed a new high priest, and violently silenced any who opposed them. The deposed high priests tried to counteract this new threat by "scolding the people of Jerusalem for their sluggishness; in the assemblies, they incited them against the Zealots, for that was what they called themselves, as if they were zealous for noble pursuits, rather than being zealous for the worst labors" (Josephus, *Jewish War* 4.160-161).

The primary reason that the Zealots are treated as a Jewish sect is because of Josephus' writings. Yet, some scholars wonder if Josephus invented this group in order to create a scapegoat that could be blamed for the Jewish revolt. Josephus writes his *Jewish War* with Roman funding and support, and he is at pains to show that the rebels are not representative of all Jews. Hence, he describes the "philosophies" of the Pharisees, Sadducees, and Essenes in an attempt to set these more mainstream groups apart from the violent and distasteful (and imaginary?) "fourth philosophy" of the Zealots

(Josephus, *Jewish Antiquities* 18.9). According to Josephus, the Zealots were led by a "sophist" who led "his own sect and had nothing at all in common with the other sects" (Josephus, *Jewish War* 2.118). Josephus wants to pin the blame on these Zealots, presenting the rest of his (non-Zealot) fellow Jews as innocent bystanders.

Jews and Gentiles and Gentiles-becoming-Jews?

Presumably, whether they were Zealots or not, the Jewish rebels did have much in common with their fellow Jews. Josephus later confesses that the only difference between the Zealots and the Pharisees was the former sect's "indomitable passion for liberty" (*Jewish Antiquities* 18.23). Indeed, first-century Pharisees, Sadducees, Essenes, and Samaritans all worshiped the God of Israel, observed Torah, and lived in the same region.

But what about non-Jews who wanted to express allegiance to the God of Israel? Gentiles were welcome to worship God in the **synagogues** of the Second Temple period, but they were not considered to be Jews on this account. Again, the meaning of "Jew" involved what we would now call cultural, ethnic, and religious elements. Yet, around the time of the Maccabean revolt, new possibilities began to emerge. For instance, the book of Judith was written in the second or first century B.C.E. The author of Judith believed that it was possible for a gentile not only to worship the God of Israel, but even to join the people Israel. According to Judith, Achior the Ammonite—a gentile—did so: "When Achior saw all the things that the God of Israel had done, he believed fervently in God and circumcised the flesh of his foreskin and joined the house of Israel until this day" (Jdt 14:10). Not all scholars are convinced of the historicity of this example. Still, the fact that the author of Judith could contemplate such a conversion experience marks a major shift in thought.

While it is problematic to describe a "religion" called "Judaism" in the first century C.E., this language may be appropriate in discussions of gentile conversion to the God of Israel. As Chapter Nine will demonstrate, it is not helpful to use the language of "conversion" when an individual moves from one Jewish sect to another.

An even clearer example of conversion is found in Josephus, whose *Jewish Antiquities* includes a lengthy narrative of Izates of Adiabene, a gentile convert to Judaism in the first half of the first century C.E. According to Josephus, a Jewish merchant named Ananias first introduced Izates to Jewish customs, and Izates was quickly persuaded to be circumcised. His mother Helena stopped him:

> But when his mother learned of his decision, she tried to stop him from following through. She explained to him that, being a king, he would face danger, for it would cause him to be greatly loathed by his subjects when they learned that he craved customs that were strange and foreign to them. They would not endure a Jew (*Ioudaios*) ruling over them as king.
>
> (Josephus, *Jewish Antiquities* 20.39)

This quote reminds us that, in the first century C.E., "Jew" was still a word that carried (what we would call) both ethnic and religious meaning. If Izates becomes a Jew, he must adopt Jewish customs like circumcision. Yet, his future subjects would interpret Izates' adoption of Jewish customs as a repudiation of his own ancestral customs—and thus a repudiation of the right to rule his own people. In keeping with this line of thought, Izates refrains from being circumcised, and his teacher Ananias encourages him to worship the God of Israel without being circumcised (*Jewish Antiquities* 20.40-42).

Then, another Jewish teacher, named Eleazar, arrives from Galilee and persuades Izates that he must be circumcised in order to observe Torah properly:

> When the king heard these things, he put off the deed no longer. Retiring to another room, he summoned his physician and accomplished what had been commanded. He then called his mother and his teacher Ananias and made known that he had done the deed.
>
> (Josephus, *Jewish Antiquities* 20.46)

Ananias and Izates' mother Helena are shocked—and frightened that this act will undermine Izates' legitimacy. If his circumcision is discovered, they fear that "the king would run the risk of losing his authority, for his subjects would not bear to be ruled by a man who was such a zealot for the customs of others" (Josephus, *Jewish Antiquities* 20.47).

This narrative brings together many of the elements discussed in this chapter. We find a man who was a "zealot" for the law, but clearly not a "Zealot" for freedom from Rome. There is an emphasis not on what we would call "beliefs" or "religion," but on religious practices or customs (to be discussed further in Chapter Eleven). Finally, note that Second Temple Jews are concerned with observing Torah. But different teachers from different sects have different interpretations. For Ananias, gentiles could worship the God of Israel without being circumcised. For Eleazar, gentiles had to be circumcised. Readers of the New Testament will find striking parallels in the dispute over the circumcision of gentile believers that resounds throughout the pages of Acts (especially Acts 15) and Galatians.

Jews and Christians

Izates the gentile hoped that, through his adoption of Jewish customs, he might be "firmly Jewish" (Josephus, *Jewish Antiquities* 20.38). Eleazar his teacher apparently thought it was possible for Izates to become fully Jewish; Ananias, on the other hand, may have harbored doubts that a gentile could ever become a Jew. The followers of Jesus engaged in this same debate, although on a much wider scale. Gentiles flooded into the early Christian community to the point that it eventually became a predominantly gentile movement.

At what point did a Jewish sect (the followers of Jesus) become a Christian church? There is no simple answer. As Jewish and gentile believers in Jesus began to worship God as part of the same community, they reached compromises and fell into conflicts. There were some major turning points, such as the destruction of the Second Temple in 70 C.E. Such a catastrophic event called for a response from all Jews—note that Jewish believers in Jesus were not quick to abandon the temple (see Luke 24:52-53; Acts 2:46; 3:1–4:2; 5:21, 42; 21:26-30). For many Jews, temple worship was replaced by the study of Torah in synagogues; this practice developed into what we now call **Rabbinic Judaism**. For other Jews (and gentile believers in Jesus), the God of Israel could be worshiped anywhere, "in spirit and in truth" (John 4:23); the Christians continued to develop their own interpretations of the scriptures and to worship Jesus as Lord.

That said, even after this so-called "Parting of the Ways" between Judaism and Christianity, Christians cannot forget their Jewish roots. Christians use the Jewish scriptures, pray Jewish prayers (using the Jewish prayer book—the Psalms), continue to conceive of God as "Father," and worship the God who became a Jewish man. With greater knowledge of Second Temple Judaism, we can begin to understand how the complexity of being Jewish *then* should shape our reading of the New Testament *now*.

Bibliography and suggestions for further reading

Shaye J. D. Cohen. *The Beginnings of Jewishness: Boundaries, Varieties, Uncertainties.* Berkeley: University of California Press, 1999. (Cohen's often-cited monograph addresses questions related to Jewish identity, translation of the word *Ioudaios*, and conversion to Judaism, with keen attention to historical development.)

John J. Collins and Daniel C. Harlow, eds. *The Eerdmans Dictionary of Early Judaism.* Grand Rapids: Eerdmans, 2010. (Already mentioned in an earlier chapter, this reference work is an excellent guide to key concepts, people, places, and writings of the Second Temple period, including helpful summaries of "Pharisees," "Sadducees," and "Samaritanism.")

Luke Timothy Johnson. "The New Testament's Anti-Jewish Slander and the Conventions of Ancient Polemic." *Journal of Biblical Literature* 108 (1989): 419–441. (Johnson demonstrates the importance of reading the New Testament in its literary and historical context; often, what looks like "anti-Jewish slander" to modern eyes is better characterized as intra-Jewish polemic.)

Amy-Jill Levine and Marc Zvi Brettler, eds. *The Jewish Annotated New Testament: New Revised Standard Version Bible Translation.* New York: Oxford University Press, 2011. (This helpful volume offers the complete New Revised Standard Version [NRSV] text of the New Testament, with annotations and essays by Jewish biblical scholars. Of special importance is Levine's essay, "Bearing False Witness: Common Errors Made About Early Judaism.")

Jodi Magness. *Stone and Dung, Oil and Spit: Jewish Daily Life in the Time of Jesus.* Grand Rapids: Eerdmans, 2011. (Magness draws on a wide array of literary and archaeological sources to shed light on various aspects of daily life in the Second Temple period, including ritual purity, meal customs, sabbath observance, clothing, and burial practices.)

James VanderKam and Peter Flint. *The Meaning of the Dead Sea Scrolls: Their Significance for Understanding the Bible, Judaism, Jesus, and Christianity.* New York: HarperCollins, 2002. (Of special interest is Chapter 10, which describes the process of "Identifying the Group Associated with Qumran.")

9

"I am a Jew": Saul, or Paul

Guiding Questions

Who was Paul?

How do Paul's letters compare and contrast to other ancient letters?

What was imprisonment like in the Greco-Roman world?

I am a Jew, born in Tarsus of Cilicia, raised in this city, educated at the feet of Gamaliel strictly according to the ancestral law, being a zealot (*zēlōtēs*) for God, just as all of you are today.

(Acts 22:3)

But when he who set me apart from my mother's womb and who called me by his grace was pleased to reveal his son to me, so that I might bring the good news about him to the gentiles . . .

(Gal 1:15-16)

Paul the Jew

According to the author of Acts, Paul was a **Jew** (*Ioudaios*). Within the narrative of Acts, Paul (also known as "Saul") of Tarsus begins as a violent persecutor of **Christians** (see Acts 7:58; 8:1; 9:1-2). He encounters the risen Jesus on the road to Damascus and is subsequently baptized (Acts 9:3-19). Henceforth, he will proclaim Jesus as the **Messiah** and Son of God to Jews and to **gentiles** (see Acts 9:20-22 for preaching specifically to Jews). Yet, in Acts 22, as Paul delivers a speech from the steps of the fortress Antonia, he claims to be a Jew. How can this be? Did Paul not convert to Christianity?

Figure 9.1 Fortress Antonia alongside Temple Mount (scale model) This scale model of first-century Jerusalem accurately depicts the proximity of the fortress Antonia (right) to the Temple Mount (left). Model © Holyland Tourism 1992, Ltd.

Saul is a Hebrew name; the first king of Israel was named Saul (1 Sam 9-11). The author of Acts continues to refer to Saul of Tarsus as "Saul" until Saul encounters a proconsul named Sergius Paulus in Acts 13:7. Then, in Acts 13:9, we are notified that Saul was also called "Paul." (*Paulus* is a Roman surname.) The use of the Roman name "Paul"/*Paulus* begins at this point in the narrative when Paul first encounters a representative of Roman rule.

How could Paul be both Jewish and Christian? In the twenty-first century, this perplexing question springs to mind. In the first half of the first century (when Paul had his vision of the risen Jesus), and even in the second half of the first century (when Acts was written), the question might still be perplexing, but for different reasons. Paul the follower of Jesus, after all, is clearly a Jew. In addition to the portrait of Paul in Acts, we also have evidence from Paul's letter to the Philippians, where he affirms his identity as Jew:

Circumcised on the eighth day, from the people of Israel, the tribe of Benjamin, a Hebrew from Hebrews, according to the law a Pharisee, according to zeal, persecuting the assembly (*ekklēsia*), according to righteousness in the law, I am blameless.

(Phil 3:5-6)

If we compare this passage with Acts 22:3, the parallels are striking. Paul is a circumcised, **Torah**-observing male (Phil 3:5); he is a Jew (Acts 22:3). Moreover, he is a member of the Pharisaic **sect** of Judaism (Phil 3:5). The phrase in Acts 22:3 translated "strictly according to the ancestral law" includes the word *akribeia*, which also suggests Paul's Pharisaic affiliation; Josephus, for example, describes a certain individual as being "of the sect of the Pharisees, who are supposed to distinguish with more strictness (*akribeia*) than others in their interpretation of their country's law" (Josephus, *Life* 191). Also, Gamaliel, who is identified as Paul's teacher in Acts 22:3, belonged to the Pharisaic sect, as mentioned in Chapter Five. Finally, we may note that Paul is described as "zealous" in both Acts and Philippians; as discussed in the previous chapter, the word *zēlōtēs* refers to his whole-hearted desire to follow Torah, not to his political affiliations. Paul, then, was a Pharisaic Jew. Assuming his birth in Tarsus (see Map 1), we can also consider him a **Diaspora** Jew. Based on his claims about Jesus, we can say that Paul was a Jew whose beliefs about Jesus the Messiah led him to open conflict with Jewish authorities.

Nonetheless, labeling Paul a "convert to Christianity" is a mistake. First, if Paul were to "convert" to Christianity, then Paul presumably would "convert" away from Judaism. Paul may question the value of some of his Jewish practices (Phil 3:7), but nowhere do we find Paul renouncing his identity as a Jew. Second, what is "Christianity"? We find three references to "Christians" in the New Testament (in Acts 11:26; 26:28; 1 Pet 4:16), but the term *Christianismos* first appears in the writings of Ignatius of Antioch, in the early second century. Nowhere is this word found in the New Testament. The narrative of Acts tells of Paul preaching in **synagogues** (e.g., Acts 9:20), of the followers of Jesus meeting in the Jerusalem **temple** (e.g., Acts 2:46; 5:12, 42), and of outsiders considering them to be Jews (e.g., Acts 16:20; 18:15; 25:19). Third, despite the fact that Paul's transformative experience of Jesus on the road to Damascus has been held up as a premier example of "conversion," this experience is better described as a "call" rather than a "conversion."

Oddly, in the narrative of Acts, none of Paul's letters is mentioned. We find letters being written by the "apostles and elders" in Acts 15:22-29 and by Claudius Lysias in Acts 23:25-30, but none by Paul. On the other hand, 2 Pet 3:15-16 betrays awareness of several letters by Paul—and, in a provocative statement, appears to place Paul's letters on the same level as "the other **scriptures**." (If this interpretation is accurate, then 2 Peter would be among the earliest texts to attribute the authority of "scripture" to writings of the New Testament.)

If we look at Paul's own writings, we find him describing that experience with the language of "calling." Paul does not claim to have converted away from a religion called "Judaism" to a religion called "Christianity." Paul did experience a profound change, but he frames this turning point in his life with language reminiscent of earlier prophetic figures. Compare Gal 1:15-16 with Jeremiah's call:

Gal 1:15-16	Jer 1:5 LXX
But when he who set me apart from my mother's womb (*koilia*) and who called me by his grace was pleased to reveal his son to me, so that I might bring the good news about him to the gentiles (*ethnē*) . . .	Before I formed you in the womb (*koilia*), I knew you, and before you came out from your mother, I sanctified you. I appointed you to be prophet to the nations (*ethnē*).

The similarities are striking. Both Paul and Jeremiah claim to be set apart by God from the very beginning of their earthly lives. And both are appointed to bring God's word to all the nations, or gentiles—the Greek word *ethnē* can mean "nations" or "gentiles." As with Jeremiah, Paul's call will lead him to be at odds with his fellow Jews, and like Jeremiah, Paul will be persecuted (compare Jer 20:1-3 with Acts 22:30–23:5).

According to Acts, Paul encounters Jesus on the road to Damascus; Jesus calls Paul to follow him and to preach the good news. According to the **gospels**, various first-century Jews encounter Jesus in various places; Jesus calls them to follow him and commissions them to preach the good news. If we do not label the twelve **disciples** "converts," why do we insist on labeling Paul a "convert"?

To question whether Paul was "converted," then, is not at all to question whether Paul experienced a deep change that put him at odds with his fellow Jews. The difference between Paul the Jew and the Jews who persecuted and prosecuted him is neatly summed up in the words of Porcius Festus in Acts 25. Festus here sets out the case against Paul to "King" Herod Agrippa II (who was actually not a king, but rather a **tetrarch** appointed by the emperor; he was also the son of Agrippa I, whose demise is detailed in Acts 12). According to Festus (or, according to what the author of Acts says that Festus said), the dispute between the Jerusalem Jews and Paul is a dispute within a religious group: "They had certain points of dispute with him regarding their own religious customs (*deisidaimonia*) and regarding a certain Jesus, who was dead, but whom Paul was claiming to be alive" (Acts 25:19). Paul has not ceased to be a Jew; he has developed an allegiance to this "certain Jesus" that many of his fellow Jews do not share.

Most English translations say that this dispute is about "their own religion," but the Greek word *deisidaimonia* does not perfectly align with our modern concept of religion. Not only does *deisidaimonia* often have the same negative connotations as "superstition," but *deisidaimonia* more literally means "fear of divine beings" (*daimones* include a wide variety of divine beings, not just "demons"). In the first-century Mediterranean world, we should think about "god(s)-pleasing practices" rather than formal religions (see Chapter Eleven for further thoughts on Greco-Roman "religion").

Paul the Jew is a Diaspora Jew. Although his letters never identify his home town, we find the identification of Tarsus as Paul's birthplace throughout the book of Acts. If Paul received any of his formal education in Tarsus, then we should not be surprised to find him quoting poetry to the philosophers in Athens (see Acts 17:28). A Diaspora Jew educated in Tarsus would have access to a first-rate Greek education:

The people at Tarsus have devoted themselves so eagerly, not only to philosophy, but also to the whole round of education in general, that they have surpassed Athens, Alexandria, or any other place that can be named where there have been schools and lectures of philosophers. But it is so different from other cities that there the men who are fond of learning are all natives, and foreigners are not inclined to sojourn there; neither do these natives stay there, but they complete their education abroad; and when they have completed it they are pleased to live abroad, and but few go back home . . . Further, the city of Tarsus has all kinds of schools of rhetoric; and in general it not only has a flourishing population but also is most powerful, thus keeping up the reputation of the mother-city.

(Strabo, *Geography* 14.5.13; *LCL* translation [H. L. Jones])

The Roman geographer Strabo (ca. 64 B.C.E. – after 21 C.E.) identifies Tarsus as a hotbed of learning, famous for its homegrown intellectuals. Paul may have been one of them; like his fellow citizens, however, he appears to have also completed his education abroad. This typical study abroad program finds an interesting parallel in the *Life of Apollonius of Tyana*, a work by L. Flavius Philostratus written in the late second or early third century C.E.:

When [Apollonius] reached fourteen his father took him to Tarsus to study with Euthydemus of Phoenicia. Euthydemus was a good orator and began to teach him . . .

(Philostratus, *Life of Apollonius of Tyana* 1.7.1; *LCL* translation [C. P. Jones])

At age fourteen, Apollonius leaves his native Tyana—a Greek city in Asia Minor—to go to Tarsus—another Greek city in Asia Minor, where he begins his studies under the guidance of the rhetorician Euthydemus. According to Acts 22:3, Paul left his native Tarsus to go to Jerusalem, where he would go on to study with Rabbi Gamaliel. For both Apollonius and Paul, their education-inspired journeys mark only the beginning of their travels.

Paul the letter-writer

In Acts, we meet Paul the itinerant preacher. In Paul's letters, we meet Paul the master of first-century social media. In the ancient world, there were limited means of communication beyond verbal address. Stone inscriptions could serve to announce the generosity of benefactors or to warn trespassers. But those who wanted to convey a more particular message to a distant audience were limited to three options: sending a letter, sending a messenger, or going in person. Often, the first two options were combined; in Acts 15, for example, the Jerusalem leadership sends a letter with two trusted delegates (see Acts 15:22-23). Such a practice had multiple advantages. In addition to assuring the transmission of the message, the sender could also ensure that the letter could be read aloud to the audience; moreover, the messenger could answer questions and help to interpret the meaning of any disputed points.

> The frequency with which Paul sends letters and delegates suggests that his social network was not composed entirely of lower-class laborers and slaves. Funding Paul's travels and the travels of his agents probably required financial support from other members of the community—perhaps wealthier individuals like the merchant Lydia (Acts 16:14) or Philemon (discussed below).

Paul's letters typically follow the arrangement of ancient letters, which can be illustrated in the following first-century C.E. letter discovered in Egypt:

> Sarapion to Justus his son. Greetings. I sent you by Papirios four drachmas and two obols, which you are to pay on behalf of Hermes and Achilles, and you are to let me know when you receive them. Greet your brothers. Farewell to you and to them.
>
> (P. Oxy. 2786)

Sarapion begins his letter by identifying himself as the sender. He then names the recipient, "Justus his son." After the greeting, Sarapion moves on to the body of his letter: he has sent money with Papirios, so that Justus can pay Hermes and Achilles. In closing, Sarapion sends greetings to Justus's brothers (or perhaps to his siblings—the Greek is ambiguous), and bids them all "Farewell." This basic letter-writing format is used throughout the ancient Greco-Roman world, by Sarapion of Egypt and Paul of Tarsus, as well as by military officials (Acts 23:25-30), high priests (1 Macc 12:5-18), and kings (2 Macc 11:22-26).

Paul's letters are the earliest Christian writings that we can date with any confidence. They are thus the primary sources for exploring the early development of Christian beliefs and practices. In addition to shedding light on early Christian theology, the letters are integral to our understanding of early Christian communities. The letters demonstrate Paul's frequent communications with his fellow believers. His letters also provide further evidence of his ever-growing address book (e.g., Romans 16). Paul might write to a distressed **church** to resolve conflicts (e.g., 1 Corinthians, Galatians, etc.). Paul also would write to a distant church to introduce himself (e.g., Romans). And Paul writes to individuals to sort out interpersonal relationships.

A prime example of this lattermost case is Paul's letter to Philemon, the master of the slave Onesimus. Paul's brief letter to Philemon can be read in a few minutes' time (I would encourage the reader to take a few moments to do so now). There is another letter from the ancient world that deals with a situation startlingly similar to that of Paul, Philemon, and Onesimus. This letter is written by Pliny the Younger, whose correspondence has already appeared in Chapter Three. A comparison between Paul's letter to Philemon and Pliny's letter to Sabinianus reveals striking resemblances, and equally striking divergences. The opening lines are similar, as we would expect. Each writer follows the basic template of Greco-Roman letter-writing, beginning with the name of the author, followed by the name of the recipient (Paul and Timothy to Philemon; Pliny to Sabinianus):

Philemon 1, 3	Pliny, *Letters* 9.21
Paul, a prisoner of Christ Jesus, and Timothy the brother, to Philemon our beloved fellow worker: . . . Grace to you and peace from God our Father and the Lord Jesus Christ . . .	Gaius Plinius greets his friend Sabinianus. Your freedman, whom you said has angered you, has come to me . . .

However, the following lines begin to diverge. Paul wishes Philemon **grace** and peace; Pliny launches into his tirade without any such niceties.

Even though both Paul and Pliny write to bring about reconciliation between master and (former) slave, the tone of their letters differs rather sharply. I reproduce here the rest of Pliny's letter:

> . . . he [Sabinianus's freedman] threw himself at my feet and clung there with as much submission as he could have done at yours. He earnestly requested me with many tears, and even with the eloquence of silent sorrow, to intercede for him; in short, he convinced me by his whole behavior that he sincerely repents of his fault. And I am persuaded he is thoroughly reformed, because he seems entirely sensible of his delinquency.
>
> I know you are angry with him, and I know too, it is not without reason; but clemency can never exert itself with more applause, than when there is the most just cause for resentment. You once had an affection for this man, and, I hope, will have again: in the meanwhile, let me only prevail with you to pardon him. If he should incur your displeasure hereafter, you will have so much the stronger plea in excuse for your anger, as you show yourself more exorable to him now. Allow something to his youth, to his tears, and to your own natural mildness of temper: do not make him uneasy any longer, and I

will add too, do not make yourself so; for a man of your benevolence of heart cannot be angry without feeling great uneasiness.

I am afraid, were I to join my entreaties with his, I should seem rather to compel, than request you to forgive him. Yet I will not scruple to do it; and so much the more fully and freely as I have very sharply and severely reproved him, positively threatening never to interpose again on his behalf. But though it was proper to say this to him, in order to make him more fearful of offending, I do not say it to you. I may, perhaps, again have occasion to entreat you on his account, and again obtain your forgiveness; supposing, I mean, his error should be such as may be fit for me to intercede for, and for you to pardon. Farewell.

(Pliny the Younger, *Letters* 9.21; *LCL* translation [W. Melmoth and W. M. L. Hutchinson], modified)

Both Paul and Pliny write to reconcile two other parties. Both Paul and Pliny coax and cajole their recipients to pardon a social inferior. Both men accept the existence of slavery as part of the fabric of society. Both men are comfortable with using the cultural currency of honor and shame to motivate, rather than using threats of force.

Although careful study of the two letters reveals other similarities, major differences quickly become obvious. Pliny is quick to tell Sabinianus what to do. Paul takes time to thank God for Philemon before turning to imperatives. Pliny appeals to Sabinianus's magnanimity with rhetorical gusto. Paul likewise makes a rhetorical appeal, but he also builds a theological argument. This theological element reveals the gaping difference between the worldviews of Paul and Pliny. Pliny is a ruler, Sabinianus is a friend of Pliny's, and the unnamed freedman is an inconvenience. For Paul, though, the three parties involved are family—despite the complete absence of any genealogical or biological ties. In **Christ**, Philemon is Paul's brother (Philm 20), and Onesimus may well become much "more than a slave, a beloved brother" of Philemon (vs. 16).

Paul the prisoner

Paul and Pliny were, of course, writing from very different social positions. Pliny writes letters as a member of the Roman elite. Paul retains his Roman citizenship, but he writes multiple letters as a prisoner of Rome (see, e.g., Phil 1:13). According to the book of Acts, he is arrested and imprisoned on multiple occasions for a variety of reasons (for details, read Acts 16:19-39;

21:33-40; 22:24-30; 23:10; 24:23-27; 25:9-27; 26:31-32; 28:16; see also 2 Cor 11:23). What did it mean to be a prisoner in the first century C.E.? In the twenty-first-century Western world, prisoners can typically write letters, receive mail, and count on three square meals a day. In the first-century Roman world, prisoners could write and receive letters, but their postal service and meals were not state-provided services. One had to get by with a little help from one's friends.

Lucian of Samosata (born ca. 120 C.E.) offers an illuminating view of the treatment of prisoners in the Greco-Roman world. His satirical *Passing of Peregrinus* tells an embellished story of a mid-second-century C.E. philosopher-turned-Christian named Peregrinus, or Proteus (Lucian uses the two names interchangeably). Formerly a Stoic philosopher, Peregrinus becomes a Christian and, according to Lucian, is imprisoned for this reason:

> Then, at length Proteus was arrested for this and thrown into prison, which itself gave him no little reputation as an asset for his future career and the charlatanism and fame-seeking that he was so fond of. Well, when he had been imprisoned, the Christians (*Christianoi*), regarding the incident as a calamity, left nothing undone in the effort to rescue him. Then, since this was impossible, every other form of attention was shown to him, not in any casual way, but with diligence. From the very break of day, aged widows and orphan children could be seen waiting near the prison, while their officials even slept inside with him after bribing the guards! Then elaborate meals were brought in, and sacred books of theirs were read aloud, and excellent Peregrinus—for he still went by that name—was called by them 'the new Socrates'.
>
> (Lucian, *The Passing of Peregrinus* 12; *LCL* translation
> [A. M. Harmon], modified)

Lucian considers Peregrinus to be a charlatan interested only in becoming a public celebrity; hence, his description should be read accordingly. Still, we can draw conclusions in two areas of interest. First, the second-century Christian community that ministers to Peregrinus resembles the first-century Christian communities described in the New Testament. For example, there is a wide array of social classes represented, both elite Christians, who can afford "elaborate meals" (compare the passage above with 1 Cor 11:20-34), and marginalized believers, including widows and orphans (see Acts 6:1; 9:36-42; 1 Cor 7:8; Jas 1:27). Also, we find that Christians are still focused on two primary activities: eating together and reading "sacred books" (compare Acts 2:42 and the Justin Martyr citation in the Post-Script). Second, Lucian's account of the imprisonment of Peregrinus is unrecognizable and even risible to anyone who has visited a maximum-security prison in the United States. With no set visiting hours, Peregrinus can receive guests at any time. He can accept entire meals. Books can be brought inside the prison. And, as the following passage shows, he can receive money:

> Indeed, people came even from the cities in Asia, sent by the Christians at their common expense, to support and defend and encourage the hero. They show incredible speed whenever any such public action is taken; for in no time they lavish their all. So it was then in the case of Peregrinus; much money came to him from them by reason of his imprisonment, and he gained no little profit from it. The poor wretches have convinced themselves, first and foremost, that they are going to be immortal and live for all time, in consequence of which they despise death and even willingly give themselves into custody, most of them. Furthermore, their first lawgiver persuaded them that they are all brothers of one another after they have transgressed once for all by denying the Greek gods and by worshipping that crucified sophist himself and living under his laws. Therefore they despise all things indiscriminately and consider them common property, receiving such doctrines traditionally without any definite evidence. So if any charlatan and trickster, able to profit by occasions, comes among them, he quickly acquires sudden wealth by imposing upon simple folk.
>
> (Lucian, *The Passing of Peregrinus* 13; *LCL* translation
> [A. M. Harmon], modified)

In this passage, Lucian reveals how at least one learned gentile viewed the second-century Christians. For Lucian, Christians were known for their belief in immortality (compare Rom 6:23; Gal 6:8), for conceiving of themselves as brothers and sisters (compare Acts 13:15; Rom 1:13; etc.), for their atheism (or disbelief in the Greco-Roman gods; compare condemnations of **idolatry** in Acts 17:16; 1 Cor 10:14; 1 John 5:21; etc.), for their worship of a crucified leader (compare 1 Cor 1:23; 2:8), for their sharing of property and possessions (compare Acts 2:44-45; 4:32) … and for their gullibility. Lucian has a rather low view of these practices and of their practitioners. He sees the sharing of possessions as the basis for an easy get-rich-quick scheme.

But food and money were not luxury items for Roman prisoners. There is a reason why those who visit prisoners are blessed, according to Matt 25:31-46. Prisoners in the ancient Mediterranean world were not guaranteed nutritious food and clean clothing. They were not literally starved to death, but prisoners who did not have outside support were left with a meager diet. In a literary work dating to roughly 200 C.E., a particularly ascetic philosopher is described as partaking "daily from the following: one loaf of white bread

… and a cup of water." The narrator then labels these rations "a prison diet" (Athenaeus, *Deipnosophistae* 4.161c). However accurate this account may be, the point is clear: prisoners were not guaranteed anything more than subsistence.

In the end, the book of Acts reports that Paul the prisoner successfully reaches Rome (Acts 28). Under house arrest, he continues to preach the kingdom of God. According to later tradition, both Peter and Paul were executed in Rome, by Rome. Eusebius of Caesarea (ca. 260 – ca. 340 C.E.) claims that Paul (the Roman citizen) was beheaded, but that Peter was crucified (*Ecclesiastical History* 2.25.5). Whether or not the traditions that Eusebius reports are reliable, the different modes of execution—beheading for the Roman citizen, **crucifixion** for the non-citizen—fit Roman practice of the time, as will be discussed in the following chapter.

Bibliography and suggestions for further reading

Paula Fredriksen. "Mandatory Retirement: Ideas in the Study of Christian Origins Whose Time Has Come to Go." *Studies in Religion/Sciences Religieuses* 35.2 (2006): 231–246. (Fredriksen presents compelling arguments for why scholars of Christian origins should abandon the terms "conversion," "nationalism," *religio licita*, and "monotheism.")

Hans-Josef Klauck. *Ancient Letters and the New Testament: A Guide to Context and Exegesis.* Translated by Daniel P. Bailey. Waco: Baylor University Press, 2006. (This English translation of Klauck's 1998 German book includes analysis and discussion of ancient Greco-Roman letters and New Testament letters; it also includes exercises for student readers.)

Jerome Murphy-O'Connor. *Paul: A Critical Life.* Oxford: Clarendon Press, 1996. (Murphy-O'Connor offers a thorough scholarly biography of Paul, with careful attention both to ancient primary sources and to modern scholarship.)

Brian Rapske. *The Book of Acts and Paul in Roman Custody.* Vol. 3 in *The Book of Acts in Its First Century Setting.* Grand Rapids: Eerdmans, 1994. (Rapske includes chapters on the conditions of prison life and on Paul's custody in Rome.)

N. T. Wright. *Paul and the Faithfulness of God.* Minneapolis: Fortress, 2013. (Wright's massive two-volume treatment of Paul includes illuminating comparative analysis of Paul's letter to Philemon and Pliny's letter to Sabinianus about the freedman on pp. 3–22.)

Part III

Reading Old Words

10

The *Crux* of the Matter

Guiding Questions

Beyond its practical function as a means of capital punishment, how did the cross function symbolically in the first-century world?

What sorts of people were crucified?

What is ordinary about Jesus' **crucifixion**, and what is unique?

How might the evangelists have interpreted Psalm 22 in light of Jesus' crucifixion?

Therefore, because we are surrounded by such a great cloud of witnesses, let us lay aside every burden and sin that so easily ensnares, and let us run with endurance the course set before us, fixing our gaze on Jesus, the founder and perfecter of faith, who—for the sake of the joy set before him—endured the cross, despising its shame, and is seated at the right hand of the throne of God.

(Heb 12:1-2)

Honor, shame, and crucifixion

Even in our post-modern age, the language of right and wrong is still pervasive, as is the concept of guilt. We advertise "guilty pleasures" and "guilt-free" desserts. A key tool for goading people into action is the "guilt trip." Cultural anthropologists label cultures that use guilt to motivate behavior "guilt cultures." For a member of a guilt culture, outsider perceptions are less important than our own self-evaluation (e.g., a seven-year-old who accidentally breaks her neighbors' window while they are on vacation might feel guilty, even though nobody else knows what she has done).

In a "shame culture," on the other hand, members are more motivated by shame and more preoccupied with outsider evaluations. If an individual did not commit a disgraceful action, yet outsiders believe that the individual did commit that action, then the individual will be more likely to feel shame, rather than the righteous indignation that a member of guilt culture might feel (e.g., if the seven-year-old in the earlier example had an older brother, and if he was falsely accused of breaking the window, he would—as a member of a guilt culture—probably respond defensively, instead of accepting his shame quietly). Nowadays, shame culture is often associated with Eastern cultures (including those influenced by Confucianism and Islam), and guilt culture is linked particularly to Western cultures (especially to the United States).

While "shame culture" and "guilt culture" are helpful concepts, it is important to keep in mind that members of a guilt culture can feel shame, and that members of a shame culture can feel guilt. These terms are intended to emphasize dominant and distinctive influences on behavior, not to imply that Westerners, for example, cannot feel shame.

From a cultural anthropological perspective, the ancient Mediterranean world can be characterized as a shame culture. Individuals in such a culture derive their worth more from outsider perceptions; thus, they seek "honor" in the public sphere. The Greek language reflects this mindset. The Greek word *timē* ("honor") also means "worth" or "value." In this culture, a person's worth is determined by the degree to which they are honored, glorified, and praised.

Honor and shame are not simply individual possessions, though; they are closely linked to one's social group (e.g., one's family or city). The public sphere is an arena where the stakes are high—words and deeds can bring honor or shame not only to an individual, but also to that individual's family members or fellow citizens. Gaining honor and avoiding shame were thus primary motivators in the Greco-Roman world (for an example of how Paul uses the threat of public shame to influence behavior, see Acts 16:37-40). As Seneca (ca. 4 B.C.E. – 65 C.E.) once wrote, "The one fixed point, from which our arguments will proceed on to other things, is this: that which is honorable is cultivated for no other reason than because it is honorable" (*On Benefits* 4.16.2). The cultivation of honor provides its own reward.

> For Seneca, honor tops the hierarchy of goods. Aristotle agrees—in his *Nicomachean Ethics*, the Greek philosopher declares honor (*timē*) to be the "greatest of all external goods" (4.3, 1123b20-21). For Dio Chrysostom (also known as Dio Cocceianus, ca. 45 C.E. – after 110 C.E.), honor was only slightly less important. In an oration on the subject of pain, Dio lists the worst misfortunes: death and illness are at the top of the list, but the very next item on the list is *adoxia* ("being obscure" or "having no reputation"), which precedes other calamities like financial catastrophe. For at least these ancient thinkers, honor gleamed more brightly than gold.

In a world that prized honor and avoided shame, the author of Hebrews announces the "founder and perfecter of faith," Jesus, who willingly exposed himself to the public shame of **crucifixion**, yet who was rewarded with the highest honor: being "seated at the right hand of the throne of God" (Heb 12:2). In this chapter, we will begin by exploring the shameful character of crucifixion; an ancient Roman would be shocked to see an individual wearing a gold or silver cross (*crux* in Latin), or displaying a cross tattoo. After investigating the function of crucifixion in the first-century world, we will close with a brief look at the transformation of the cross from symbol of terror into sign of victory. (That the cross has undergone a further transformation into a sort of good luck charm or fashion accessory will have to await a different chapter in another book.)

The shame of the cross

The New Testament writings recognize that the cross is something more than a charm to be worn around the neck. When Jesus issues a call for followers, he promises a way of self-denial: "If anyone wants to follow me, let them deny themselves and take up their cross and follow me. For whoever wants to save their life will lose it, but whoever loses their life for my sake and for the sake of the good news will save it" (Mark 8:34-35). Jesus promises salvation and life, but the way to salvation and life is the way of the cross—a way marked with pain and suffering . . . and shame.

A crucified savior did not serve as a helpful recruiting tool for early **Christians**. In the previous chapter, we discussed Lucian of Samosata's second-century account of the imprisonment of a certain Peregrinus. Before Lucian describes the imprisonment, he explains how Peregrinus first became a Christian:

> It was then that Peregrinus learned the wondrous wisdom of the Christians, by associating with their priests and scribes in Palestine. And how else could it be? In a short time he made them all look like children, for he was prophet, cult-leader, head of the synagogue, and everything, all by himself. He interpreted and explained some of their books and even composed many, and they revered him as a god, made use of him as a lawgiver, and set him down as a protector, next after that other, to be sure, whom they still worship, the man who was crucified in Palestine because he introduced this new cult (*teletē*) into the world.
>
> (Lucian of Samosata, *The Passing of Peregrinus* 11; *LCL* translation [A. M. Harmon], modified)

As Lucian mocks both the charlatan Peregrinus and the gullible Christians, he reveals an outsider's view of second-century Christian communities. Lucian appears to confuse **Jews** and Christians, given his descriptions of "priests and scribes" and the identification of the Christian Peregrinus as a revered "lawgiver" (a title generally applied to Moses). Still, Lucian recognizes that the Christians worship "the man who was crucified in Palestine because he introduced this new cult into the world." Based on his other references in *The Passing of Peregrinus*, Lucian appears to know two things about Jesus: (1) he was crucified in Palestine, and (2) he founded a new "cult" (the Greek word *teletē* is usually used to describe the rites of initiation into cultic mysteries).

In a culture where "new" things were regarded with suspicion, the founding role that Jesus played for the Christians would bring him no honor. Even worse, the means of his execution would bring only shame. The ranks of the crucified were filled with all manner of villains. For example, the first-century B.C.E. Greek historian Diodorus Siculus records how Dionysius of Syracuse conquers a Carthaginian outpost and takes many of the defeated as captives. Dionysius sells some of the captives into slavery, but he punishes more harshly his fellow Greeks who fought against him: "having captured Daïmenes and some other Greeks who had fought alongside the Carthaginians, he crucified them" (*Library of History* 14.53.4). Daïmenes and company are crucified as traitors.

In the Greco-Roman world, crucifixion was also seen as an appropriate penalty for fugitive slaves. The first-century C.E. novelist Chariton of Aphrodisias describes a scene where Chaereas, the story's protagonist, is enslaved and chained with fifteen other men in the estate of a wealthy man named Mithridates. Some of Chaereas's companions decide to escape:

> Some of those chained with Chaereas (sixteen in all shut up in a gloomy cell) broke through their chains in the night, murdered the overseer, and then attempted a getaway. But they did not escape, as the dogs' barking betrayed them. They were discovered and all securely fastened in the stocks for the night, and when day came the estate manager told Mithridates what had happened. Without even seeing them or listening to their defense he immediately ordered the sixteen cell-mates to be crucified. They were duly brought out, chained together at foot and neck, each carrying his own cross. The executioners added this grim public spectacle to the requisite penalty as a deterrent to others so minded.
> (Chariton of Aphrodisias, *Callirhoe* 4.2.5-7; *LCL* translation [G. P. Goold])

Chariton shows us how crucifixion could be used both as a shameful penalty for the victim and as a "deterrent" for any onlookers.

In his autobiographical *Life*, Josephus tells of a journey he made to a village named Tekoa during the Jewish revolt. As he returns from the journey, he sees crucified rebels (Josephus, *Life* 420). The Romans commonly crucified rebels in public places, especially along roads. Such positioning achieved the maximum deterrent effect. In perhaps the most infamous case, Crassus successfully quelled the slave revolt led by Spartacus. To discourage future slave revolts, Crassus crucified some six thousand rebel-slaves along the road from Capua to Rome (Appian of Alexandria, *Civil Wars* 1.120). These grisly human billboards undoubtedly had the desired effect.

Josephus presents other examples that demonstrate how crucifixion could be used as a warning. Josephus describes the crucifixion of rebels against the Roman empire. During the siege of Jerusalem in the final days of the Jewish revolt, for instance, a Jewish attempt to burn Roman siege equipment failed. The Roman general (and future emperor) Titus used crucifixion as a warning to the rest of the Jewish rebels:

> It happened that, in the course of this fight, a certain Jew was captured alive. Titus commanded that he be crucified before the city wall, to see whether the rest of them would become terrified at this spectacle and surrender.
>
> (Josephus, *Jewish War* 5.289)

Nevertheless, the rebels refused to be intimidated, continuing their resistance. The Romans continued this strategy as the siege took its toll on the Jewish population of Jerusalem:

> The famine made them bold in their sorties, so that even if they escaped notice on the way out, they ended up being captured by their enemies. As they were being taken, they had to defend themselves, and after such conflict it seemed like bad timing to plead for mercy. They were flogged and then tortured with every torment to the point of death; finally, they were crucified in front of the city wall.
>
> So, their suffering seemed to Titus worthy of pity, with five hundred or more being captured every day, but he saw that it was not safe to release those whom he had captured by force. And watching over so many prisoners would be the same thing as leaving his guards under guard! His chief reason for not stopping was that he hoped that maybe, at such a sight, they would give up, realizing that they would suffer a similar fate if they did not surrender.
>
> The soldiers, out of rage and hatred, nailed their captives to the crosses in various positions, as a cruel joke. On account of the multitudes, they ran out of space for the crosses, and out of crosses for the bodies.
>
> (Josephus, *Jewish War* 5.449-451)

As this quotation demonstrates, the form of crucifixion was not standardized. Seneca also testifies to numerous possibilities for the positioning of crucified bodies—the possibilities include not only the upside-down crucifixion of the victim, but also various forms of impalement (Seneca, *Dialogues* 6.20.3).

Unfortunately, the large-scale operation of Titus lacked neither parallel nor precedent. Alexander Jannaeus—a *Jewish* ruler who committed atrocities against *fellow Jews*—might be guilty of the worst instance:

> After taking the city and gaining control over the men, he led them up to Jerusalem. He then committed the most savage deed of all. While feasting with his concubines in the sight of all, he ordered that about eight hundred of them be crucified, and that—while they were still living—their children and their wives be slaughtered before their eyes.
>
> (Josephus, *Jewish Antiquities* 13.380)

Both the "most savage deed" of Alexander Jannaeus (who ruled from 103 to 76 B.C.E.) and the large-scale executions under the Roman general Titus demonstrate that crucifixion was a punishment designed not simply to do away with victims, but to make an example of them.

Still, as scary as crucifixion was, not everyone needed to fear this fate. Most of the time, Roman citizens were spared the gruesome torments of crucifixion. There were, however, rare exceptions:

> Altogether, the number of those killed on that day, with their wives and children (for they did not spare even the infants), was around six hundred and thirty. The latest innovation of Roman savagery made this calamity even harder to bear, for Florus dared to do then what no one had done before. He had men of the equestrian order flogged and nailed to the cross in front of his tribunal; these men, even if they were Jews by birth, were still of Roman dignity.
>
> (Josephus, *Jewish War* 2.307-308)

For Josephus, what was so terrible about the crucifixions carried out by Gessius Florus was that they involved Roman citizens—and elite Roman citizens at that. It was no small thing to be a Roman citizen. Rome extended the privilege of citizenship to children of Roman parents, to those who served in the Roman legions, and to other groups loyal to Rome; only in the early third century C.E. did Rome declare all free persons in the empire to be citizens. Citizens were supposed to receive favorable tax status and freedom from barbaric punishments like crucifixion (see Acts 16:37-38 and 22:25-29 for examples of the protections granted to Roman citizens).

The famous orator (and lawyer) Marcus Tullius Cicero (106 – 43 B.C.E.) composed an oft-cited speech against Verres, who had been governor of Sicily. In this speech, Cicero condemns the many abuses committed by Verres, including the sentencing of Roman citizens to the "most cruel and shocking punishment" of crucifixion (Cicero, *Against Verres* 2.5.165). As in the time of Josephus, so in the time of Cicero, the crucifixion of a Roman citizen is seen as an appalling breach of the social order.

In sum, crucifixion was generally reserved for extreme circumstances, for times when the authorities wanted to send a strong message. Traitors could be crucified by victorious generals (as Diodorus Siculus reports), violent runaway slaves could be crucified by their owners (as Chariton presumes), and rebel soldiers could be crucified as warnings for the populace (as

Josephus records). The crucifixion of Roman citizens made headlines; the crucifixion of turncoats and violent criminals was more typical. To look at one last example, we can take up another first-century C.E. novel. In his *Satyricon*, Petronius (who died in 66 C.E.) includes a story within the story about a woman of extraordinary virtue whose husband has died. Ever faithful, she sits in her husband's underground tomb, weeping over him. With the stage thus set, the story takes a sudden turn:

> At this moment the governor of the province gave orders that some robbers (*latrones*) should be crucified near the small building where the lady was bewailing her recent loss. So on the next night, when the soldier who was watching the crosses, to prevent anyone taking down a body for burial, observed a light shining plainly among the tombs . . .
>
> (Petronius, *Satyricon* 111; *LCL* translation [M. Heseltine])

This soldier quickly becomes distracted and devotes his efforts to seducing the mourning wife; as he does so, the parents of one of the crucified men remove their son's body. This tale again confirms the importance of the spectacle of crucifixion. The soldier is there to ensure that the bodies remain upon the crosses, deterring future criminal activity by this very public example. Yet these robbers (*latrones*, a Latin word that can mean "robber," "bandit," or "brigand") are common criminals, not rebels threatening the Roman empire.

Crucifixion is not unique to the Romans. We have already seen examples of Greek (Dionysius of Syracuse) and Jewish (Alexander Jannaeus) crucifixions. What is more, some form of crucifixion, impalement, or bodily suspension appears to have been practiced by many ancient cultures, including Persians, Assyrians, Celts, and Carthaginians.

To close this section, we might begin to draw some preliminary conclusions about the crucifixion of Jesus in its Greco-Roman context. First, crucifixion shames the crucified and all those associated with him. Close examination of the canonical **gospel** narratives of Jesus' crucifixion show that the entire process of interrogation and beating and procession is intended to shame the victim (e.g., see Mark 14:65; 15:15-20), and thus to warn would-be imitators of Jesus. Second, crucifixion alone does not necessarily mark Jesus out as a political rebel; we have seen examples where the crucified are rebels against Rome (most clearly in Josephus, *Jewish War* 5.289), and we have seen examples where the crucified have no political aims (see the examples in the novels of Chariton and Petronius). That said, the sign over Jesus' head ("King of the Jews" in Mark 15:26 and parallels) certainly lends credence to the view that—from a Roman perspective—Jesus was executed as a political subversive. Third, we see multiple connections between the accounts of Jesus' crucifixion and other narrative accounts from the first century: the scourging of the victim prior to the crucifixion (compare Josephus, *Jewish War* 5.449 with Mark 15:15 and parallels), carrying the cross to the site of execution (compare Chariton, *Callirhoe* 4.2.7 with John 19:17), and a guard over the crucified body (although in Petronius, *Satyricon* 111, the guard is charged with keeping the body on the cross, whereas the soldiers in Matthew 27:62-66 are charged with keeping the body in the tomb).

The glory of the cross

Against this violent background, some parts of the New Testament appear to be making ludicrous claims. For instance, the fullness of God is said to dwell in Jesus ". . . and through [Jesus] to reconcile to himself all things—whether things on earth or things in heaven—making peace through the blood of the cross" (Col 1:20). How could God reconcile everything to himself through crucifixion? Crucifixion does not make peace! Crucifixion threatens, tortures, intimidates. Such means can bring about a brutally efficient *Pax Romana* (= Roman peace), but surely Paul had a different peace in mind when he wrote of "the peace of God that surpasses all understanding" (Phil 4:7).

Paul understands the brutal meaning of crucifixion, yet Paul is also convinced that the crucifixion of Jesus has given a brand-new meaning to the cross: "For the word of the cross is foolishness to those who are perishing, but to us who are being saved it is the power of God" (1 Cor 1:18). What was a symbol of shameful death has become "the power of God." This power does not come from a glorious military victory, but from the humiliating death on a cross. Or, to use the language of the Gospel of John, we may remember that Jesus equates his death with his exaltation: "And I, when I am exalted from the earth, will draw all people to myself" (John 12:32). John adds, "He said this to explain by what manner of death he was going to die" (John 12:33). Jesus' crucifixion is thus his exaltation, the revelation of Jesus' true glory.

One of the clearest instances of this inversion of the honor-shame system with respect to the life and death of Jesus may be found in Phil 2:5-11. In these verses, Jesus, the one "being in the form of God" (2:6) goes on to exchange that honorable status for a much lower position: "he emptied himself, taking the form of a slave" (2:7). However, this humiliation to the point of death leads to a counter-intuitive outcome: "and every tongue will confess that Jesus Christ is Lord, to the glory of God the Father" (2:11). This pattern of self-abasement leading to glory is an element of Christian theology that clashes with cultures of self-promotion both ancient and contemporary.

In the canonical gospels, the glory of Jesus is regularly referenced, but rarely visible (the accounts of the Transfiguration in Mark 9:2-8 and parallels are an exception). Later writings about Jesus give evidence that not all early Christians were satisfied with this reticence about the glory of their Lord. For example, there was at least one second-century author who was not satisfied with previous accounts of Jesus' death and **resurrection**. In this ostensibly new-and-improved version, known as the "Gospel of Peter," the resurrection does not take place behind the scenes, as it does in the New Testament writings. Instead, we find an impressively embellished account of the actual resurrection of Jesus, with sky-high angels and a speaking cross taking the stage:

Early in the morning, when the sabbath was dawning, a crowd from Jerusalem and the surrounding region came to see the sealed tomb. But in the night on which the Lord's day dawned, when the soldiers were keeping watch, on guard-duty two at a time, there was a great noise in heaven. And they saw the heavens opened, and two men, who were very radiant, came down from there and approached the tomb. That stone, the one placed at the entrance, was rolled by itself and moved over to one side. And the tomb was opened, and both the young men entered. Seeing this, therefore, those soldiers woke up the centurion and the elders – for they were also there keeping watch. While they were reporting what they had seen, again they saw three men coming out of the tomb, and the two supported the one and a cross followed them. And the heads of the two reached up to heaven, but the one being led by their hand went beyond the heavens. And they heard a voice from heaven, saying, "Did you proclaim to those who have fallen asleep?" And an answer was heard from the cross, "Yes."

(*Gospel of Peter* 9:34-10:42)

Figure 10.1 Tomb with stone rolled away
This tomb, with its stone rolled away, lies near Megiddo. According to
Rev 16:16, Megiddo (Hebrew *har Megiddo*, which comes into Greek as
Armagedon) will be the site of a great battle.

In the New Testament, the cross of Jesus is both an instrument of lethal
torture and a symbol of the victorious death of the Son of God. In this "Gospel
of Peter," the cross of Jesus becomes a character who can walk ("a cross
followed them") and talk ("Yes"). To be sure, this later work was not written by
the apostle Peter, and its account of a walking, talking cross does not seem
historically reliable. Still, we see how important the cross became in the early
Christian imagination. A former symbol of shame, terror, and torture has
been transformed into a sign of glory, hope, and salvation. The ancient
equivalent of the noose, of the electric chair, of the lethal injection, now can
be seen dangling from the necks of archbishops and priests, monks and nuns,
faithful believers and many unbelievers. Cicero and Seneca would be baffled.

Epilogue

The majority of this chapter has been devoted to reading Jesus' crucifixion
against its cultural background in the larger Greco-Roman world. In closing,

it will be helpful to remind ourselves of some important Jewish influences in the passion narratives. I would like to offer one particularly compelling example.

According to Mark, Jesus uttered his final words, gave a "loud cry," and then breathed his last breath (Mark 15:34-37). Jesus' last words are a question, spoken in **Aramaic**: "*Eloi, Eloi, lema sabachthani?*"—Mark helpfully translates the question for his Greek audience: "My God, my God, why have you forsaken me?" (Mark 15:34). How are we to understand this question? According to Mark, Jesus' Jewish hearers confuse *Eloi* ("my God") for *Eli* ("Elijah"), mistakenly assuming that Jesus is calling on Elijah. Non-Jewish hearers in the first and twenty-first centuries can easily come to the conclusion that Jesus has hit bottom: even God has turned his back on Jesus.

Did Jesus give in to despair? What does his question mean? Christian readers often assume that Jesus is fully God and fully human—how could God abandon God? Or does Jesus here reveal that he is just human after all, bereft of any sense of the divine presence?

These questions generally assume that Jesus' last words in Mark (and in Matthew) are simply a cry of despair. But what if there is more to these words than despair? What if they are closer in meaning to Jesus' last words in Luke's Gospel: "Father, into your hands I entrust my spirit" (Luke 23:46)? Now, the parallels in wording between Mark 15:34 and Luke 23:46 are few. But, more strikingly, Mark 15:34 and Luke 23:46 appear to be (slightly modified) quotations from the book of Psalms.

The surrounding context hints that "My God, my God, why have you forsaken me?" might be read as a biblical quotation, not an improvised cry of dereliction. These words closely approximate the beginning of Psalm 22 (= Psalm 21 LXX). Both Mark and Matthew allude to or quote Psalm 22 multiple times in their passion narratives (compare Ps 21:9 LXX with Matt 27:43; Ps 21:19 LXX with Mark 15:24 // Matt 27:35; Ps 21:8 LXX with Mark 15:29 // Matt 27:39). What are we to make of this awareness of Psalm 22? How does it affect our reading of the last words of Jesus?

As noted above, Psalm 22 begins with this same cry of abandonment. As the psalmist cries out in lament, so the crucified Jesus cries out in lament. But that is not the whole story. Psalm 22 tells a story of hope and lament. The psalmist laments God's distance (22:1-2), praises the past deeds of God (22:3-5), declares himself a miserable "worm" (22:6-8), issues an earnest plea for help (22:9-11), describes his perilous state (22:12-18), calls upon God to act (22:19-21), and concludes with extensive praise to God for God's apparent response to his cry for help (22:22-31). The psalm thus begins with a desperate cry for help, then oscillates wildly between faithful hope and bitter lament, and finally ends with a grateful declaration of praise.

I do not claim to read the mind of Jesus on the cross. But I think we can make some educated guesses about how Mark wanted us to read Jesus' quotation of the words of Psalm 22. Jesus' deep suffering and loud cry dispel any notions that Jesus should be seen as a divine being who is simply passing time on the cross, waiting until the resurrection. The words of Psalm 22 give voice to Jesus' agony. But the number of allusions to Psalm 22 in Mark's narrative suggests that Mark wants the reader (or hearer) to know that Jesus' words are not the end of the story, but the beginning. The story that begins with lament will conclude not with shame for the sufferer, but rather a very public praise of the God who delivers in the end: "I will declare your name to my brothers; in the midst of the assembly (*ekklēsia*) I will praise you" (Ps 21:23 LXX = Ps 22:22). From the shameful cross, God is honored as the one who is faithful.

Bibliography and suggestions for further reading

David W. Chapman. *Ancient Jewish and Christian Perceptions of Crucifixion*. Grand Rapids: Baker Academic, 2010. (This book was first published in 2008 by Mohr Siebeck in the WUNT series; now, it is available from Baker Academic. Chapman offers a thorough overview of how ancient Jews and Christians perceived crucifixion.)

Everett Ferguson. *Backgrounds of Early Christianity*. Third edition. Grand Rapids: Eerdmans, 2003. (This comprehensive volume is a rich resource for students of the New Testament. Ferguson offers a concise treatment of honor and shame in the midst of a larger chapter on society and culture.)

Martin Hengel. *Crucifixion: In the Ancient World and the Folly of the Message of the Cross*. Philadelphia: Fortress, 1977. (Hengel has written the classic reference work on crucifixion in the ancient world. This little book is still cited constantly by scholars today.)

Jerome H. Neyrey. *Honor and Shame in the Gospel of Matthew*. Louisville: Westminster John Knox, 1998. (Neyrey argues that Matthew was well versed in the conventions of rhetoric, and that the gospel-writer used the rhetoric of praise and blame to fashion his portrayal of Jesus. Neyrey also draws heavily on cultural anthropology in his interpretation of this Gospel.)

Matthew S. Rindge. "Reconfiguring the Akedah and Recasting God: Lament and Divine Abandonment in Mark." *Journal of Biblical Literature* 131.4

(2012): 755–774. (Rindge argues for the importance of reading Mark 15:34 against the background not of Psalm 22, but of Genesis 22, where Abraham comes close to sacrificing his son Isaac—a scene often referred to as the binding [*aqedah* in Hebrew] of Isaac.)

11

Faith(fulness)

Guiding Questions

What are some of the problems of applying our modern notions of "religion" to texts from the ancient Mediterranean world?

What can the Greek word *pistis* mean?

Who is faithful, according to ancient Greeks, Romans, and **Jews**?

How are **faith** and **resurrection** connected?

If any consider themselves to be devout (*thrēskos*), and do not bridle their tongue, but rather deceive their heart, then their worship (*thrēskeia*) is useless. Worship (*thrēskeia*) that is pure and undefiled before our God and Father is this: to look after orphans and widows in their distress, and to keep oneself unstained from the world.

(Jas 1:26-27)

Religion, then and now

Are you "religious"? Or do you consider yourself "spiritual but not religious"? Or are you neither spiritual nor religious? Or both spiritual and religious?

While the "neithers" and the "boths" have been around for centuries in Western society, the "spiritual but not religious" tag has become popular in recent years. In contemporary parlance, claiming to be "spiritual" acknowledges that our lives run deeper than what can be seen on the surface. Adding "but not religious" attempts to contrast this deeper life with the (perceived) stodgy and oppressive nature of religious institutions. The "spiritual but not religious" person wants to recognize transcendence, avoid organized religion, and chart his or her own individual course through the deep waters of life.

I have yet to meet a person claiming to be "religious but not spiritual." Historically, though, the words "spiritual" and "religious" have typically served as synonyms rather than antonyms. Among those who claim to be "spiritual but not religious," these words function as placeholders. "Spiritual" implies "liberating freedom to pursue my own inner life." "Religious" entails "stultifying conformity to groupthink." You will not find these sorts of definitions in a twentieth-century dictionary, but familiarity with the twenty-first-century context enables us to understand the connotations of these contemporary identity claims.

It gets more complicated when we turn to a first-century context. In the above quotation from James 1, almost every modern English translation renders the Greek word *thrēskos* as "religious." To avoid importing our modern understanding of "religious" into James 1:26, I translate *thrēskos* as "devout." This passage is talking about *thrēskeia* (usually translated as "religion"), a Greek word that was in use long before the time of Jesus. This word was used with the meaning of "worship," "ritual," or "divine service." So, "religion" is not a bad translation of *thrēskeia*, but such a translation can mislead modern readers.

When we see the word "religion," many of us have a set of connotations in mind: a person's "religion" is chosen by that individual; a person can convert from one "religion" to another; "religion" is something that is more private than public; "religion" involves going to weekly communal gatherings of fellow believers, praying, and maybe the occasional service project or charitable donation. This modern (primarily but not exclusively Christian) understanding of "religion" incorporates several assumptions that do not hold true in the world of Pliny, Paul, and Cicero.

Ancient **polytheism** and contemporary religious pluralism share the concept of multiple, legitimate approaches to the divine (or to transcendent experience). However, the recognition and encouragement of diversity in religious pluralism encompasses the widely divergent beliefs and practices of Christianity, Judaism, Hinduism, Confucianism, Islam, and many other religions. In comparison with this bewildering variety, the "religious" beliefs and practices of various polytheistic cultures in the ancient Mediterranean world appear relatively homogeneous.

First and foremost, it is not very helpful to think of individually-chosen religious affiliations. Almost everybody in the Greco-Roman world practiced ancestral customs that involved the worship of certain gods. If you were born in Ephesus, you offered **sacrifices** to the goddess Artemis, who boasted a magnificent shrine in the city. If you lived in Athens, you cultivated a particular devotion to the goddess Athena; the entire city would participate in the great Panathenaea. This festival featured athletic games, a major procession to the altar of Athena, the sacrificial slaughter of scores of heifers, and feasting—the meat from the sacrifices was distributed to the general public. This distribution of sacrificial meat has no regard for our modern categories: should we call such activity "participating in a ritual meal" or "grocery shopping"? Our modern tendency to compartmentalize and individualize is nowhere to be found.

> This interweaving of "religious" customs and daily life created problems for the followers of Jesus. If one opposed the worship of "idols" (e.g., the cult statue of Athena), should one avoid meat that had been sacrificed to idols? Answers varied. According to the book of Acts, the Jerusalem leadership condemned the eating of sacrificial meat (Acts 15:20, 29; 21:25; compare Rev 2:14, 20), but Paul developed a more nuanced view that weighed individual conscience alongside respect for the convictions of other believers (1 Cor 8:1-13; 10:18-21).

Individuals did not choose their ancestral customs as we choose religious affiliations; after all, how does one choose ancestors? These customs were woven into the fabric of life in antiquity. Hence, we need to re-think "conversion" in the ancient world. Conversion posed a threat to the very fabric of life; it is no wonder that the charge of "not believing the gods that the city (*polis*) believes" may have helped to condemn Socrates to death (Plato, *Apology* 24B). Moreover, in a society where many people worship a broad **pantheon** of gods, "conversion" is not the right word for adding or subtracting gods to be worshiped. (Of course, if a polytheist abandons his ancestral customs and is circumcised and begins to worship the God of Israel, then we may talk about "conversion.")

In a book on the interpretation of dreams written between the mid-second century and the early third century C.E., the author declares that the "common customs" are the following: "to worship and honor the gods. For no human culture is without a god, just as no culture is without a king. Different cultures honor different gods, but they all refer to the same one" (Artemidorus, *Oneirocritica* 1.8.14). According to Artemidorus, a culture loses coherence in the absence of gods and kings, and we again see the role of honor in structuring a society. This writer recognizes the many different forms of worship, yet he still acknowledges an element of unity within the diversity.

In the Roman world, as in many societies ancient and modern, there was no separation of **church** and state. Where the head of the state (the emperor) is viewed as a (soon-to-be) divinized being, there is little room for such distinctions. The emperor himself offered sacrifices, built **temples**, and prayed to the gods. These acts might be labeled "religious," but they could also be labeled as "civic duties." (Magnificent festivals like the above-mentioned Panathenaea were organized by public officials.) To abandon the ancestral customs, after all, would be an affront to the ancestral gods, an act that could imperil the empire. Religion was no private matter, but rather an affair of utmost public importance.

When James writes about pure worship (*thrēskeia*) that is acceptable to God the Father, then, we need to put away thoughts about individually-chosen religious affiliations and private religious beliefs. James has in mind a true worship that involves personal discipline (bridling the tongue), care for the marginalized (caring for widows and orphans), and avoiding evil (preserving oneself from being "polluted" or "stained" by "the world"). For James, this range of practices should shape one's life, showing that one is a truly devout (*thrēskos*) person.

Have I abandoned the word "religion" too hastily? Our English word "religion" comes from the Latin word *religio* and thus has ancient roots, does it not? Yes, it does. But even closely-related words can evolve in different directions over time. Back in the early fifth century C.E., the African theologian Augustine of Hippo (354 – 430 C.E.) could speak about *religio* as follows:

The word 'religion' (*religio*) would seem, to be sure, to signify more particularly the 'cult' offered to God, rather than 'cult' in general; and that is

why our translators have used it to render the Greek word *thrēskeia*. However, in Latin usage (and by that I do not mean in the speech of the illiterate, but even in the language of the highly educated) 'religion' is something which is displayed in human relationships, in the family (in the narrower and the wider sense) and between friends; and so the use of the word does not avoid ambiguity when the worship of God is in question. We have no right to affirm with confidence that 'religion' is confined to the worship of God, since it seems that this word has been detached from its normal meaning, in which it refers to an attitude of respect in relations between a man and his neighbor.
(Augustine, *City of God* 10.1; H. Bettenson translation [Penguin, 1972])

Augustine is sampling different Latin and Greek words, trying to figure out which are best suited for talking about the worship of God. He considers *religio*, but he is not satisfied with a word that can mean vague "respect for the sacred," "superstition," or "worship" (the verb *religo* means "tie," "fasten," or "connect"). For Augustine, *religio* applies to a wide range of relationships: between humans and God, between family members, or between friends. Any relationship which involves respect can fall under the category of *religio*; hence, Augustine abandons this overly-broad term.

To sum up the above discussion, talking about religion is complicated. It is not helpful to talk about any ancient "religion" as if it could be extricated and placed in its own compartment, separate from ancient culture, from ancient politics, or from ancient philosophy. Thinking in terms of a "religious affiliation" is particularly unhelpful, because most inhabitants of the ancient Mediterranean world would not have thought in terms of "religious affiliation." Rather, they would generally adopt (or unconsciously absorb) the beliefs, practices, and customs of their family and of their city. Instead of trying to disentangle "religion" from ancient life, let us instead talk about Greek and Roman gods, about the customary rites offered to these gods, about the places where these gods received worship, or about the ways in which humans modified their behavior in order to please the gods.

On faith and faithfulness

If we abandon the loaded language of "religion," how can we talk about the interactions and relationships between mortals and gods in the ancient world? We could follow the lead of the Letter of James; immediately following the definition of true worship (*thrēskeia*) in 1:27, the author mentions the "faith (*pistis*) of our Lord" (2:1). The language of faith (*pistis* in Greek) pervades the pages of the New Testament. The familiarity of faith in today's world, however, has bred misunderstanding, so we will need to address once more the issue of semantic stretch. On the one hand, today, the word "faith" peppers daily conversation: "keeping the faith," "breaking faith with someone," "blind faith," and the "leap of faith." On the other hand, when I ask a group of students to define the word "faith," the most common answers revolve around "belief" and "trust." Students have a terribly difficult time coming up with any other words to use in a definition. Why? Because many of us tend to associate the concept of faith with cognitive assent: I believe that something is true; therefore, I have faith.

The ancient words for faith (Greek *pistis* and Latin *fides*) certainly can include the idea of assenting to a proposition. But this assent hardly exhausts the meaning of faith. Think back to the closing lines of the previous chapter, where I spoke of the psalmist honoring God as "faithful." What does it mean to speak of a "faithful" God—or a "faithful" friend or a "faithful" spouse? Does such faith belong strictly to the realm of cognitive assent? Or does this faith fit more with the realm of promise-keeping and marital fidelity?

In fact, the Greek word *pistis* and the Latin word *fides* can each be translated as "faith" or as "faithfulness" (or "trustworthiness," "loyalty," or "fidelity"). In English, we have to make a choice between "faith"/"belief" on the one hand, and "faithfulness"/"loyalty" on the other. In Greek and Latin, we are spared the choice. A single word expresses both meanings, and they cannot always be separated.

> Dio Chrysostom (ca. 45 C.E. – after 110 C.E.) wrote an entire discourse called "On Faith (*pistis*)." Or perhaps it should be called "On Trust" or "On Trustworthiness" (either would be a legitimate translation of *pistis*). The discourse is largely a blistering exhortation on why one should *not* attempt to be trusted. Why? Dio's oration is directed to an audience that is considering taking on an additional responsibility, and Dio describes this responsibility as a "trust" or "deposit"—that is, as *pistis*. For Dio, whether one is entrusted with an army or with money (*Discourses* 73.1), such a responsibility is sure to bring trouble, anxiety, and even danger (73.4). For Dio, *pistis* was not at all restricted to "faith" in a god.

That is not to say that Greek- and Latin-speakers used and understood the words *pistis* and *fides* in the same way; language is limited and often

creates barriers to understanding (see Gen 11:1-9). The Greek historian
Polybius (ca. 200 B.C.E. – ca. 118 B.C.E.) provides an excellent example of
cross-cultural confusion. In Book 20 of his *Histories*, Polybius describes a
conflict between the Romans and the Aetolians. The Aetolians quickly
realize that they are powerless to oppose the Romans, and so they ask for
peace. Polybius narrates the misunderstanding that takes place between the
Greek-speaking Aetolians and the Roman representative Manius Acilius
Glabrio:

> The Aetolians, after some further observations about the actual situation,
> decided to refer the whole matter to Glabrio, committing themselves "to the
> faith" (*pistis*) of the Romans, not knowing the exact meaning of that phrase,
> but deceived by the word 'faith' as if they would thus obtain more complete
> pardon. But with the Romans to commit oneself to the faith of a victor is
> equivalent to surrendering at discretion.
>
> (Polybius, *Histories* 20.9.10-12; *LCL* translation [W. R. Paton])

For the Aetolians, "committing themselves to the faith (*pistis*) of the Romans"
meant "deciding to trust the Romans." Apparently, they hoped that trusting
the powerful Romans might inspire the Romans to trust the Aetolians and
grant them clemency. They were not aware that the Latin phrase *dedere se in
fidem* was a technical term with the meaning "to surrender unconditionally."
As Polybius explains in a different context:

> Those who thus commit themselves to the faith (*epitropē*) of Rome surrender
> in the first place the whole of their territory and the cities in it, next all the
> inhabitants of the land and the towns, male and female, likewise all rivers,
> harbors, temples, tombs, so that the result is that the Romans enter into
> possession of everything and those who surrender remain in possession of
> absolutely nothing.
>
> (Polybius, *Histories* 36.4.2-3; *LCL* translation [W. R. Paton])

Here it is clear that "committing oneself to the faith of the Romans" is the
equivalent of handing oneself over to the Romans—and handing over all of
one's land, people, and possessions.

By initiating hostilities with Rome, the Aetolians had proven themselves
to be unfaithful. When they committed themselves to the "faith" of the
Romans, they hoped for clemency. Instead, the Aetolians now found
themselves in Roman chains.

Translating "faith" across linguistic borders involves challenges. The
Greek-speaking Aetolians struggled to understand the Latin *fides*. Modern
German- and English-speakers have lately been wrestling with the Greek

pistis. For a prime example, consider the last few decades of scholarly debate over the meaning of the phrase *pistis Christou* (Gal 2:16; Phil 3:9; etc.). Most translations read "faith in **Christ**." But the Greek is open to a wide variety of readings, including "belief in Christ," "faithfulness to Christ," "Christ's faithfulness," and "Christ's trustworthiness." Which one is right?

Some scholars argue that *pistis Christou* refers to our faith in Jesus (this view is known as the "objective genitive" interpretation), and others believe that *pistis Christou* refers to the faithfulness of Jesus himself (the "subjective genitive" interpretation). If you are a translator trying to render *pistis Christou* into English, then you have to make a choice. In some cases, one meaning or the other might make more sense. But, recalling our earlier discussion of the term *basileia* in Chapter Two, I again would argue that understanding a concept does not always require us to choose one meaning at the expense of another meaning. Sometimes, to understand *pistis* in a given context, you need to take into account both senses of the word: faith and faithfulness.

Faithful humans, faithful God

For further insight into the meaning of *pistis*, we can turn to Philo of Alexandria, who wrote a treatise on Abraham in the first half of the first century C.E. In the previous chapter, we spoke of the Greco-Roman prioritization of honor, which various authors placed above all other worldly goods. For Philo, there is something better than honor: "Faith (*pistis*) in God, then, is the one sure and infallible good" (*On Abraham* 268; *LCL* translation [F. H. Colson]). Here, Philo is clearly talking about human trust in God. What does it mean to trust God? According to Gen 15:6 (quoted by Philo in *On Abraham* 262), Abraham "trusted in God and it was credited to him as righteousness." Commenting on this passage, Philo adds that Abraham " 'trusted in God.' Now that is a little thing if measured in words, but a very great thing if made good by action. For in what else should one trust? In high offices or fame and honors or abundance of wealth and noble birth or ... strength and beauty of body?" (*On Abraham* 262-263; *LCL* translation [F. H. Colson]). Philo discards trust in fleeting honor or in bodily strength as shoddy substitutes for trust in God.

Philo goes on to connect the various senses of *pistis*, showing how faith relates to faithfulness: "That God, marveling at Abraham's faith (*pistis*) in him, repaid him with faithfulness (*pistis*) by confirming with an oath the gifts that he had promised, and here he no longer talked with him as God with a human, but as a friend with a familiar person" (*On Abraham* 273; *LCL* translation [F. H. Colson], modified). Abraham's trust in God leads God to trust and reward Abraham, which leads to a close relationship between God and Abraham. Put another way, Abraham's conviction that God is trustworthy leads God to believe that Abraham is trustworthy, and so God entrusts gifts to Abraham and treats him as a friend. According to Philo the truly "faithful" fall into two categories: "God" and "the friend of God" (*Allegorical Interpretation* 3.204). Is this "religious" language? Or is this language appropriate for any relationship between persons? To say that Abraham is faithful is simply to say that Abraham can be trusted, that Abraham is loyal, that Abraham is worthy of friendship.

Abraham served as a model of faith in **Second Temple** Judaism. While the nineteenth-century philosopher-theologian Søren Kierkegaard has influenced many to link Abraham's faith with the binding of Isaac in Genesis 22 (following Heb 11:17-19), Gen 15:6 looms large in ancient discussions of Abraham's faith. This latter verse is quoted in 1 Macc 2:52; Rom 4:3; Gal 3:6; Philo, *On Abraham* 262; and many later Christian and rabbinic Jewish writings. James 2:21-23 combines the two scenes into a unified affirmation of Abraham's faith.

Later Jewish writings continued to reflect on the faithfulness of Abraham, including the *Mekhilta de Rabbi Ishmael*, a work that was edited in the fourth century C.E. yet contains traditions from the second century C.E. and earlier. The *Mekhilta* interprets the book of Exodus, but like most rabbinic works, its interpretive technique requires drawing on other biblical texts in order to explain the text at hand. The following quotation comments on the Israelites' belief in God in Exod 14-15, linking the presence of the **Holy Spirit** with the practice of faith. As in other Jewish and Christian sources, we find a high value placed on faith in God:

Great indeed is faith before Him who spoke and the world came into being. For as a reward for the faith with which Israel believed in God, the Holy Spirit rested upon them and they uttered the song; as it is said: "And they believed in the Lord . . . Then sang Moses and the children of Israel" (Exod 14:3; 15:1). Rabbi Nehemiah says: How can you prove that whoever accepts even one single commandment with true faith is deserving of having the Holy Spirit rest upon him?

> (*Mekhilta de Rabbi Ishmael*, tractate *Beshallah* 7; J. Z. Lauterbach translation 1:167, modified)

Rabbi Nehemiah hails the importance of faith and provides evidence that **Christians** were not the only believers to revere the Holy Spirit. He links the presence of the Holy Spirit with the inspired song of the Israelites in Exod 15. The following passage shows that faithfulness is rewarded with divine blessing, including the gift of the Holy Spirit, the inheritance of the present world and the world to come, and the exodus from Egypt:

> We find this to have been the case with our fathers. For as a reward for the faith with which they believed, they were considered worthy of having the Holy Spirit rest upon them, so that they could utter the song, as it is said: "And they believed in the Lord … Then sang Moses and the children of Israel." And so also you find that our father Abraham inherited both this world and the world beyond only as a reward for the faith with which he believed, as it is said: "And he believed in the Lord," etc. (Gen 15:6). And so also you find that Israel was redeemed from Egypt only as a reward for the faith with which they believed, as it is said: "And the people believed" (Exod 4:31). And thus it says: "The Lord preserves the faithful" (Ps 31:24)—He keeps in remembrance the faith of the fathers.
>
> (*Mekhilta de Rabbi Ishmael*, tractate *Beshallah* 7; J. Z. Lauterbach translation 1:167, modified)

In the *Mekhilta*, Moses and the Israelites join Abraham as models of belief, and these faithful people are rewarded by their faithful God.

Turning back to the New Testament, the Letter to the Hebrews praises the faith of Moses and the faith of Abraham (for Moses, see Heb 3:1-5). The author describes how Abraham obeyed God's call, left his homeland, and settled in a foreign land through faith, a "conviction about things not seen" (Heb 11:1). Through the lens of faith, the unseen things (a promised land in an unknown place and a promised child from an infertile womb) became visible; faith transformed old Abraham and his barren wife Sarah into the father and mother of all nations (Heb 11:8-12). Why were they faithful? Because they believed "that the one who had promised was faithful (*pistos*)" (11:11). Human faithfulness blossomed when rooted in the conviction that God is faithful (*pistos*).

While the ancients sometimes questioned the reliability of the gods, many Greeks believed that the gods were nonetheless faithful. We might extract a sort of polytheist's creed out of the lines of the Greek poet Pindar (ca. 518

B.C.E. – after 446 B.C.E.): "the tribe of the gods is faithful (*pistos*)" (*Nemean Odes* 10.53). Similarly, the New Testament writings affirm the reliability of the God of Israel time and again: "God is faithful (*pistos*)" (1 Cor 1:9; 10:13; 2 Cor 1:18; 2 Thess 3:3; etc.). A striking passage in 2 Timothy underscores the faithfulness of Jesus: "The word is reliable (*pistos*): for if we have died with him, we will also live with him. If we endure, we will also reign with him. If we deny him, he will also deny us. If we are faithless, he will remain faithful (*pistos*), for he is not able to deny himself" (2 Tim 2:11-13). For the inalienably faithful Jesus, being faithless would amount to a denial of self.

> For Jesus and for Abraham, being faithful is only "religious" in the sense given by Augustine, who refers to *religio* as the set of bonds that bind persons together. Being faithful means being trustworthy, being loyal, being worthy of relationship, friendship, and love. This concept, then, belongs neither to the religious realm nor to the secular realm, but to the human realm.

This faithful Jesus reflects the character of the faithful God of Israel, and the followers of Jesus held high expectations of their God. They interpreted Jesus' resurrection as evidence that the faithful God keeps promises—even promises made in generations past (Acts 13:30-37). God's raising of Jesus from the dead also testified to God's power over death (1 Cor 15:12-20). Hence, these faithful ones expected their God to keep faith beyond the grave: "If we have died with him, we will also live with him" (2 Tim 2:11; see also Rom 6:5-11). As God faithfully raised Jesus, so God would bring about the resurrection of the faithful. Or, as Paul puts it, "Since we have the same spirit of faith (*pistis*) according to what was written, 'I believed, therefore I spoke,' we also believe, therefore we also speak, knowing that the one who raised the Lord Jesus will also raise us with Jesus" (2 Cor 4:13-14; see also 2 Cor 1:22).

This Christian conviction aligned with the expectations of other Second Temple Jews. The book of Daniel already expects that the righteous will awake to "eternal life" (12:2). According to 2 Maccabees, one of the Maccabean martyrs declared with his final breath, "Because we have died on behalf of his laws, the king of the universe will raise us up to live again eternally!" (2 Macc 7:9). The late first- or early second-century C.E. *2 Baruch* likewise affirms that the righteous will rise from the dead. In this text, the coming of the **messiah** coincides with the resurrection of those "who have fallen asleep," that is, of the dead:

And it will be after these things, when the time of the appearance of the Messiah is fulfilled, that he will return in glory. Then all who have fallen asleep in hope of him will rise. And it will happen at that time that the treasuries in which the number of the souls of the righteous are kept will be opened, and they will come out, and the multitude of souls will be seen together in one assembly, of one thought, and the first will rejoice and the last will not be grieved.

                    (*2 Baruch* 30.1-2; D. M. Gurtner translation [T&T Clark, 2009])

First Thessalonians 4:15-17 presents a strikingly similar account of the last days, when the glorious appearance of Jesus will also bring the resurrection of those who have fallen asleep, "the dead in Christ" (4:16). The God who raised Christ from the dead will be faithful to raise the dead in Christ, and so faithful Christians should remain "firm up to the end" (Heb 3:14; compare John 13:1).

In closing, too many contemporary readers of the New Testament underestimate the potency of the word "faith" in phrases like "faith in God" or "faith in Christ." Too often, these phrases take on a simple meaning of "belief," somewhat like a "belief in fairies." Such belief assents to the existence of the thing believed. One can "hold" such a belief and "have" such a faith. But when Philo, Paul, and other ancient authors express their admiration for faithful humans and faithful deities, they praise not cognitive assent, but loyalty, allegiance, or fidelity in the face of adversity. According to the author of Hebrews, "anyone who draws near to God must believe that he exists and that he rewards those who seek him" (Heb 11:6). So, faith does assume the existence of the one being trusted ("believe that he exists"). But faith also carries a conviction that the one being trusted is worthy of such a trust ("and that he rewards those who seek him"). So convinced, the one who has faith continues to keep faith, enduring "as if seeing one who is invisible" (Heb 11:27). Faith, then, or faithfulness, is indeed a conviction with regard to things unseen—a conviction that motivates action (see Heb 11 and Jas 2:15-24).

Bibliography and suggestions for further reading

E. Badian. *Foreign Clientelae (264-70 B.C.)*. Oxford: Clarendon, 1958. (Badian addresses the wide range of patron-client relationships that took shape during the rise of Rome. Badian has helpful comments on the role of *fides* ("faith") in these relationships.)

F. Gerald Downing. "Ambiguity, Ancient Semantics, and Faith." *New Testament Studies* 56 (2010): 139–162. (Downing argues against both sides of the *pistis Christou* debate as too polarized, pointing to the ancient evidence for preserving ambiguity.)

Daniel M. Gurtner. *Second Baruch: A Critical Edition of the Syriac Text: With Greek and Latin Fragments, English Translation, Introduction, and Concordances.* Jewish and Christian Texts in Contexts and Related Studies 5. New York: T&T Clark, 2009. (Gurtner's sub-title sums up the contents of this useful edition. Scholars and students alike will profit from a close look at *2 Baruch*, a fascinating Second Temple Jewish apocalypse.)

Richard B. Hays. *The Faith of Jesus Christ: The Narrative Substructure of Galatians 3:1-4:11.* Second edition. Grand Rapids/Dearborn: Eerdmans/Dove, 2002. (Although Hays' primary aim is to explicate Paul's Letter to the Galatians, this book is famous for advancing the thesis that *pistis Christou* means "the faithfulness of Jesus" rather than "faith in Jesus.")

Jacob Z. Lauterbach, ed. *Mekhilta de-Rabbi Ishmael: A Critical Edition, Based on the Manuscripts and Early Editions, with an English Translation, Introduction, and Notes.* Two volumes. Second edition. Philadelphia: The Jewish Publication Society, 2004. (This commentary on the book of Exodus reveals numerous insights into early Jewish biblical interpretation (*midrash*).)

Simon Price. *Religions of the Ancient Greeks.* Cambridge: Cambridge University Press, 1999. (Price expertly navigates the gods, shrines, and cultic practices of the ancient Greeks, ranging from the eighth century B.C.E. to the fifth century C.E.)

12

Apocalypse Then

Guiding Questions

What is an "**apocalypse**"?

Why is it important for interpreters to consider the genre of a text?

How does apocalyptic literature function?

How can knowledge about a text's context inform our interpretation?

The revelation (*apokalypsis*) of Jesus Christ, which God gave him in order to show his servants the things that must soon take place, and which he made known by sending it by means of his angel to his servant John, who testified to the word of God and to the witness of Jesus Christ—everything that he saw.

(Rev 1:1-2)

What apocalyptic literature is

Apocalyptic literature reveals, discloses, unveils. If all the world is a stage, then apocalyptic thinkers report on the hidden actors who govern the main plot. Some apocalyptic literature issues a backstage pass, allowing readers and hearers an opportunity to go behind the scenes and see what is really happening from a heavenly perspective. Other apocalyptic writings present a preview of future events. If the audience is living in the midst of the fourth act of human history, then the apocalyptic author lifts the curtain for a look into the decisive fifth and final act.

The apocalyptic book of Revelation has perplexed generations of readers, many of whom wonder if the book's fantastic visions offer an accurate "sneak preview" of the end times. Scholars have argued more recently that Revelation offers more of a "sneak peek" at the behind-the-scenes action in the first-century. Either way, the book of Revelation is designed to reveal something to someone. The book derives its name from the Latin *revelatio*, a translation of the Greek word *apokalypsis* that appears in 1:1. Both words mean "revealing," "unveiling," or "uncovering." What does it reveal? Is it a sneak preview of future events, or sneak peek into a present, hidden reality?

Apocalyptic texts can pull back the curtain on the present and the future, yet the visions so offered do not always beget clarity. Apocalyptic literature brims over with paradox, revealing and obscuring. The revelation of secrets often takes a form so bizarre that the modern reader looks up from the page more puzzled than she was beforehand. More so than narrative histories or occasional letters, apocalyptic literature requires both careful scrutiny of the complex imagery and frequent recourse to exegetical aids. Before diving into the world of apocalyptic thought, we must take up the word "**apocalypse**" itself, as well as its cognate terms.

Scholars tend to use the word "apocalypse" to describe a literary genre. Hence, the book of Revelation can be labeled an apocalypse, as can the book of Daniel, *2 Baruch, 1 Enoch, 4 Ezra*, the *Sibylline Oracles*, and the *Shepherd of Hermas*. This label helpfully isolates a body of literature defined by the following elements: (1) a revelation (2) mediated by an angel or other nonhuman being, (3) dealing with both eschatological events (= events in the "end times") and (4) an unseen spatial reality. So, the book of Daniel qualifies as an apocalypse: (1) the prophet Daniel witnesses revelatory visions (throughout Dan 7-12); (2) otherworldly beings explain the meaning of these visions to Daniel (e.g., Dan 7:16; 8:17-26; 9:21-27; etc.); (3) these explanations include descriptions of "the time of the end" (e.g., 8:17); and (4) Daniel witnesses events that take place in an alternate spatial reality (e.g., 7:13-14).

Angels fascinate many of us. In spite of our interest in angels, biblical texts tend not to delve into the details of angelic existence. Texts like Daniel and Revelation focus on the function of angels as **heaven**-sent messengers and divine agents. The word "angel" (*malakh* in Hebrew, *angelos* in Greek) simply means "messenger," and it can also refer to human messengers. Jacob sends messengers (*malakhim*) to Esau in Gen 32:4. John the Baptist sends two **disciples** (*mathētai*) to Jesus in Luke 7:19, and these "messengers" (*angeloi*) return to John in Luke 7:24. More often, the "messengers" are otherworldly beings, sent by God for a purpose, whether to reveal a message from God (e.g., Gen 16:7-12), to rescue a servant of God (e.g., Acts 12:7-12), to interpret a vision (e.g., Dan 8:16-26), or to execute divine judgment (e.g., Rev 20:1-3). Jude 6 depicts fallen angels, whose failed rebellion culminated in "eternal chains" and "darkness."

Both Daniel and Revelation meet these four criteria and are considered to be apocalypses. But the two books differ from each other with regard to the content of the visions. Moreover, they each lack internal consistency. Daniel begins with six chapters of narratives about Daniel and his companions; these stories show little interest in expounding on secret matters or prophesying future events. In addition to vision sequences and angel-mediated interpretations, Revelation includes seven letters to seven churches in Rev 2-3; in fact, the entire text of Revelation is framed as a letter from "John to the seven churches in Asia" (Rev 1:4). On a smaller scale, the lengthy conclusion to *2 Baruch* takes the form of a letter:

> These are the words of that epistle which Baruch son of Neriah sent to the nine and one half tribes. Thus says Baruch, son of Neriah, to the brothers who were taken into captivity, "Grace and peace be with you. I remember, my brothers, the love of him who created me, who loved us from the beginning and never hated us, but above all instructed us."
> (*2 Baruch* 78.1-3; D. M. Gurtner translation [T&T Clark, 2009])

The opening of Baruch's letter sounds less like an apocalypse and more like a hybrid of a Pauline letter and the first lines of the letter of James. Given the diversity of content in these apocalypses, I generally prefer the label "apocalyptic literature" as a way of acknowledging that many of our so-called "apocalypses" comprise a variety of genres.

To some degree, the limitations of labels like "apocalypse" are offset by their usefulness in facilitating and furthering discussion. Such disparate writings as the *Sibylline Oracles*, the book of Daniel, and Revelation diverge in numerous ways, but the many points of connection can illuminate literary influences and obscure imagery. In the context of the New Testament writings, Revelation can stand out like an ugly duckling. Reading Revelation alongside other apocalypses restores this book to a more natural habitat.

Not only do apocalyptic works include non-apocalyptic material, but various **gospels** and letters of the New Testament also contain some apocalyptic elements—not enough to classify these works as "apocalyptic literature," but enough to remind us that apocalyptic thought is not limited to one book of the New Testament. In the previous chapter, we discussed 1 Thess 4:15-17, where Paul reveals "the word of the Lord" about the eschatological coming of Jesus, the heavenly trumpet call, and the airborne reunion between the followers of **Christ** and Jesus himself. When Jesus proclaims that "the time is fulfilled, and the kingdom of God has come near" (Mark 1:15), he heralds a new epoch of human history. Later in Mark's Gospel, Jesus delivers a lengthy apocalyptic prophecy about "the end" (Mark 13:5-37), incorporating catastrophic images from earlier prophetic books (compare Mark 13:14 with Dan 11:31 and 12:11, or Mark 13:24-25 with Isa 13:10—as well as Rev 6:12). In Matthew's Gospel, Jesus utters another apocalyptic discourse about an eschatological judgment, when the righteous "sheep" will be separated from the cursed "goats" (Matt 25:31-46).

The menagerie of apocalyptic literature runs wild with such imagery (see Dan 7:2-7; 8:2-12, 20-22; etc.). Perhaps the best example is the Animal Apocalypse, one component of a larger apocalyptic work known as *1 Enoch*. The various visions and traditions of *1 Enoch* were composed and collected between the fourth and first centuries B.C.E., and fragments of the ancient **Aramaic** text have turned up at **Qumran** among the **Dead Sea Scrolls**. The Animal Apocalypse (= *1 Enoch* 85-90) engages animals to tell a story familiar to readers of the Jewish **scriptures**:

> When those twelve sheep had grown up, they handed over one of themselves to the wild asses, and those wild asses, in turn, handed that sheep over to the wolves, and that sheep grew up among the wolves. And the ram led forth the eleven sheep to dwell with it and to pasture with it among the wolves. And they multiplied and became many flocks of sheep. And the wolves began to fear them and oppress them until they did away with their young, and they cast their young into a river of much water. And those sheep began to cry out because of their young and to make complaint to their Lord.
>
> (*1 Enoch* 89:13-15; G. W. E. Nickelsburg and J. C. VanderKam
> translation [Fortress, 2004])

Before reading further, look over the above quote again. Do you recognize the storyline? The twelve sheep are the twelve sons of Jacob, Joseph is the sheep sold to the Ishmaelites (Gen 37:25; compare Gen 16:12), and the ram who leads the eleven sheep is Jacob. The Israelites, or sheep, multiplied in this new land (compare *1 Enoch* 89:14 with Exod 1:7). The Egyptian "wolves," however, turned on the Israelites; *1 Enoch* 89:15 parallels Exod 1:8-22. In the following lines of the Animal Apocalypse, a sheep (Moses) will escape from the wolves (89:16), another sheep (Aaron) joins him in confronting the wolves (89:18), and the sheep eventually escape across a "swamp of water" that is "split apart" by the Lord (89:23-27). Throughout this text, symbolic animals act out a familiar script.

What apocalyptic literature does

The Animal Apocalypse retells the story of Israel. But why does it tell this story as a series of animal escapades? The roughly contemporary book of *Jubilees* retells these same events, using the same faces and places familiar from the **Pentateuch**. Whether an apocalypse retells the past, reveals the truth behind present events, or foretells the future crisis, why do apocalyptic texts so often utilize such bizarre imagery? The Animal Apocalypse and book of Daniel, like the book of Revelation, achieve a range of goals through their use of strange beasts and vivid images. Before turning to Revelation, let us show how apocalyptic imagery addresses past, present, and future.

First, although apocalyptic imagery tends to mystify modern readers, the images follow conventions and traditional usages. Ancient readers would find much of the imagery familiar, not strange. For example, the book of Revelation reuses the bestiary of Daniel. In Rev 13:1, the seer witnesses a "beast coming up out of the sea." Whence do the four beasts of Daniel 7 emerge? The sea (Dan 7:3). Three of these four beasts are compared to animals: the first to a lion, the second to a bear, and the third to a leopard (Dan 7:4-6). The beast of Rev 13 resembles "a leopard, and its feet are like those of a bear, and its mouth like the mouth of a lion" (13:2). Likewise, the Animal Apocalypse labels the Israelites "sheep," in keeping with longstanding biblical tradition (see Num 27:17; 1 Kgs 22:17; Ps 44:11, 22; 74:1; 78:52; etc. For God as shepherd, see Gen 48:15; 49:24; Ps 23:1; etc.)—and with the canonical gospels (see Matt 9:36; 25:31-46; etc.). This recycling of prophetic imagery stems not from laziness or dullness, but from a desire to tap into this venerable tradition. By rewriting history as a tale of wandering sheep and ravenous lions, apocalyptic writers gain the ability to draw on the authority invested in earlier sacred texts. They can then use this ability to highlight and shape the history of the past in keeping with their vision of the present and future.

Second Temple Jewish apocalyptic authors enjoyed multiple means to draw on the authority of the past. In addition to borrowing prophetic imagery, the authors often borrowed the prophets themselves, or at least their names. Scholars believe that the two earliest Christian apocalypses (Revelation and the *Shepherd of Hermas*) are attributed to their true authors: John and Hermas, respectively. (Little is known about these two figures.) Yet, most scholars are convinced of widespread **pseudonymity** among the authors of Jewish apocalypses in this time period. That is, the Enoch of Gen 5:18-24 did not write *1 Enoch*. Ezra the scribe did not write the first-century C.E. book of *4 Ezra*. The prophet Jeremiah's scribe Baruch (see Jer 36:4) did not write the late first- or early second-century C.E. Syriac apocalypse of Baruch (*2 Baruch*). And despite the Babylonian setting of the book of Daniel, most historical-critical scholars believe that the book attained its current form in the second century B.C.E.

Second, once an apocalyptic (or non-apocalyptic) text is tied into the tradition by using the symbols of the tradition, the text can comment on the present situation with the authority of the tradition. The Animal Apocalypse does not stop short at the end of the exodus from Egypt; it retells the story of God's people from the creation of Adam and Eve in 85:3, to events closer to the author's time (which are harder to identify from the descriptions given), to the eschatological judgment (90:20-27). The late first-century or early second-century C.E. *Shepherd of Hermas* speaks to present concerns far more than questions about the future. By sharing his visions with the larger community, Hermas hopes to convert his audience to live lives of greater faithfulness; like the letter of James, Hermas exhorts his audience to whole-hearted **faith** and opposes "double-mindedness" (*dipsychia*)—this word and its cognates appear over fifty times in the *Shepherd* (compare Jas 1:7; 4:8). Similarly, the book of Revelation employs a panoply of prophetic images to comment on the true meaning of present (and future) circumstances, as we will soon explain.

Third, apocalyptic literature does indeed deal with future events, especially events of the end times. Readers tend to fixate on the eschatological aspects of books like Revelation. The problem with such a focus on the last days becomes clearer when compared to modern views of Jewish and Christian prophecy; the working definition of a "prophet" in most twenty-first-century minds is "one who predicts the future." Actually, the Greek word *prophētēs* does not at all mean "one who predicts the future." Instead, a *prophētēs* is "one who speaks on behalf of a god" or "one who interprets the will of a god." If the god wants to convey information about the future, the prophet will foretell future events. But the God who spoke to (and through) Isaiah, Jeremiah, and Amos showed little interest in forecasting world events, stock market futures, or later fashion trends. Even when prophets are technically predicting the future, their intentions usually lie in the present or very near future. Yes, Jonah predicts the destruction of Nineveh, but God seeks to turn the Ninevites to immediate repentance through this message of coming doom (Jonah 1:2; 3:1–4:11). In the same vein, John the Baptist combines an exhortation to repentance with an announcement of the coming wrath (Luke 3:7-9). Like John and other prophetic figures, apocalyptic writers earnestly paint pictures of eternal reward and everlasting damnation. While their eyes may seem set on the future, their words are directed towards the present, encouraging the faithful and forewarning the wicked. Reflection on the end aims to transform the present.

The analogy between apocalyptic writing and prophecy can be pushed further. If apocalyptic literature's essential function is to reveal a divinely-inspired vision of an otherworldly and eschatological nature, then apocalyptic literature can be viewed as a sub-type of prophecy (= the words and deeds of the one who speaks on behalf of a god). In fact, we find John describing himself as being "in the spirit on the Lord's day" (Rev 1:10); prophets are often described as being filled with the Holy Spirit (for a dramatic example, see 1 Sam 10:6-10). The book of Daniel presents an even clearer example: this apocalyptic work is attributed to a prophet (see Matt 24:15). For further evidence, see the pervasive use of prophetic imagery in later apocalyptic works, noted above.

Scenes from an apocalypse

So far, we have discussed broadly what apocalyptic literature is, and what it does. In this final section, we will zoom in for a closer look at certain passages in the book of Revelation. The most popular of the ancient apocalypses, Revelation has been read, interpreted, and hazardously misinterpreted for centuries. (I once heard a professor suggest to his students that all copies of the book of Revelation should come with a warning label, given its history of use and abuse. They laughed, but I am not sure that he was joking.) In the following pages, we will look at four scenes from the book of Revelation, showing how our more theoretical discussion can influence the interpretation of individual texts. The first two texts reflect more of the first-century Roman context of the book of Revelation; the last two, the Jewish (scriptural) roots of Revelation. (Author's note: In the following section, readers will profit from reading the relevant passage in Revelation prior to reading my treatment of that passage.)

As the previous two sections suggest, the best preparation for reading Revelation would be a careful reading of relevant Old Testament texts, including Genesis, Exodus, Psalms, Isaiah, Jeremiah, Ezekiel, and (of course) Daniel.

Scene 1: Laodicea (Rev 3:14-22)

Earlier, back in Chapter Three, we deciphered the clues in Rev 17 that link the "great prostitute" seated on "seven mountains" with Rome, "the great city that holds royal authority (*basileia*) over the kings of the earth" (Rev 17:2, 9, 18). We will return to that sort of detective work later; first, let us take up a more straightforward example. In Revelation 2-3, we find seven letters to seven churches; the seven churches (or "assemblies") are located in seven cities in Asia Minor (= modern-day Turkey): Ephesus, Smyrna, Pergamum, Thyatira, Sardis, Philadelphia, and Laodicea (See Map 1). The last of the letters reveals the Spirit's words to "the angel of the church (*ekklēsia*) in Laodicea" (Rev 3:14). The Spirit berates the "lukewarm," "poor," and "naked" Laodiceans (Rev 3:16-17). The spirited scolding makes clear that the Spirit is displeased, but stepping into the world of the first-century Laodiceans can further illuminate the Spirit's scalding words. Fortunately, we have access to an ancient account of Laodicea, courtesy of the Roman geographer Strabo (ca. 64 B.C.E. – after 21 C.E.). Strabo describes Laodicea as follows:

> Laodicea, though formerly small, grew large in our time and in that of our fathers, even though it had been damaged by siege in the time of Mithridates Eupator. However, it was the fertility of its territory and the prosperity of certain of its citizens that made it great ... The country round Laodicea

produces sheep that are excellent, not only for the softness of their wool, in which they surpass even the Milesian wool, but also for its raven-black color, so that the Laodiceans derive splendid revenue from it.

(Strabo, *Geography* 12.8.16; *LCL* translation [H. L. Jones], modified)

According to Strabo, Laodicea is a prosperous city, renowned for its production of black wool. He went on to note the Laodiceans' proximity to a respected medical school (*Geography* 12.8.20). Other comments by Strabo imply deficiencies in Laodicea's water supply; their water is drinkable, although very rich in minerals (*Geography* 13.4.14). Scholars have suggested that this hard water may have originated from nearby hot springs. If so, the water may not have cooled down by the time it reached the city.

When read against this background, the letter to the Laodiceans comes into focus for the twenty-first-century reader. (Keep in mind, of course, that first-century Laodicean readers would already know much more about their black sheep and hard water than we could ever learn from our reconstructions.) Like their tepid water, the Laodiceans themselves are nauseatingly "lukewarm" (Rev 3:16). The other admonitions, though, reveal a trenchant reversal of expectations. The affluent Laodiceans are "miserable and pitiable and poor" (3:17). The traders in luxuriant black wool are commanded to "purchase ... white garments" so as to cover "the shame of [their] nakedness" (3:18). While they are shopping, they should also pick up some of the Spirit's eye ointment, so that they can see (3:18). The region in which Laodicea was located possessed not only a fine medical school but also a reputation for healing eye powders. In short, the vivid imagery of the letter debases every Laodicean boast, calling a proud and supposedly independent people to repentance and humility (3:19). The letter reveals weakness in place of strength, judgment in place of approval, and in the end, opportunity to sit with God the Father for those who hear and obey (3:21-22).

Scene 2: On the right hand or the forehead (Rev 13:11-18)

In Revelation 3, the Spirit directly and openly rebukes the **church** in Laodicea. Ten chapters later, plain talk disappears, replaced by a beast with characteristics of a lamb, and of a dragon (13:11). This beast takes the stage as the latest member of a cast of apocalyptic villains, a cast featuring both human evil-doers (e.g., the Nicolaitans of 2:6 and 2:15 and the woman

Jezebel of 2:20-23) and the otherworldly enemies of the righteous: Satan (2:9, 13), the devil (2:10), Death and Hades (6:8), scorpion-like locusts and their ringleader Abaddon-Apollyon (9:3-11), four killer angels (9:14-15), the beast from the abyss (11:7), the seven-headed, ten-horned red dragon with a star-scattering tail (12:3-4)—who is later identified as the "ancient serpent," the "devil," and "Satan" (12:9), and the earlier seven-headed, ten-horned beast that emerges from the sea and works with the dragon (13:1-4). This beast "from the earth" (of Rev 13:11) teams up with the beast "from the sea" (of Rev 13:1-4) to take over the world. The earth-beast works miracles, creates a speaking simulacrum of the sea-beast, and forces all the people of the world to get "a mark on their right hand or on their forehead" (Rev 13:17); this beastly mark is "the name of the beast or the number of its name" (Rev 13:17). What is the beast's name? "Let the one who has understanding calculate the number of the beast, for it is the number of a man, and his number is six hundred sixty-six" (13:18). How do we get from a name to a number?

The concept of identifying people by a mark on the forehead comes from Ezekiel 9, where those marked with the name of the Lord are spared deadly judgment. This beastly mark on the forehead parodies the earlier prophecy, as the beast subverts the ways of God and leads the people of the world into idolatrous worship. The mark of the lamb in Rev 14:1 opposes the mark of the beast in 13:16-17.

Names become numbers through **gematria**, the Jewish practice of biblical interpretation through the numerical value of words. Nowadays, we use Arabic numerals to count (1, 2, 3, etc.). Earlier, Roman numerals were used (I, II, III, etc.). Like Rome, many ancient cultures employed their alphabets both to write and to count. The Greek and **Hebrew**-Aramaic alphabets thus provided both letters and numbers (by the first century C.E., Hebrew was written using **Aramaic** letters). The first letter of the alphabet (Greek *alpha* and Hebrew *aleph*) could also stand in as the number "one." The next nine letters served as 2-10, and the eleventh letter of the alphabet equaled 20. So, for example, King David's name in Hebrew adds up to 14—interestingly, we find Matthew's **genealogy** of Jesus the "son of David" organized into three groups of 14. But who adds up to 666?

Jesus, or *Iēsous* in Greek, adds up to 888 (10 + 8 + 200 + 70 + 400 + 200). An unknown second-century Christian editor of the *Sibylline Oracles* probably added the following lines to an earlier Jewish text: "Then indeed the son of the great God will come, incarnate, likened to mortal men on earth, bearing four vowels, and the consonants in him are two. I will state explicitly the entire number for you. For eight units, and equal number of tens in addition to these, and eight hundreds will reveal the name" (*Sib. Or.* 1.324-329; *OTP* translation). The *Sibylline Oracles* also include a review of Roman history, where emperors are referred to by the numerical value of the first letter of their name (5.1-42).

We have at least two available alphabets (Greek and Aramaic), multiple mathematical possibilities, and almost two thousand years of hermeneutical creativity. Who is 666? Answers vary. The most popular solution is the emperor Nero. If the Greek for "Nero Caesar" is transliterated into Hebrew, then the resulting *qsr nrwn* adds up (100 + 60 + 200 + 50 + 200 + 6 + 50 = 666). Other theories have yielded more or less credible hypotheses: one scholar has shown how an abbreviation of emperor Domitian's name could yield 666; a more dubious conspiracy theory once proposed Ronald Wilson Reagan (six letters in each of his three names!). If the "Nero Caesar" reading is correct, then we should read this part of Revelation as condemning the first-century Roman imperial cult, particularly the idolatrous Roman worship of Nero (recall the enmity between Nero and **Christians** in Tacitus, *Annals* 15.44, cited in Chapter Three).

Do these calculations imply that Nero is the "Antichrist" of popular Christian lore? No. Revelation offers no hints to the identity of someone named the "Antichrist." If you read the book of Revelation, you will find that the word "antichrist" (*antichristos*) never appears. The only New Testament discussion of an "antichrist" is in the letters of John, not the Revelation of John. In 1 John 2:18, we are told that "antichrist is coming" and that "many antichrists have come." What or who is the antichrist? Literally, *antichristos* means "one who is against Christ" or "a counterfeit Christ," but these precise meanings are not reflected in 1 or 2 John. "This is the antichrist, the one who denies the father and the son"

(1 John 2:22). Also, regarding "those who do not confess the coming of Jesus Christ in flesh," the author confirms that "this one is the deceiver and the antichrist" (2 John 7). "Antichrist" functions as more of a label for those whose beliefs about Christ (or "Christology") do not conform to the author's beliefs.

Symbolic numbers litter the landscape of Revelation; this particular number reveals the true identity of the opponent of the Lamb. If our interpretation is accurate, then Revelation 13 may or may not forecast a future showdown between the Antichrist and Jesus. That scenario cannot be ruled out, given the polyvalent nature of apocalyptic literature. We can infer with more confidence, however, that the bestial imagery and number play function to reveal the true nature of the Roman imperial cult, which opposes the worship of the Lamb of God (see Rev 14).

Scene 3: By the sea of glass (Rev 15:1-8)

Although Rome lurks in the background of Revelation, this apocalypse relies even more heavily on imagery and themes from the Jewish scriptures. To understand the "seven plagues" of Revelation 15, we need to hearken back to an earlier story of plagues. Exodus 7:14-12:32 recounts ten plagues instead of seven; Revelation tends to prefer groups of seven (compare Gen 1). The plagues, narrated in Revelation 16, resemble the earlier plagues on the Egyptians (compare Rev 16:2 with Exod 9:8-11; Rev 16:3-6 with Exod 7:17-21; Rev 16:10-11 with Exod 10:21-23; Rev 16:13 with Exod 8:1-6; and Rev 16:18-21 with Exod 9:22-25). Beyond a set of numbered plagues, other facets of Revelation 15 call to mind the story of the Israelite exodus. The gathered people alongside the "sea of glass" are singing "the song of Moses" (Rev 15:2-3). This scene evokes another festive sea-side gathering, when Moses and the Israelites sang a song to God immediately after their sea-crossing departure from Egypt (Exod 14:30-15:21; compare also Isa 11:15-12:6). The harp-playing, singing people of God give thanks with this new song of Moses after their deliverance. Their presence alongside a "sea of glass" may reflect a later Jewish interpretation of Exod 15:8, where the sea turns into glass: "The sea congealed on both sides and became a sort of glass crystal, as it is said: 'The deeps were congealed in the heart of the sea'" (*Mekhilta de Rabbi Ishmael*, tractate *Beshallah* 5; J. Z. Lauterbach translation 1:149). The plagues, crossing of the sea, and triumphant song are all transposed from Egypt to heaven.

Unlike the Animal Apocalypse, which retells history sequentially, Revelation shows no interest in retelling ancient history. Revelation instead draws potent images of salvation from Jewish tradition and recasts them, linking God's past acts of salvation with God's future acts of salvation. The great future deliverance of the people of God is described in language that recalls the greatest past deliverance of the people of God. The message for first-century readers? As God was faithful, so God will be faithful; therefore, take heart!

Scene 4: New heavens and new earth (Rev 21:1-22:5)

As future deliverance mirrors past salvation, so the end reflects the beginning. Revelation does not end with the souls of the righteous flying away to heaven. Rather, John sees "a new heaven and a new earth" (Rev 21:1), as well as a "new Jerusalem descending out of heaven from God" (21:2). In this penultimate chapter of Revelation, we are reminded of the first chapter of the Jewish and Christian **Bibles**, which tells how, in the beginning, God created heaven and earth (Gen 1:1). Revelation 21-22 narrates a new creation that echoes the creation narratives of Gen 1-2.

Revelation has been labeled an anti-Semitic or anti-Jewish work, based on two worrying references to a "**synagogue** of Satan" (see Rev 2:9 and 3:9). If a twenty-first-century Christian were to label the synagogue down the street as a "synagogue of Satan," that individual could be rightly labeled as anti-Jewish. Leveling the same charge at John is problematic, for a variety of reasons. First, John was most likely Jewish, as his deep familiarity with scriptural imagery suggests. Second, John specifies in both cases that he is concerned with "those who say that they are Jews but who are not" (Rev 2:9; compare Rev 3:9). John specifies that his critique is not aimed at Jews, but at those who falsely claim to be Jews. What we have here is an argument over Jewish identity; John condemns those who claim to be Jewish, yet who do not meet John's criteria for being Jewish. An in-house quarrel over what it means to be Jewish produces sharply-worded condemnation ("synagogue of

Satan"), but this dispute should not be confused with modern religious hate speech—even if they use the same words.

No knowledge of the Roman empire is required to see these parallels. On the one hand, the new creation differs from the old: in this new creation, there is no sea (Rev 21:1), neither sun nor moon (21:23), no night (22:5), and no more weeping, pain, or death (21:4). On the other hand, we do find a river (Rev 22:1 // Gen 2:10), the tree of life (Rev 22:2 // Gen 2:9), and a garden setting (Rev 22:2 // Gen 2:8). Compare this Christian vision of life in the city of God and the Lamb with an earlier Jewish vision of the end:

> On that day, I shall make my Chosen One dwell among them, and I shall transform heaven and make it a blessing and a light forever; and I shall transform the earth and make it a blessing. And my chosen ones I shall make to dwell on it, but those who commit sin and error will not set foot on it. For I have seen and satisfied my righteous ones with peace, and have made them to dwell in my presence. But the judgment of the sinners has drawn near to me, that I may destroy them from the face of the earth.
>
> (*1 Enoch* 45:4-6; G. W. E. Nickelsburg and J. C. VanderKam translation [Fortress, 2004])

This oracle of *1 Enoch* aligns precisely with the final visions of the book of Revelation, including the following details: a new **heaven** and earth (Rev 21:1), "light forever" (compare Rev 21:23-24), exclusion of and judgment on the wicked (Rev 20:14-15; 21:8, 27), and a double blessing on the righteous of peace and the presence of God (Rev 21:3-4, 7; 22:3-4). Second Temple **Jews** expected to see the beginning in the end.

The apocalypse: a final word

Apocalyptic texts emerge from a worldview that prizes revelatory visions (usually mediated by angels), recognizes a heavenly realm, and expects an eschatological crisis. Interpreters of texts emerging from such a worldview should not try to pry apart these elements. The eschatological crisis regularly involves actors from the heavenly realm, and the visions narrate both heavenly journeys and scenes from the "last days" or "end of days." Jewish and Christian apocalypses employ these visions for a variety of purposes. They give hope to the faithful, consolation to the persecuted, exhortation to those who waver, and warning to those who have fallen away. As radical as these visions may seem to the modern reader, apocalyptic literature often retains a conservative character, recycling earlier prophetic images and themes in the oracles of what is to come.

> Throughout this chapter, I have discussed the form, function, and content of apocalyptic literature. I have left its origins unaddressed. We can comment about how literature works, but we are in a poor position to attempt an evaluation of whether a given text (1) originated in an actual revelatory experience, (2) was composed by an imaginative individual, or (3) was rooted in a vision of some sort, yet assumed a later form through literary revisions. The final option seems most likely.

Readers have long looked into the visions of future things as a means of gaining special knowledge about the future. For instance, when exactly will the world end? That is easy: shuffle the prophecies around, blend together **gematria** and astronomic observations, and voilà, Jesus is coming soon. The practitioners of end-time hype perform an ironic service. After all, the New Testament writings exhort readers to be faithfully vigilant, lest the end of the age catch them unawares: "Behold, I am coming soon!" (Rev 22:12; see also Matt 24:43; 1 Thess 5:2; 2 Pet 3:10; Rev 3:3). The eschatologically-minded radio broadcasts and blog posts that blare "The end is near!" echo the urgency of this announcement. Both first-century apocalypse and twenty-first-century bullhorn serve to encourage vigilance and preparation. Still, the constant claims to have discerned the imminent date of Jesus Christ's return can rightly be criticized, if only for being so reliably inaccurate.

Among the crowd of critics we might bump into two noteworthy figures: Jesus and Paul. To the televangelist who announces that Jesus is coming back next week, Jesus might respond, "But about that day or that hour, no one knows, not even the angels in heaven, nor the Son, but only the Father" (Mark 13:32). If the Bible is your source for figuring out the date of the end times, then you should read Mark 13:33, too: "For you do not know when the time will come." On a more general note, we might turn to Paul, who wrote to a Corinthian audience that obsessed over esoteric knowledge: "Knowledge puffs up, but love builds up. If someone seems to know something, they do not yet know as they should. But if someone loves God, that person is known by God" (1 Cor 8:1-3). Facing an audience that yearns for esoteric knowledge, Paul promotes an alternative option: love.

Bibliography and suggestions for further reading

David E. Aune. "The Apocalypse of John and the Problem of Genre." *Semeia* 36 (1986): 65–96. (Aune summarizes previous scholarship on the genre of the book of Revelation and contributes a more detailed treatment of how apocalypses function literarily and socially. Aune has also authored a valuable three-volume commentary on Revelation in the Word Biblical Commentary series.)

John J. Collins. *The Apocalyptic Imagination: An Introduction to Jewish Apocalyptic Literature.* Second edition. Grand Rapids: Eerdmans, 1998. (Collins' introduction provides a standard overview of apocalyptic literature, including discussions of the various sub-categories of apocalyptic texts.)

George W. E. Nickelsburg and James C. VanderKam. 1 Enoch: *A New Translation.* Minneapolis: Fortress, 2004. (This short book reproduces the translation of *1 Enoch* used in the two-volume Hermeneia commentary on *1 Enoch*. This translation of the pseudonymous apocalypse has a helpful introduction and includes textual notes.)

Carolyn Osiek. *The Shepherd of Hermas: A Commentary.* Minneapolis: Fortress, 1999. (For readers interested in the *Shepherd of Hermas*, this commentary includes a fresh translation and expert commentary.)

Robert Louis Wilken. *The Spirit of Early Christian Thought: Seeking the Face of God.* New Haven: Yale University Press, 2003. (This erudite and beautifully-written introduction to early Christian thought includes an entire chapter—"The End Given in the Beginning"—on the connections between the creation of the world and the **eschaton**.)

Post-Script: Loose Canons

Guiding Questions

What did Marcion believe?
How did Irenaeus respond to Marcion?
How did the Christian canonical process work?

One of the scribes came and heard them arguing with one another, and seeing that he answered them well, he asked him, "Which commandment is first of all?"

Jesus answered, "The first is, 'Hear, Israel: the Lord our God, the Lord is one; you shall love the Lord your God with all your heart, and with all your soul, and with all your mind, and with all your strength.' The second is this, 'You shall love your neighbor as yourself.' There is no other commandment greater than these."

(Mark 12:28-31)

Marcion, Irenaeus, and the Two-God Hypothesis

What does God call humans to do? In a word, love. Love God. Love neighbor. In the passage above, Jesus articulates the twofold divine command to love. Many **Christians** (and non-Christians) have perceived this message of love as Jesus' rebuke to a legalistic Jewish religion. According to this line of thought, Jesus was a breath of fresh air after centuries of stifling legalism. The Old Testament god was cruel and exacting, they say, but Jesus brought a god-who-is-love.

So they say. Or don't say—more often than not, they leave unspoken this belief in an Old Testament god of wrath and a New Testament god of love. Yet, drawing from my experience with a fairly broad swath of American Christianity, I have heard this belief expressed regularly by university students, by various **church** members, and in popular blog posts and viral videos. These individuals do not announce that they worship two gods, or that they worship one god while disavowing another god. If you ask a group of twenty-first-century Christians how many gods they worship, the answer is typically "one"—according to Trinitarian belief, the three divine persons, Father, Son, and **Holy Spirit**, are understood as being one, triune God. But if you ask the same group of Christians about the "Old Testament god," you will generally find more than one eager to explain their puzzlement at that deity's wrath, vengeance, anger, or cruelty.

How do these two ideas co-exist in the Christian mind? Two reasons seem likely. First, many Christians have not read much of the Old Testament, but what they do know about the actions of God in the Old Testament concerns them. Why was Abraham told to offer up Isaac? Why did God command the slaughter of the Canaanites? It is much easier to dismiss such a god as barbaric, savage, and cruel than it is to grapple with the Old Testament writings themselves. The "Old Testament god" is the bad cop; Jesus plays the good cop. The "Old Testament god" caricature is thus a short-cut that frees us from having to deal with the challenge presented by the slaughter of the Canaanites or the binding of Isaac.

As support for this hypothesis, we might note that those who maintain this notion of an inferior "Old Testament god" generally do not subject this idea to careful scrutiny. If one does take time to think about it, disturbing implications begin to arise. As discussed above, what Christians call the "Old Testament" is usually the same group of writings that **Jews** call "the **scriptures**." Thus, the vengeful, cruel "Old Testament god" might also be called the "God of the Jews." So, a dismissal of the "Old Testament god" equals a dismissal of the God of Judaism. If one believes that Jews worship an inferior god, then what opinions will one form about Jewish people? Might this line of thinking begin to explain the prevalence of anti-Jewish (and anti-Semitic) prejudice among Christians past . . . and present? If this idea of an inferior "Old Testament god" has anything to do with the horrific atrocities that have been committed in the name of **Christ**, then it merits more than a second thought.

Second, this mindset did not spring full-formed from the twenty-first-century mind. It actually has far deeper roots, going back at least to the second century C.E. Once upon a time, in a city of Asia Minor, there lived a man named Marcion. In the first half of the second century, he encountered the writings of Paul, and he was captivated by Paul's presentation of salvation by **grace** through **faith**. Marcion was impressed with the apparent novelty of this God of grace announced by Paul. He concluded that Jesus was the anointed one of a brand-new god. According to Marcion, this new good god opposed the old god, who had created the world, chosen the Jews, and given the **law**. This older god prized justice; the newer god brought mercy. To show how the good god brought by Jesus was better than the old creator god, Marcion drew up a series of statements illuminating the contradictions between the two deities. This series of statements, known as Marcion's *Antitheses*, uses the **Gospel** of Luke and the letters of Paul to show the superiority of the new god of Jesus over the old god of the Jews:

> 2. The Creator did not even know where Adam was, so he cried, "Where are you?" But Christ knew even the thoughts of men [cf. Luke 5:22; 6:8; 9:47].
>
> 18. The Jewish Christ was designated by the Creator solely to restore the Jewish people from the Diaspora; but our Christ was commissioned by the good God to liberate all mankind.
>
> 29. The Christ [of the Old Testament] promises to the Jews the restoration of their former condition by return of their land and, after death, a refuge in Abraham's bosom in the underworld. Our Christ will establish the Kingdom of God, an eternal and heavenly possession.
>
> 30. Both the place of punishment and that of refuge of the Creator are placed in the underworld for those who obey the Law and the prophets. But Christ and the God who belongs to him have a heavenly place of rest and a haven, of which the Creator never spoke.
>
> (Marcion, *Antitheses*; W. A. Meeks translation [Norton, 2007])

The creator god loses track of people (#2), shows concern only for Jews (#18), and offers an inferior afterlife (#29, #30). The good god, on the other hand, reads minds, loves all of humanity, and offers eternal life in **heaven**.

Marcion's proposal entices with its simplicity and straightforward logic. In the world of Marcion, bad things happen because of the ineptitude of the creator god. The good god, on the other hand, is innocent of any complexity and loves all of humanity. Who does not want a loving god who offers rest and peace to all?

Of course, some aspects of his presentation are questionable. For example, when Adam hides from God in Genesis 3, and God calls out in search of him, it is possible to assume that God has lost track of Adam (*Antithesis* #2). But might there be another explanation for why the God who just created the universe calls out to his newly-fallen creature?

The **Hebrew** alphabet consists only of consonants, and most Hebrew writing uses only these consonants. Vowels can be added through a system of points and lines. Because most texts existed only in consonantal form, creative interpreters could supply different vowels to derive a different meaning. Some rabbis applied this method to the underlying Hebrew of Gen 3:9; instead of the curious "Where are you?" they read God's call as a compassionate "How are you?" to a disobedient and frightened Adam.

Likewise, in *Antithesis* #18, Marcion argues that the **messiah** of the creator god is only concerned with saving Jews. Yet Marcion's own heroes Luke and Paul severely undercut his case. In Luke's Gospel, a citation from Isaiah is extended to include the phrase, "all flesh will see the salvation of God" (Luke 3:6, quoting Isa 40:5). And Paul argues that God had promised salvation for all the **gentiles** (see Gal 3:8, quoting Gen 12:3). Thus, both Luke and Paul cite *Old Testament* promises of a salvation available to everyone, both Jew and gentile.

Marcion quotes Luke and Paul extensively in his *Antitheses*. Why, when Luke and Paul repeatedly undermine Marcion's arguments? Irenaeus, the bishop of Lyons, explains. In his five-volume *Against Heresies*, written in the late second century C.E., Irenaeus takes on a variety of opponents, including Marcion. Irenaeus accuses Marcion of doctoring the evidence:

> . . . Marcion and his followers have mutilated the scriptures. They do not acknowledge some books at all, and, curtailing the gospel according to Luke and the epistles of Paul, they assert that these are alone authentic, which they have themselves thus shortened.
>
> (Irenaeus, *Against Heresies* 3.12.12; *ANF* translation, modified)

Assuming the accuracy of this report, Marcion's "mutilation" constitutes the earliest known attempt to establish a **canon** of authoritative writings. As discussed earlier, a canon enumerates a list of writings that "measure up" to a certain standard. For Marcion, the Gospels of Matthew, Mark, and John apparently failed to measure up. Acts and Revelation must have also fallen short. According to Irenaeus, Marcion preserved only the Gospel of Luke and the letters of Paul, and even these writings he edited heavily.

So, if certain passages in Luke and Paul proved inconvenient, Marcion may have felt free not only to ignore them, but even to cut them out. Where he perceived inconsistency, he created coherence—at the cost of his sources' integrity. Given the frequency with which Luke and Paul quote earlier scriptures, Marcion's sustained endeavor to purge their writings from Jewish influence must have required Herculean effort.

In response to Marcion, Irenaeus underscores the unity between the Jewish scriptures and the Christian writings. For Irenaeus, Jesus did not herald the arrival of a brand-new god. Rather, Jesus came as the messiah promised by the same God who created the heavens and the earth. A careful reading of the New Testament reveals its deep indebtedness to the Old Testament. Take, for instance, the passage that opened this chapter, where Jesus announced the commandment to love God and neighbor. Jesus was by no means innovating here. Instead, as the following chart demonstrates, he was quoting:

Mark 12:29-31	Deut 6:4-5 & Lev 19:18
Jesus answered, "The first is, 'Hear, Israel: the Lord our God, the Lord is one; you shall love the Lord your God with all your heart, and with all your soul, and with all your mind, and with all your strength.'" (Mark 12:29-30)	"Hear, Israel: The Lord our God, the Lord is one. You shall love the Lord your God with all your heart, and with all your soul, and with all your might. (Deut 6:4-5)
"The second is this, 'You shall love your neighbor as yourself.' There is no other commandment greater than these." (Mark 12:31)	You shall not avenge yourself or bear a grudge against any of your people, but you shall love your neighbor as yourself. I am the Lord. (Lev 19:18)

Jesus' words in Mark 12:29–31 constitute a pair of citations from the books of Deuteronomy and Leviticus. The commandment to love God and neighbor is entrenched in the heart of the Jewish scriptures, in the first five books which are known as the **Pentateuch** or **Torah**.

Irenaeus notes this connection in his *Against Heresies*, and he uses it to launch his response to Marcion:

> Because in the law and in the gospel, the first and greatest commandment is to love the Lord God with the whole heart, and then there follows a similar commandment, to love one's neighbor as oneself, the creator of the law and the gospel is shown to be one and the same.
>
> (Irenaeus, *Against Heresies* 4.12.3; *ANF* translation, modified)

Marcion's textual manipulations yield two gods, one inferior and one superior. For Irenaeus, on the other hand, the "creator of the law and the gospel is ... one and the same." The argument of Irenaeus carried the day, and Christians have affirmed that the Old and New Testaments combine to tell one story about one God.

From Marcion to the Council of Trent

This process of putting early Christian writings on an even par with the Jewish scriptures began prior to Irenaeus. In 2 Pet 3:16, the letters of Paul are compared to the "other scriptures." For the author of 2 Peter, the letters of Paul—written in the middle of the first century C.E.—were considered to be "scripture." The early second-century bishop Polycarp of Smyrna makes his high view of the early Christian writings even more obvious in his *Letter to the Philippians*, where he cites Ps 4:5 and Eph 4:26 and identifies them both as "sacred letters" (Polycarp, *To the Philippians* 12.1). A bit later in the second century, Justin Martyr provides evidence that early Christians were giving some Christian writings the same respect that they gave to the Jewish scriptures:

> And on the day called Sunday there is a meeting in one place of those who live in cities or the country, and the memoirs of the apostles or the writings of the prophets are read as long as time permits. When the reader has finished, the president in a discourse urges and invites [us] to the imitation of these noble things.
>
> (*First Apology* 67; E. R. Hardy translation [Touchstone, 1996])

The Sunday meeting begins with a lengthy reading; "the memoirs of the apostles or the writings of the prophets" presumably indicates that the reading was taken either from a gospel like Matthew or from a prophet like Isaiah. A reading from Isaiah would simply form part of the second-century Christian routine. Whether the reader chose a reading from Matthew or from Isaiah seems immaterial to Justin Martyr. Gospels and letters are treated as sacred texts, even if there is no official canon.

The *First Apology* of Justin Martyr gives a detailed description of early Christian worship, beginning with the readings—which apparently continued for quite some time ("as long as time permits"). Next, the leader of the group would preach on the readings. Then, the people prayed, shared bread and wine, and collected contributions to take care of those in need. These practices overlap both with summary statements in the book of Acts (e.g., 2:42–47) and with modern Christian practices.

Back in the first chapter, we discussed the Muratorian fragment and its controversial dating. While our first complete canonical lists are fairly late, we do find early evidence that Jews and Christians had working lists of authoritative Jewish scriptures. In the first decade of the second century C.E., Josephus claims that the Jews have twenty-two books, including the five books of Moses, thirteen prophetic books, and four books of "hymns" and "counsels" (*Against Apion* 1.38-40). (Do not read too much into these numbers, since ancient Jews counted the books differently; for instance, Josephus would have counted the twelve "minor prophets" as one book.) In the late second century, Melito, the Christian bishop of Sardis, also supplies a list of "books of the old covenant" in a letter to his associate Onesimus (*Fragment* 3). By the end of the second century, Christians and Jews had a relatively settled understanding as to which Jewish scriptures "measured up."

Widespread agreement about certain books of the Jewish scriptures (e.g., the Pentateuch, the historical books, the major prophets, and Psalms) did not extend to every book that now forms part of the **Tanakh** or Christian Old Testament. The book of Esther lingered on the edge for centuries; Melito does not mention Esther, and Athanasius excludes it from the canon. Fragments of every book of the Jewish scriptures have been found at **Qumran**—every book but Esther, that is. Rabbinic writings report that the famous rabbis Shammai and Hillel appear to have agreed that Esther was a sacred text (Babylonian Talmud, *Megillah* 7a), but this notice suggests that debates over Esther continued among some first-century B.C.E. Jews.

The official process of settling upon a Christian canon was much more drawn-out. Even though Marcion may have catalyzed a more serious discussion, the process moved slowly. Contrary to popular belief, there was no hidden conspiracy to purge "heretical" writings from recorded history, no campaign to burn heretical authors at the stake. (In these early centuries, you might find Christians being executed by the state, but you will not find church authorities wielding secular power against dissidents.) On the other hand, never did a church council gather all available texts, establish proper criteria for evaluation, and promulgate an official canon. Rather, as Justin Martyr testifies, local Christians met together to worship, and at these meetings they publicly read both Jewish scriptures like the book of Isaiah and Christian texts that were linked with apostles like Paul and John. This local usage of apostolic texts laid the foundation for future decision-making on a larger scale. In short, the canonical process happened more like the biological theory of evolution than the cosmic Big Bang theory.

In the early texts, then, what we find has the character of a research report, rather than an "official church teaching." Eusebius of Caesarea (ca. 260 – ca. 340 C.E.) preserves an illuminating account of how one contested text was excluded from canonical consideration. In his *Ecclesiastical History*, Eusebius reproduces an account written in the late second-century or early third-century by Serapion, bishop of Antioch. Serapion visited one of the churches under his supervision—the Greek word for "bishop" (*episkopos*) means "overseer"—and found them reading a certain "Gospel of Peter" (probably the same text cited above in Chapter Ten). Unfamiliar with this work, Serapion encouraged the local church to read it. Later, Serapion is warned by individuals who are familiar with this text. He acquires a copy, reads it, and concludes, "We find many things that accord with the true teaching of the savior, but some things that are added on, which we have appended below" (*Ecclesiastical History* 6.12.6). To summarize, someone wrote the "Gospel of Peter," presumably in the second half of the second century. (Serapion provides our earliest reference to it.) A group of Christians near Antioch then accepted this text as authoritative. The visiting Serapion was not alarmed to find Christians reading a gospel that he did not know. When Serapion learned by word of mouth that this gospel was associated with deviant beliefs, he obtained a copy, read it carefully, and then passed judgment. Even then, Serapion did not condemn the Gospel of Peter to a banned books list; he simply pointed out ways in which it strays from the "true teaching of the savior."

Around 170 or 180 C.E., we find Irenaeus arguing strenuously for a fourfold gospel: no more and no less (*Against Heresies* 3.11.8). This bishop cannot simply declare that Matthew, Mark, Luke, and John are "canonical." He must make an argument. Obviously, not everyone agreed: witness the thoughtful procedure of Serapion a few decades after Irenaeus. About one century later, Eusebius of Caesarea provides his list of New Testament books, informed by "the testimony of the ancient ones" (*Ecclesiastical History* 3.24.18). Eusebius recognizes the same four gospels as Irenaeus, but he admits uncertainty with regard to certain writings: James, Jude, 2 Peter, 2 John, and 3 John (3.25.3). He is also unsure about Revelation, given the divided opinions with regard to this work (3.24.18). To Eusebius, consensus matters.

Twenty-first-century Christians may or may not be surprised to see that the Revelation of John stirred up different opinions. Interestingly, Revelation was not the only **apocalypse** to encounter a mixed reception. The *Shepherd of Hermas* enjoyed popularity among many Christians. Athanasius, a fourth-century C.E. bishop of Alexandria, quotes Hermas with approval in his Festal Letter of 339; in 367, though, he classifies the *Shepherd* with Esther and Sirach as books that can be read privately but not publicly. Even more strikingly, the mid-fourth-century C.E. *Codex Sinaiticus* testifies to the popularity of certain books at a relatively late period. This massive biblical manuscript includes not only familiar books from the Old and New Testaments, but also 1 Maccabees, 4 Maccabees, Wisdom of Solomon, Sirach, and two Christian works that are now excluded from the canon: the *Epistle of Barnabas* and the *Shepherd of Hermas*. (The placement of these two works at the very end of the **codex** implies their liminal status.)

The first somewhat official list of twenty-seven books referred to as the "New Testament" appears in a letter sent by Athanasius, bishop of Alexandria, in 367 C.E. Yet even this letter does not spell the end of the canonical process. The New Testament portion of the canon may have attained its final form, but Athanasius excludes both Esther and certain books that came to be known as **apocrypha**, including the Wisdom of Solomon and Sirach. In spite of the spirited defense of apocryphal works by figures like Priscillian of Avila (died ca. 386 C.E.), many communities continued to exclude them. The Catholic Church includes apocrypha as "deuterocanonical" works; they form part of the canon officially promulgated at the Council of Trent in 1546. This Council supplied the first official Christian canon, even though the majority of books had been largely agreed upon by Christians for centuries.

To return to the beginning, we can recall that "Christian Scriptures" is not another name for the New Testament. The Christian **Bible** is composed of Old and New Testaments. Even if twenty-first-century Christians have theological convictions that differ from those of twenty-first-century Jews, Christians must remember that Jesus was a Jew, that Paul was a Jew, and that the earliest Christians used the same scriptures as their fellow first-century Jews. Unfortunately, over the centuries, some Christians have followed Marcion's lead in dismissing the Old Testament and its deity as inferior. In the twentieth century, some of these Christians shamefully and tragically collaborated in the fratricidal execution of millions of Jews. In the aftermath of this catastrophe, Christians have begun to realize how much can be learned from Jews, from Judaism, and from the Jewish scriptures. Far from dismissing Judaism as an inferior religion, Christians must learn about and from Jews (both ancient and contemporary) in order to understand their own religion. And Christians and Jews together must never forget the command, and invitation, to love God and to love neighbor.

Bibliography and suggestions for further reading

Codex Sinaiticus. (High-resolution photographs of this codex are available online at http://codexsinaiticus.org/en/manuscript.aspx [accessed 27 May 2014].)

Irenaeus, *Against Heresies.* (A free online translation is available at http://www.ccel.org, but this very antiquated translation comes from the late nineteenth century. A new translation is gradually coming out in the *Ancient Christian Writers* series.)

Bart D. Ehrman and Andrew S. Jacobs. *Christianity in Late Antiquity, 300–450 C.E.: A Reader.* New York: Oxford University Press, 2004. (In this useful reader, Jacobs includes a rare English translation of Priscillian's *On Faith and Apocrypha.*)

Wayne A. Meeks and John T. Fitzgerald, eds. *The Writings of St. Paul.* Second edition. New York: W. W. Norton, 2007. (Meeks and Fitzgerald include a complete listing of Marcion's *Antitheses* on pp. 286–288, followed by illuminating excerpts from Adolf von Harnack's monograph about Marcion.)

Glossary

apocalypse: from the Greek word *apokalypsis*, meaning "revelation" or "unveiling." As a literary genre, an apocalypse consists of a mediated revelation dealing with eschatological events and an unseen spatial reality.

apocalyptic: literally, "revelatory," but often carries eschatological and catastrophic connotations.

apocrypha: usually refers to writings that were valued by ancient Jews and Christians, yet were not canonized; can also refer specifically to the books of the Roman Catholic Bible that Protestants do not accept as canonical (e.g., Tobit, Judith, and 1 Maccabees).

Aramaic: from the sixth to the fourth century B.C.E., the most widely-used language in the Near East; also adopted by Jews and Christians who lived in this region. See also ***targumim.***

asceticism: from the Greek word *askēsis*, meaning "training" or "discipline." Those who practiced asceticism typically disciplined themselves through fasting and other means of self-denial.

Bible: from the Greek word *biblia*, meaning "books." The Bible is a collection of sacred texts. For Christians, the Bible consists of the Old and New Testaments; for Jews, the Bible is the **Tanakh**.

canon: from the Greek word *kanōn*, meaning "reed" or "measuring stick." A canon is a list of authoritative texts. Different religious groups often have different canons; for example, Protestants, Roman Catholics, and Eastern Orthodox agree on the books of the New Testament, but they vary with respect to the books of the Old Testament and the status of the **apocrypha**.

Christ: from the Greek word *christos*, which translates the Hebrew word *mashiach*. Both words mean "anointed one" or "**messiah**."

Christians: from the Greek *christianoi* and the Latin *christiani*, this term was probably derogatory in its earliest usage, when it would have been applied as an outsider's label for followers of Jesus Christ; in the modern period, usually identified by baptism (for Catholics, Orthodox, and some Protestant denominations) or a public profession of faith (for many Protestants and Pentecostals).

church: English translation for the Greek *ekklēsia*, which means "assembly." In the New Testament, a "church" consists of the followers of Jesus, gathered in a given location; nowadays, "church" can mean "local group of Christians," "building with a steeple," or "organized religious body."

codex: from the Latin word for "book," a new technology that began to replace scrolls in the late first or early second century C.E.

covenant: a binding agreement between two or more parties, often solemnized through blood **sacrifice**. The New "Testament" would be more accurately translated as the New "Covenant."

crucifixion: a means of execution used in the ancient world, most famously by the Romans; the victim was typically nailed or tied to a wooden cross, where they hung until they could breathe no more.

Dead Sea Scrolls: a collection of Greek, **Aramaic**, and (mostly) Hebrew texts discovered in the region around the northwestern coast of the Dead Sea in the 1940s and 1950s. These texts include ancient biblical commentaries, documents regulating the communal life of an ancient Jewish sectarian group, and our earliest known manuscripts of the Jewish scriptures. See also **Qumran**.

diaspora: from the Greek word *diaspora*, meaning "scattering" or "dispersion." Diaspora Jews were spread throughout the Mediterranean world and beyond through conquest and, eventually, emigration. Scholars typically differentiate between Palestinian Jews (= Jews who lived in Judea and the surrounding regions) and Diaspora Jews (= Jews who lived anywhere else) in the Second Temple period.

disciple: from the Latin word *discipulus*, meaning "learner" or "student."

election: choosing; used in theological discussions to speak of God's mysterious preference or selection of one particular person or group.

epitaph: inscription on a grave marker, serving to memorialize the deceased.

eschaton: transliteration of the Greek word for "end," often used to refer to an ultimate future crisis or to the "last days."

Essenes: a Jewish **sect**, usually considered to be the group responsible for writing or copying many of the Dead Sea Scrolls.

eunuch: a castrated male; because castrated males frequently functioned as trusted court officials in the ancient world, the term later applied also to officials who were not castrated.

evangelist: in popular use, refers to a preacher; in scholarly use, refers either to a preacher of good news or to the author of a written **gospel**.

faith: often understood as a cognitive property; the Greek word *pistis* and Latin *fides* can refer to belief or to loyalty. Apart from context, one cannot distinguish between these meanings of "faith" and "faithfulness."

Fall, the: theological label for the beginning of human sin, as described in Genesis 3.

fasting: abstaining from food (or from particular foods) for a sustained period of time.

gematria: the Jewish practice of biblical interpretation through the numerical value of words.

genealogy: an account of one's family line or ancestral origins.

gentile: from the Latin *gens* meaning "people" or "nation," this label can be applied to anyone who is not Jewish.

gospel: literally, "good news" or "favorable message." This meaning was later expanded to include the writings about Jesus and his good news.

grace: literally, "free gift," often used to speak of God's voluntary extension of benefits to humans.

Hasmonean: any member of the family of Mattathias (who descended from a certain *Asamōnaios*), the leader of the **Maccabean revolt**. The Hasmonean dynasty ruled from 135 to 36 B.C.E.

heaven: often perceived as the dwelling place of God. The Greek *ouranos* can be translated as "heaven" or "sky"; for ancients, the two would not differ significantly in meaning.

Hebrew: a person descended from Abraham—who was a descendant of Eber (see Gen 11:10-26). Such a person would typically self-identify as an "Israelite" or "child of Israel," so "Hebrew" may have been more of an outsider's term (see Gen 39:14). The language spoken by Hebrews (= Israelites) was also known as "Hebrew."

Hellenism: a combination of Greek customs, Greek language, and Greek thought.

Holy Spirit: a divine being, often indistinguishable from God. The Holy Spirit is said to speak through the prophets. For Christians, the Father, Son, and Holy Spirit make up the **Trinity**.

idolatry: the worship of images or representations. Jews, Christians, and Muslims believe that God alone is to be worshiped; therefore, the worship of anything else on earth or in heaven is condemned as idolatry.

incarnation: the act of becoming human or, more literally, taking on flesh. Christians believe that Jesus existed with God prior to being conceived in the womb of Mary.

Jews: initially, a term used to describe the residents of Judea. It came to mean "any descendant of Israel (= Jacob)." Later on, this genealogical definition of Jewishness was expanded, as conversion to Judaism became possible.

law: in Jewish and Christian literature, usually refers to Torah. See **Torah**.

literary form: a term used by scholars to describe the sub-types of genre that make up a literary work; in the present book, this term is used as a catch-all to describe any category of writing associated with certain structural features or interpretive expectations.

liturgy: from the Greek word *leitourgia*, originally meaning "public service." Ancient Jews and Christians came to use this word to refer to public worship. Nowadays, "liturgy" more frequently refers either to communal worship, or to the order of service used in communal worship.

Maccabean revolt: a Jewish uprising against **Seleucid** rule, reacting against the actions of Antiochus IV Epiphanes in 167 B.C.E.; the revolt concluded in 164 B.C.E. with the rededication of the Jerusalem temple, now celebrated as the feast of Hanukkah.

martyrdom: from the Greek word *martys*, meaning "witness." Martyrdom is the ultimate act of bearing witness, through death.

messiah: from the Hebrew word *mashiach*, meaning "anointed one." Throughout the Jewish scriptures, kings and priests are anointed. Hence, when Second Temple Jews hoped that God would send one or more anointed ones to deliver the people of God, their expectations often involved royal and priestly figures.

miqveh: a Hebrew word meaning "reservoir," a site for ceremonial bathing to restore ritual purity.

Mishnah: a Hebrew word meaning "oral teaching"; a collection of Jewish oral law that was compiled around 200 C.E., but contains earlier traditions.

Nicene Creed: statement of Christian belief that emerged from the Council of Nicaea in 325 C.E. It affirms the divinity and humanity of Jesus and offers a detailed description of Christian belief in the Trinity. When Christians nowadays recite the "Nicene Creed" together, they are usually saying the slightly longer "Nicaeno-Constantinopolitan Creed" that emerged from the Council of Constantinople in 381 C.E.

pantheon: from Greek words meaning "every god" or "all gods," often used to label a **temple** dedicated to all the gods.

patriarch: a founding father, usually with reference to Abraham, Isaac, or Jacob.

Pentateuch: from a Greek word meaning "five scrolls," the first five books of the Jewish and Christian Bibles.

Pharisees: a Jewish **sect** of the Second Temple period, noteworthy for belief in **resurrection** and angels, strict adherence to **Torah** (both written and oral), and a commitment to integrating Torah into every facet of daily life.

polytheism: belief in more than one god. Nowadays, the polytheism/monotheism distinction has fallen out of favor, given the frequent references to other divine beings in both Jewish and Christian scriptures. (See, e.g., Zeph 2:11 and John 10:34.)

promised land: in the biblical narratives, the land of Canaan (= modern Israel-Palestine) is granted to Abraham and his descendants.

pseudonymity: the phenomenon of false attribution of a written text (e.g., *1 Enoch*).

Ptolemies: the descendants of the general Ptolemy, a successor of Alexander the Great who was granted rule over Egypt.

Qumran: more fully, Khirbet Qumran was a site where an ancient Jewish community lived; this community has been identified with the **Essenes**

and linked to the writing and copying of the documents known as the **Dead Sea Scrolls**.

Rabbinic Judaism: the movement that emerged after the destruction of the Jerusalem **temple** in 70 C.E. and produced the **Mishnah**, Talmud, and other important writings. It most closely aligns with Pharisaic Judaism of the Second Temple period.

resurrection: being raised from the dead.

sacrifice: from a Latin word that literally means "to make holy," usually refers to an offering made by a priest to a deity on behalf of an individual or group.

Sadducees: a Jewish **sect** of the Second Temple period that was closely aligned with the leadership of the Jerusalem temple; this group rejected oral law and belief in resurrection.

Samaritans: inhabitants of Samaria, a city in northern Israel. Over time, Samaritans became a Jewish **sect**, arguing that God should be worshiped at Gerizim, not Jerusalem. From the second or first century B.C.E. onward, they began to use a sacred text (the Samaritan **Pentateuch**) containing readings that differ from the Jewish scriptures; eventually, Samaritanism developed into a religion separate from Judaism.

scriptures: sacred, authoritative writings.

Second Temple: the Jerusalem temple, rebuilt and dedicated in the late sixth century B.C.E., then destroyed in 70 C.E. This time period is known as the Second Temple period.

sect: although a derogatory term in popular use, scholars use this term to describe an organized sub-group within a larger religious (or philosophical) group or school of thought.

Seleucids: the descendants of the general Seleucus, a successor of Alexander the Great who was granted rule over Syria and the surrounding regions. For Jews, the most noteworthy Seleucid was Antiochus IV Epiphanes, whose actions in 167 B.C.E. set off the **Maccabean revolt**.

Septuagint: from the Latin word for "seventy" (reflecting a tradition reported in the *Letter of Aristeas*), Greek translations of the Jewish scriptures.

sign prophets: refers to individuals who won adherents through their promises to liberate the people by working signs and wonders.

signs: in biblical texts, another word for "miracles." A sign always points to something else.

sin: the Greek word *hamartia* means "missing the mark," and sin can be defined (for Jews and Christians) as any departure or straying from the will of God, or any failure to love God and neighbor.

synagogue: from the Greek word *synagōgē*, meaning "gathering place." In the Second Temple period (and beyond), the synagogue functioned for Jews as a place of worship and Torah study.

Tanakh: a Hebrew acronym that stands for the major divisions of the Jewish Bible: *Torah* ("law"), *Nevi'im* ("prophets"), and *Ketuvim* ("writings").

targumim: Aramaic versions of the Jewish scriptures, part translation and part paraphrase, the result of Aramaic replacing Hebrew as the mother tongue of Jews in the ancient Near East.

temple: a building where a deity is considered to be especially present; hence, also a place of worship.

tetragrammaton: The Greek word *tetragrammaton* means "four letters" and refers to the sacred four-letter name of God ("YHWH" or "Yahweh").

tetrarch: from a Greek word meaning "ruler of a fourth," this term is used in the New Testament to describe rulers granted authority by Rome over smaller regions (but not necessarily a literal "fourth" of a larger area).

Torah: the Hebrew *torah* is usually translated as "law," but more literally means "instruction" or "teaching." The Torah is given to Moses on Mount Sinai as part of the covenant between God and Israel, according to the latter half of the book of Exodus. Later, Torah came to include both written and oral instruction.

Trinity: from the Latin word *trinitas*, meaning something like "three-ness." This word is intended to capture both the oneness of the God of the Christians, and the presence of three persons—Father, Son, and Holy Spirit—who are of the same essence.

Zealots: a group of Jews that opposed Rome and promoted violent revolution; Josephus blames this "fourth philosophy" for the Jewish revolt against Rome; given these apologetic motives, scholars question whether they existed as a distinct group.

Index of Ancient Sources

1:1	34	24:3	63
1:1-17	2	24:15	187
1:3	74	24:23-26	63
1:5-6	74	24:43	195
1:16	73–4, 76	25:31-46	149, 184, 185
1:20	2, 34, 74	26:20	118
1:21	74	27:6	86
1:23	25	27:25	121
2	81	27:35	164
2:2-4	76	27:37	102
2:16	76	27:39	164
3:2	23	27:43	164
3:11	58	27:62-66	161
4:1-10	68	28:7	45
4:11	68		
4:17	23	Mark	
4:23	35–6	1:1	40–41
5-7	25	1:4-6	57
5:17	130	1:7	57–8
5:21-47	130	1:9	57
5:44	2	1:13	68
6:10	25	1:14	57–8
6:24-33	112	1:14-15	24
8:25	117	1:15	184
9:14	117	1:16-20	107, 110
9:36	185	1:35	68
10:2	118	2:18	117
10:9-10	111	2:23-28	130
11:2	117	4:10	118
11:7-14	63	6:3	91, 99
11:11	58	6:8	111
11:14	63	6:10-11	112
12:28	25	6:14	91–2
13:55	92, 99	6:14-29	81
14:12	117	6:17-29	58
19:23-24	24	6:29	117
19:24	25	6:30	118
19:28	118	8:14-16	117
21:42	3	8:22-25	98
22:15-16	117	8:29	91
22:21	51	8:34-35	155
22:44	102	9:2-8	162
22:49	3	10:2-12	88
24-25	63	10:29	35–6

Index of Subjects

prophet 36, 57, 63, 96–7, 100–1, 104,
    108–10
  definition 186–7
pseudonymity 186
Ptolemies 31–2, 40
Ptolemy I 40
purity 58, 64–5, 128–9

Qumran
  community 16–17, 64–8, 101–2, 119,
    131–2
  Khirbet Qumran 16–17, 65–6, 114,
    131, 203

Rahab 74
Reagan, Ronald W. 191
Red Sea (Sea of Reeds) 12, 62
Rehoboam 124
religion 15, 50, 124, 126, 133, 135–7, 143,
    167–71
resurrection, ancient belief in 16,
    177–8
Rome 32, 34, 37, 40–7, 50–3, 87, 103–4,
    113, 117, 134, 147, 150, 157–61,
    173, 188
  citizenship 49, 159
  Roman numerals 190
  socio-economic status 72, 159
Romulus 43–4
Ruth 74

sabbath 32, 91, 121, 127–8, 130, 162; see
    also Jews, practices
sacrifice 11, 49, 60, 84, 102, 125, 127–8,
    169
Sadducees 83, 98, 113, 115–16, 119,
    130–1, 134–5
salvation 40–1, 45, 67–8, 74, 101, 155–6,
    193, 200
  by grace through faith 198–9
Samaria 37, 80, 85, 107, 133
Samaritans 86, 113, 132–5
Samuel 100
Sanhedrin 99, 131

Sarah 176
Sardis 188
Satan 68, 190
Saul (king) 100, 124, 140
Saul of Tarsus see Paul
Second Temple 9, 31, 37, 77, 122; see also
    Jews, Second Temple Judaism
sect 14; see also Jews, sects
Seleucids 31–2, 37, 40, 128
Seleucus I 40
semantic stretch 3–4, 14, 19, 172
Septuagint 5, 31
Serapion of Antioch 204
Sergius Paulus 140
shame 35, 147, 153–7, 160–3, 165
  shame culture 154
Shammai 87, 203
Sidon 82
sign prophets 62–3, 68
signs see miracles
Simon, son of Mattathias 15
Simon Peter see Peter
sin 11, 13, 23, 57–9, 65–8, 74, 101–2, 105,
    153, 194
slavery 3, 11, 35, 49, 72, 88, 145, 146–7,
    156–7, 159, 162
Smith, Morton 93
Smyrna 188
Socrates 110–12, 116–17, 148, 169
Solomon 37, 100, 124
Spartacus 157
speeches 9–10
"spiritual but not religious" 167–8
Stoicism 116, 148
synagogue 3, 92, 135, 137, 141
  of Satan 193–4
Syria 31, 84

Talmud 88
Tamar 74
Tanakh 3, 11, 15, 203
targum 5
Tarsus 139–41, 143–4
Tekoa 157

temple *see* Elephantine; Jerusalem,
    temple; Second Temple
Temple Mount 77–8, 123, 140
tetragrammaton 25–6, 67
tetrarch 52, 58, 80–1, 143
Theudas 62, 67
Thomas 45
Thyatira 188
Tiberius 43, 47, 52–3, 85, 87
Tigris River 29
Timothy, 146
Titus (emperor) 53, 157–8
Torah 12, 15, 32, 67, 73, 79, 85, 88,
    125–30, 132, 134–7, 199, 201
    dietary laws 80, 126, 128
    strict interpretation of 87, 115, 141
Trajan 47–50, 53
Trinity 13, 198
Tyre 82

Varro 42
Vespasian 18, 41, 52–3, 98
virtue 72, 112–14, 160
Vitellius (emperor) 41, 53
Vitellius (governor of Syria) 84, 87
voluntary associations 48–50

wilderness *see* desert

Xenophon, son of Gryllus 110–12

Yahweh *see* tetragrammaton
Yom Kippur 84

Zadok 100
zealot (*zēlōtēs*) 64, 134, 136, 139,
    141
Zealots 134–6
Zeus 40, 41, 44; *see also* Jupiter